THE BLACK PEARL

THE BLACK PEARL

Spiritual Illumination in Sufism
and East Asian Philosophies

Henry Bayman

MONKFISH BOOK PUBLISHING COMPANY
RHINEBECK, NEW YORK

Printed in the United States of America
Book and cover design by Georgia Dent
Seated Dervish
Riza Abbasi, Iranian, ca. 1565-1635
Iran, 1626
Ink on paper; 21.0 x 14.0 cm
Art and History Collection. Photograph courtesy of the Arthur M. Sackler Gallery, Smithsonian Institution, Washington, D.C.: LTS1995.2.79.

Library of Congress Cataloging-in-Publication Data

Bayman, Henry, 1951-
   The black pearl : spiritual illumination in Sufism and East Asian philosophies / by Henry Bayman.-- 1st impression.
      p. cm.
   ISBN 0-9749359-5-6
   1. Sufism. 2. God--Comparative studies. 3. Philosophy, Confucian. 4. Philosophy, Comparative. 5. Philosophy--East Asia. I. Title.
   BP189.B4 2005
   297.4'1--dc22

                                    2005010192
Bulk purchase discounts for educational or promotional purposes are available.
Monkfish Book Publishing Company
27 Lamoree Road
Rhinbeck, New York 12572
www.monkfishpublishing.com

A seeker on the path visits a true Master and asks him about various spiritual methods. The Sage replies: "Do not fear— they all belong to us! Yet you are like one who earnestly tills the soil, waiting for a shoot to grow. Then you wait for the shoot to become a tree. Then the tree must blossom. Then only finally may it yield fruit. Whereas I (and here he reaches out his hand towards the seeker), I am offering you fresh fruit—all you have to do is eat!"

CB

TABLE OF CONTENTS

PREFACE... xi

INTRODUCTION xvii
    Enlightenment And Gnosis,
    Buddhahood and Prophethood xxx
    Overview xxxiv

1. SECRETS OF THE TEA CEREMONY 1
    The Tea Ceremony.. 5
    Awakening to the One.. 7
    The Symbolism of the Tea Ceremony 9

2. A SUFI'S WORSHIP 17
    Faith.. 17
    Faith in the Master 19
    Faith in the Prophet 22
    Faith in God.. 25
    Order and Harmony.. 28
    The Importance of God for Human Beings 29
    Empiricism 30

3. ON WAR.. 32
    Kendo and the "Sword of No-Abode" 35
    War Against Oneself.. 37

4. UNITY AND ITS FAMILY 40
    Unity.. 40
    Truth, Beauty, Goodness 43
    Peace.. 47
    Harmony 48
    Love.. 49
    Equality.. 51
    Intimacy 52
    The Tree Metaphor.. 57
    The Divine Helper.. 58

5. FROM NATURE TO GOD 61

6. LIFE AFTER DEATH...68
   The Metaphor of the Garden.......................................68
   Reincarnation...71

7. GOD IN EAST ASIAN CULTURE........................78
   Tao, T'ien, Ti, Kami...78
   God in the *I Ching*...79
   The Yin and Yang of God...82
   Similarity and Incomparability.....................................84
   God and the Taoists..85
   Shinto...90
   The Sun Behind the Sun...93
   The Knowledge of No Knowledge.....................................93
   Hollow Chestnut, Delicious Walnut.................................95
   The Bobbing Melon and the New Creation............97
   The Homecoming...98
   Nirvana in Brahman...100
   No god but God...104
   The Orange and the Sage..105
   None-self but One Self...106
   The Mouse that Bit the Balloon................................108

8. EMPTINESS OR GOD?...111
   Nirvana and Nihilism...111
   Evolution of the *Sunyata* Concept..........................114
   The Problem with Emptiness.......................................120
   The *Sunyata* Shortfall..122
   Zeroing the Self..125
   The Ethics of Unity..130
   Charity Stones...132

9. CONFUCIUS: THE EXOTERIC DIMENSION.......136
   Confucian Divine Law...136
   Further Parallels...139
   Sincerity and Unity...147

10. INDRA'S NET...150
    Mutual Interdependence.......................................150

Two Different Visions..153
The Emptiness of Emptiness.......................................155
Indra's Holographic Net 157
The Room of Mirrors 160
The Mysteries of Unification......................................161

11. SELF-CULTIVATION IN SUFISM 164
The Two Restrictions...164
The Difficulty of the Way 166
The Man with Too Much Tea 166
The Cavity of the Heart 167
The Heavenly Book 169
The Way of the Prophet...171
One's own strength (*jiriki*) 172
Another's strength (*tariki*) 172
The Synthesis in Sufism 173
The Flying Frog..175
Stages of the Self 176
The Base Self 178
The Goose as Model for the Base Self 179
Namik Kemal and the Cat 181
Nitinol and the Base Self 182
Sleep Less, Wake Up to God..184
Sufism and Biotech..186
Unveiling..187
Quantum Sufism 189
Loqman's Last Lesson 191

12. THE END OF THE JOURNEY 194
The Peak of Unification...194
Formal Prayer 199
Chuang Tzu Visits a Sufi Physicist 200

CONCLUSION 204
APPENDIX (FORMAL PRAYER) 208
GLOSSARY 217
INDEX 225

PREFACE

Without our searching, You gave us this search.
—Rumi

The journey of a thousand miles begins with one step.
—Lao Tzu

In my younger days, I devoted much time to the study of Eastern philosophies—Yoga, Zen, Taoism, Buddhism. Each was an eye-opener. I learned many things from the priceless wisdom that the sages of the East had accumulated down the centuries. I can say that each of these religions/philosophies represented a stepping stone along the path I traveled, and I am forever indebted to them for providing me with an understanding of what religion and philosophy are all about.

I was not originally interested in religion very much, but found my way to it through philosophy (and to philosophy, in turn, through science). Once, when I was young, a friend asked: "What is philosophy?" I replied: "In my view, philosophy is to harvest good results from whatever happens to you, good or bad." I probably had Epictetus and the Stoics in the back of my mind when I said that. In this pragmatic approach—which I readily admit may not be shared by many philosophers—philosophy is something by which we improve ourselves. It was Eastern thought, which is philosophy on one face and religion on the other, that led me on to religion.

I started with Zen, which seemed closest to our secular world view. I remember that the earliest books I read on the subject were *The Way of Zen* by Alan Watts and *Zen Buddhism* by Christmas Humphreys. This led on to a study of Yoga (especially Hatha Yoga which is most practical), Buddhism, and Taoism.

Then I met the incomparable Sufi saint, Ahmet Kayhan. Every ideal, whether human or superhuman, I found embodied in him. But without the infrastructure provided by Eastern thought to appreciate what I was facing, I should never have recognized the Master for what he was, what he represented. That background alerted me to the mystical dimension present within Islam: its esoteric aspect, its spiritual core. Before, I had shared the widespread misconception that Islam is a solely exoteric religion based on beliefs, laws and external observances, with little regard to inner experience. Also, the appreciation that a sage is a person of great accomplishment and thus worthy of respect proved instrumental in approaching the Sufi masters with the proper courtesy.

I believe that Islamic Sufism has much in common with Buddhism, with Taoism, with Zen, and yes, even with Confucianism. At the same time, however, Sufism differs in various respects from each of these paths, to a degree that it becomes worthwhile to write a book about the subject.

At the center of the discussion is Absolute Reality: God, the Tao, Buddha-nature, the One (*al-Ahad*). Branching off from this are: exoteric Confucianism, which deals with morality; esoteric Taoism and Buddhism, and their combined form Zen, which deal with wisdom and mysticism; plus other traditions which are less widespread but nevertheless represent important aspects of Eastern thought.

Rumi, the great mystical poet, once told the following Sufi story:

> A Greek, an Arab, a Turk and a Persian once came together, and when they were hungry they pooled their money to buy something to eat. At that point a difficulty arose, because the Greek wanted to buy *stafil*, the Arab wanted to buy *inab*, the Persian wanted *angur* while the Turk wanted *uzum*. They finally began to quarrel, and at that moment a sage passing by interrupted them. "Tell me what you want," he said, and taking the money from them, soon came back with some grapes. They were amazed to see that they all had wanted the same thing.

Likewise, it appears that various traditions in the east and west have used, not merely different words, but also different *concepts*, in pointing to the same reality—illustrated by another famous Rumi story, "the elephant in the dark." Everybody has got hold of one part the truth. Once this is grasped, it becomes easier to make sense of many issues.

I find it surprising that scarcely anything has been written about Sufism in relation to Eastern philosophy. Toshihiko Izutsu's *Sufism and Taoism* (1967) is the one notable exception that comes to mind.[1] Many years ago, I ran across the book in an Istanbul bookshop. It was the original edition published at Keio University. I could not purchase it at that time, however, and when I came to read it years later, it was a copy published by the University of California. We shall always be grateful to Izutsu for having initiated a new field of study, and his influence will be seen in various places of the present work.

But of course, Izutsu confined himself to a comparison between Sufism and Taoism (more specifically, comparing the great Sufi sage Ibn Arabi with Lao Tzu and Chuang Tzu), not

---

1. Sachiko Murata's *The Tao of Islam* (1992) and *Chinese Gleams of Sufi Light* (2000) are two other exceptional studies.

East Asian thought in general. Furthermore, being an outstanding scholar, he was writing more for an academic audience.

This present work both is, and is not, a comparative study. Lest I be accused of academic pretensions, let me say at once that this is not a study of Buddhism, Taoism, Zen, or Confucianism. It is a study of Buddhism, Taoism, Zen, and Confucianism *as I have understood them to be*. I hope my readers will forgive me if they come across an occasional misunderstanding on my part. Similarly, it is not a study of Sufism in the academic sense, but of Sufism as I have seen, heard, and learned it from my Master and my own studies, to the extent of my acumen. All I can lay claim to is being a *student* of Sufism.

ോ   ോ   ോ

The juggernaut of modernization has rolled over every delicate flower of the East, until today we are faced with their imminent extinction. Attachment to the secular world, to material goods and values, has erased the sacred almost completely from our lives. To my mind, this state of affairs is deplorable. Our material wealth should cease to be a curse, a devil's trade-in, and become the springboard for doing more important things with our lives—such as perfecting ourselves, becoming what we already have the potential to be.

The world's religions are, to me, a vast jigsaw puzzle, and even if I haven't been able to advance far, it has given me great pleasure to contemplate how the pieces fit together.

Before us is a bouquet of flowers. And like a honey bee, we shall wend our way from lotus blossom to cherry blossom, guided by the evocative subtlety of the fragrances.

☙   ☙   ☙

In this book I have followed most of the conventions set forth in an earlier book, *The Station of No Station* (North Atlantic, 2001). To summarize briefly, while Ahmet Kayhan called his teaching "Islam" and I call it "Sufism," we both mean the same thing, i.e., Islamic Sufism. By Islam he meant both the exoteric and the esoteric aspects, thus using the term in a sense which many people are unaccustomed to. His use is the correct one, I believe, but then we come up against a problem of understanding. I have used the term Sufism because Eastern thought, with the exception of Confucian ethics, deals mainly with esoteric matters. But Islam is generally perceived to be an exoteric religion, and its esoteric or contemplative aspect is commonly denoted by the word "Sufism."

The gender problem is endemic to the English language. When I call God "He," this is only intended to point to God in the third-person singular. It does not mean that God, who is beyond everything and also beyond gender, is a male. Similarly when speaking of humans: unless a person is a male, or masculinity is explicitly indicated, "he" also implies "she."

I myself have translated the Turkish pieces. The translations have been done freely, with clarity foremost on my mind and aiming at accuracy only in bringing out crucial points. In transliterating the names of the ancient Chinese sages, I have mostly adhered to the Wade-Giles system rather than Pinyin as a personal preference.

Extensive use has been made of the secondary literature. I have used more sources than are indicated in the footnotes. An attempt has been made to keep them to a minimum. In speaking of Sufism I use fewer footnotes, as I am writing directly from memory or from "field notes" taken during training. When I relate a Sufi story, it is typeset differently in order to indicate its "trademark."

My gratitude and thanks to Tim Thurston and Peter Murphy, who have contributed to making this book what it is.

To err is human, and there will be errors in this book. For these, I apologize in advance.

Henry Bayman
(*hbayman@gmail.com*)

INTRODUCTION

God is beautiful, He loves beauty;
God is generous, He loves generosity;
God is pure, He loves purity.

—The Prophet

Sufism is the way of inner truth and inner purity, of sincerity, love, and compassion. It counsels selflessness and desirelessness, benevolence and forbearance. It is pluralistic, democratic, and tolerant. Its beliefs are simple, practical, and direct. It teaches faith in One God, ethical conduct, and realization of the Absolute through charity, good deeds, and straightforward practices (such as Formal Prayer and Fasting).

The parallels between Sufism and Eastern philosophies are deep and many-faceted. Below are some principles shared by Sufism and Eastern thought alike:

The original nature of man is good.

The clearest expression of this widespread Eastern perception is found in Mencius: "Human beings are inherently good."[2] In the *Great Commentary* on the *Book of Changes*, it is stated that the Tao "is good...it is the essence." The essence is that which all things are endowed with at their origin, and Richard Wilhelm observes that this was probably the passage on which Mencius based his doctrine.[3] Lao Tzu agrees that "the original nature of man is goodness." Even Hsün Tzu, the one notable exception to

---

2. *Mencius*, 6A:6.

this approach, merely claimed that human beings were *inclined* to evil,[4] and believed they could become good through education.

Sufism, too, embraces the concept of original innocence and refuses that of original sin. The Prophet said: "Every child is born according to his true nature (*fitra, hsing*)...just as animals produce their young with their limbs perfect."[5] A literal translation of verse 30:30 (Koran) reads, "God's innate nature with which He has 'natured' humankind." The natural disposition of human beings, in other words, is perfect. Likewise, the Chinese word *hsing* (essence, nature) is also translated as "human nature," indicating that *fitra* and *hsing* are one.

Look at a baby. How beautiful it is, how pure, how innocent! How can anyone even imagine that such a wonderful creature, so full of joy and so much in need of loving care, could have anything to do with evil? Everyone remembers from their early childhood how clear and untainted the world appeared before we all got sucked into its mire. Little children are already pure. Neither is the world itself bad, but it is rather tainted good or bad by the actions of human beings.

Spiritual self-cultivation is essential.

If this is the case, to what does the world owe its less-than-perfect state? According to Mencius, "the true character of man is good; however, the evil mind arises by the temptation of material desires. Therefore, man should cultivate his mind himself

---

3. *Ta Chuan* (The Great Treatise), 1.5.2, in *The I Ching or Book of Changes,* tr. Richard Wilhelm/Cary F. Baynes, Bollingen Series 19, Princeton, NJ: Princeton University Press, 1973 [1950], p. 298 and *ibid.,* n3.

4. Laurence G. Thompson, *Chinese Religion: An Introduction,* 4th ed., Belmont, CA: Wadsworth, 1989 [1979], p. 16.

5. *Bukhari,* Book 77 (Qadar):597; *Muslim,* Book 33 (Qadar):6423. The remainder of the saying states that a child grows up to become what it is, and the follower of another religion, according to the way its parents raise it.

and exhibit his own true character." Chuang Tzu, Wang Pi, and many other Eastern philosophers called for a "return to the true and natural character of man." As the *Great Learning* puts it, "From the king down to the common people, all must regard the cultivation of the self as the most essential thing."

The Prophet said, "Begin with your own self." According to Sufism, the original pearl, the pure nature, becomes encrusted with impurities in the course of time. Spiritual cultivation of the self means that the pearl should be cleansed of these barnacles and restored to its original state. The main factor responsible for this degeneration, says Sufism, is "the self that commands to evil" (*nafs al-ammara bis-sui,* 12:53), or "Base Self" for short. As the Prophet explained, "Your worst enemy is the self between your two sides." This is the source of selfishness, egotism, and impure desires. Hence it must be tamed, subdued, brought to a quiescent state, so that further spiritual progress may become possible. This need for quiescence is also recognized by the Taoists, and has been called "Quietism" in the West, though the latter term may be misleading. In Sufism, the purification of the self is a difficult and lengthy process requiring great effort; nevertheless, it is feasible. Seven basic stages can be distinguished in the development of the self, during which it rises from the Base Self at the beginning to the (wholly) Purified Self at the end. This is to climb the Cosmic Mountain in order to reach the Peak of Unification. There, looking at the horizons and in one's self (41:53), one knows that all one's troubles have been worth it. As the Sufi poet Niyazi Misri puts it:

If the emperor of the entire world heard of this
He would give his life for just a drop of it.

Human beings are the acme of creation.

The ancient Chinese recognized three realms: Heaven, Earth, and Man. (The Koran often speaks of the heavens and the earth—a plurality of heavens is also recognized in the *I Ching*.) In his ideal form, as a sage, Man would form a bridge between Heaven and Earth, and all beings would coexist in harmony. According to Tsung-mi, fifth patriarch of Huayen (Kegon) Buddhism, the human being is the highest of all existences.

> The Yellow Emperor said: 'Covered by Heaven and supported by Earth, all creation together in its most complete perfection is planned for the greatest achievement: Man.'[6]

Likewise, Islam regards the human being as "the most honorable of creatures" (*ashraf al-mahluqa*). God states in the Book that He has "honored" human beings (17:70): "Surely We created man in the best of statures" (95:4). In Sufism, Man is seen as the recipient of all the Divine Names and Attributes—he is a miniature version of the cosmos. Sheikh Galib, a leading Turkish Sufi poet, wrote the following couplet:

> *Regard yourself with favor, for you are the elect of the universe*
> *You are a human being—the pupil[7] of the universe's eye.*

But why is man so dear? Because, according to Galib, the universe is not large enough to encompass the full potentials of the

---

6. Ilza Veith (tr.), *The Yellow Emperor's Classic of Internal Medicine (Huang Ti Nei Ching Su Wen)*, Berkeley, CA: University of California Press, 1973 [1949], p. 213.
7. Or apple.

human spirit. Rarely if ever has this notion been better expressed in all the poetry of the world:

> *The candle of the soul has such a flame*
> *As will not fit under the bell jar of the heavens*

Again, here is Rumi:

> *The attribute of man is to manifest God's signs.*
> *Whatever is seen in man is the reflection of God,*
> *Even as the reflection of the moon in water.*[8]

Or, coming closer to the fount of Revelation, consider this poem by Ali, the Fourth Caliph:

> *Your pain is from you, but you see not*
> *Your cure is in you, but you know not*
> *In you has been placed the whole cosmos*
> *Yet you still deem yourself something small*

In Sufic cosmology, God formed all things out of His attributes, which are referred to by His names. Everything is an "interference pattern" of some, even many, such names. But it is the human being who is God's masterpiece, because he brings together all names and attributes within himself. As the Neo-Confucianist Chou Tun-yi expressed it, "It is man alone, however, who receives [the *yin* and *yang*] in their highest excellence and hence is the most intelligent [of all beings]."

---

8. Rumi, *Mathnawi,* http://arthurwendover.com/arthurs/islam/
mathnv10.html, accessed June 18, 2004.

Tolerance

Tolerance is an essential characteristic of Eastern philosophies. Prince Shotoku, who introduced Buddhism to Japan, wrote in the tenth article of his constitution: "Forget resentment, forsake anger, do not become angry just because someone opposes you...if you are not quite a saint, neither is he quite an idiot." In a similar vein, the Turkish Sufi poet Yunus Emre sang: "Because of the Creator, be tolerant towards what is created." The Sufi saint Ahmet Kayhan taught that even a fly or a dangerous animal should be rescued if it is in distress. The following poem by a Turkish Sufi, Father Hulusi,[9] summarizes the ethics of Islamic spirituality in a nutshell:

Don't think the world is your servant or your slave
For the sake of the Real, be the servant and slave of the world

Don't be vain or deluded by the caprices of the self
Let feet step on your chest, be the path for every foot

For the sake of God, respect everyone, love and be loved
Don't be a thorn to every eye: be their hyacinth, their rose

Serve each living thing without grudge or expectation
Be the feet and hands of the destitute and poor

Offend no one, nor be offended by them
Be of smiling mien, sweet of tongue, the honey of every mouth

Even if you wreck the Kaaba by siding with your self
Don't give offense, don't break a heart, though you be wise or mad

---

9. Mevlevi dervish from Konya (1752-1811).

Be lovingkind like the sun, modest like earth
Like water be generous, full of compassion

A dervish should be on the way, has no reputation to bolster
Forgive the guilty their crimes, be tolerant

Empty your being that you may achieve Nothingness
Speak your words truthfully, become the tongue of Hulusi.

Filial piety.

The deep reverence felt by Eastern people for their ancestors is well-known. Confucius "maintained that the best way to honor our ancestors is to honor and respect our parents, and by extension, our other blood relatives."[10] Reverence and concern for them, and fulfilling their aims while they are still alive, are better than offering sacrifice to their spirits once they are dead. The Zen priest Bankei taught that benevolence to parents was of the utmost importance: "You should respect them. This is filial piety. To follow the way of filial piety is Buddhahood. Filial piety and Buddhahood are not different." In other words, charity begins in the home; a person disrespectful of one's parents has no chance of becoming a sage, a perfect human being.

This sentiment is echoed by Sufism. In the Koran, the Heavenly Classic, it is written:

Be kind to parents
Whether one or both of them attains old age with you,
Say not a word of contempt to them, nor chide them,
But speak unto them words respectful,

---

10. Laurence C. Wu, *Fundamentals of Chinese Philosophy,* Lanham, MD: University Press of America, 1986, p. 22.

And lower to them the wing of humbleness
Out of mercy and say, "My Lord, have mercy upon them,
Even as they cherished me in childhood." (17:23-24)

We have enjoined on a human being
Kindness to his/her parents; his mother bore him painfully,
And in pain she gave birth to him.
His bearing and his weaning are thirty months.
At length, he is fully grown, and reaches forty years. (46:15)

His mother bore him
In weakness upon weakness...
Be grateful to Me, and to your parents. (31:14)

The Prophet's words: "Heaven lies under the feet of mothers," underlines the fact that only by pleasing one's mother can one enter the Pure Land. Needless to say, this does not exclude the father. According to Sufi lore, although the prophet Abraham disapproved of his father's idolatry, he would carry him on his shoulders when his father's worship was done and they were returning home. Care and concern should be extended to relatives as well: "God enjoins justice, good works, and looking after needy relatives." (16:90)

Sagehood or buddhahood.

"The sage," said Mencius, "is the acme of human relations" (*Mencius*, 4A:2), which means, literally, that the sage is the morally perfect human being. This is echoed in the Sufic concept of the "Perfect Human" (*insan al-kaamil*, called *jen ren* in Chinese). But moral perfection is a step to something higher. Mencius continues: "He who has completely developed his mind, knows his nature. He who knows his nature, knows Heaven." (7A:1) Or, in the words of the Prophet, "He who knows his self knows his Lord." The result is Enlightenment, a state where, according to the Ch'an (Zen) masters, "there ceases to be distinction between the experiencer and the experienced,"[11] between subject and object, which is Unity (*wahdah*) in Sufic terms.

According to Mencius (6B:2) as well as Sufism, all men can become sages. Every single human being has this potential, for this is the goal for which human beings were expressly designed. Not everyone will become a sage or a buddha, of course, but this has more to do with individual inclination and struggle than with innate capacity.

Optimism.

In Eastern thought, the identification of nature with the Absolute led to the appreciation that nature is beautiful and the world, a good place to live in. This is an optimistic view, also shared by Sufism. To paraphrase the Prophet, "If you know that the end of the world is tomorrow, do not hesitate to plant a tree today." One should hope for the best and be constant in Right Action just as if life will go on as usual. "What's the use" would be a gesture of hopelessness and despair. "Be hopeful, be brave," the Master always advised. We have seen above that the original nature of human beings is regarded as good, which is itself an optimistic view.

Mo Tzu and his followers regarded the universe as wonderfully good. It is, in their conception, ruled over by Shang Ti, the Heavenly Ancestor or Sovereign on High, a personal God who "loves men dearly...Heaven loves the whole world universally. Everything is prepared for the good of man."[12] According to

---

11. *Recorded Sayings of Ancient Worthies, chüan* 32, quoted in Fung Yu-lan, *A Short History of Chinese Philosophy,* Derk Bodde (ed.), New York: Macmillan Free Press, 1966 [1948], p. 262.

the Koran, "God has created all things with the greatest goodness and beauty" (32:7). The Sufi Sheikh Geylani adds: "Men use expressions such as 'good' or 'beautiful' for things relative to their selves, and things that are disagreeable they call 'evil' or 'ugly.' But for one who knows the Truth, there is no distinction whatever; all that is created is precious…It is for this reason that the one who has matured in his perception of reality does not see fault or flaws in creation."[13]

Calamities are part of life. There may come a point when even the most optimistic despair. Yet, if we persevere in patience, we will both see the end of it, and realize the fact that God transforms evil into good, just as He brings life out of death and causes death to emerge from life (3:27). To quote from Ibrahim Hakki's long poem on trusting God:

Bad things to good, God modifies
Think not He does otherwise
Always watched on by the wise—
  What God will ordain, let us see
  Whatever He does, well does He

Since matters are in God's hands, vain
Is any confusion or pain
He unfolds Wisdom divine
  What God will ordain, let us see
  Whatever He does, well does He

Do not say: "Why is this so?"
It is good that it is so
Look, see how the end will go

---

12. Quoted in Huston Smith, *The Religions of Man,* New York: Harper Perennial, 1958, p. 173.
13. Abdulqader Geylani, *Treatise on Divine Aid* (*Risala al-Gawsiyya*).

What God will ordain, let us see
Whatever He does, well does He
Just when your hopes are down to nil
Suddenly He parts a veil
He grants solace from every ill
What God will ordain, let us see
Whatever He does, well does He[14]

Good and evil, the Golden Rule, the Golden Mean.

The Taoists taught that "one must not perform evil, but do good," a path which would finally result in one's becoming a sage, a superhuman being. And Prince Shotoku stated in his 17-article constitution: "Chastise that which is evil and encourage that which is good. This was the excellent rule of antiquity." The same principle occurs in Islam as "enjoin the good and forbid the evil" (*amr bil-maruf, nahy an al-munkar*). (In a careful translation, William Chittick renders good as "honor" and evil as "dishonor," which highlights the shame of doing evil.[15])

The Golden Rule: "Do as you would be done by," is perhaps the most universal principle of ethics. It can be found in all religions and amongst all peoples. Here is how Confucius expressed it: "Do not impose on others what you yourself do not desire."[16] And the Prophet Muhammad: "No one of you is a believer until he desires for his brother what he desires for himself."

The Golden Mean (a.k.a. the Happy Medium): "Avoid excess," has been favored by Taoist and Confucianist alike. Their motto is "Never too much," reflecting the conviction that overdoing

---

14. Ibrahim Hakki of Erzurum, *Tefviizname* ("Put Your Trust in God"), stanzas 1, 7, 11, 16. I have tried to emulate the rhyme and meter of the original.
15. William C. Chittick, *Sufism: A Short Introduction,* Oxford: Oneworld, 2000, p. 55.
16. *Analects,* 15:24.

things may cause harm beyond repair, whereas it is frequently possible to increase what is insufficient. In Eastern philosophy, man and nature are not opposed to each other, but exist (or should exist) in harmony. In order to harmonize with nature and live in peace, the harmony of all beings is necessary, which leads to the idea of moderation.

In Sufism, moderation is likewise essential. "In prayer be neither loud nor hushed, but seek a middle course between." (17:110) The Prophet himself always exercised and advised moderation: "Whoever goes to extremes, is ruined." This applies to everything—even to worship, even to love. One should err neither on the side of too much (*ifrat*), nor of too little (*tefrit*). The Koran praises "those who, when they spend, are neither wasteful nor miserly." (25:67) The following verse surely has ecological import: "Eat, drink, but do not be wasteful; God does not love those who waste." (7:31)

In charity, too, one should observe the median. "Give the relatives their right, and the needy, and the traveller, but do not squander…Do not keep your hand tied, nor stretch it out widespread, or you will become blameworthy and destitute." (17:26, 29)

A tied hand means to be tight-fisted. A Turkish saying teases out the meaning of the verse. When one locks one's hand into a fist, no water can enter it. On the other hand, if one stretches out an open palm, water cannot remain in one's hand. But if one curves one's fingers to form one's palm into a cup, water can be held in it, both for one's own use and for offering those in need. If one is a tightwad, one ceases to prosper and does not benefit society; if one gives everything away, there is nothing left to support oneself and one's own family. In either case, one becomes blameworthy and destitute. Again, moderation is counseled.

The Use of Edifying Stories.

Sometimes the stories of East Asia and Sufi teaching-stories are so similar that it is difficult to tell which belongs to which. The reader is invited to guess the sources of the following tales:

The Man Born Blind: There was a man born blind. He had never seen the sun and asked about it of people who could see. Someone told him, "the sun's shape is like a brass tray." The blind man struck the brass tray and heard its sound. Later when he heard the sound of a bell, he thought it was the sun. Again someone told him, "The sunlight is like that of a candle," and the blind man felt the candle, and thought that was the sun's shape. Later he felt a big key and thought it was a sun.

The sun is quite different from a bell or a key, but the blind man cannot tell their difference because he has never seen the sun. The Truth is harder to see than the sun, and when people do not know it they are exactly like the blind man. Even if you do your best to explain by analogies and examples, it still appears like the analogy of the brass tray and the candle. From what is said of the brass tray, one imagines a bell, and from what is said about a candle, one imagines a key. In this way, one gets ever further and further away from the truth. Those who speak about Truth sometimes give it a name according to what they happen to see, or imagine what it is like without seeing it. These are mistakes in the effort to understand Truth.

The Elephant in the Dark: Some Hindus had brought an elephant for show to a town that had never seen an elephant before. As it happened, however, they arrived at night, and had to put it in a huge barn where there was no light. The people, all agog with curiosity, took turns going in. But in the darkness, they had to get by with their sense of touch. One of them happened to feel its trunk, and thought the animal was like a hose, a pipe. Another felt its ear, and thought the animal was fan-like. Another touched its back, and became convinced that it was like a saddle. Another grasped its leg, and thought of a pillar; still another felt the tusk, and thought of a rounded porcelain sword. Whereas if they had used a candle and all gone in together, they would have seen it for what it was.

Both stories, of course, are telling us about God, about Ultimate Reality, and our difficulty in comprehending Him. The first uses blindness as a metaphor for the human condition and the sun as a metaphor for God. The second uses darkness and the elephant, respectively, and it has also been retold as applying to blind men.

Only prior knowledge will help in discerning the sources of these tales: the first belongs to the Chinese poet Su Tung-po[17] and the second to the Sufi poet Rumi.[18] But if this order had been reversed, would it have made much difference?

Enlightenment And Gnosis, Buddhahood and Prophethood

The term "enlightenment" (*bodhi, satori, wu*) is called, in Sufic technical terminology, "Gnosis" (*marifa*), "union, arrival, attainment" (*wuslat*) and "union, unity" (*wahdah*). Gnosis is "knowledge that illuminates," and its full name—God-knowledge (*marifa Allah*)—is indicative of this quality.

---

17. Related in Lin Yutang, *The Wisdom of China and India,* New York: Random House, 1942, p. 1067. I have made some minor editorial changes and substituted Truth for Tao, a change suggested by Yutang himself.
18. *Mathnaiw* III, 1259-69.

Enlightenment is an eminently acceptable term from the Sufic standpoint, because God is Light (*al-Nur*). As the famous Light Verse puts it, "God is the Light of the heavens and the earth...Light upon Light!" (24:35) Since the goal in Sufism is the Summit of Unification, where only God exists, it is clear that the climb to that peak entails increasing levels of enlightenment. And indeed, Sufis speak of the appearance of various "lights" (*anwar*) during the long ascent to the top. Shihabuddin Suhrawardi used the term "sunrise, enlightenment" (*ishraq*) to describe the illumination that occurs when the Sun of the spiritual world is born in one's Heart.

Here a short digression may serve to justify the translation of "prophet" as "buddha" or "bodhisattva." "Prophet" is *nabi* in both the Semitic languages Hebrew and Arabic, and derives from *nabiim* or *naba*. "These terms come from a group of cognate words which have nothing to do with time [or prophesying the future], but rather with flowing and becoming bright."[19] In Arabic, *naba* means 1. news, message (whence "Messenger" or prophet) and 2. (sometimes rapid) elevation. Now all these concepts actually describe a spiritual Ascension (*meeraj*), for one Ascends via a beam of white light that emanates from God, who is Light (24:35). (One becomes brighter as light flows out below.) It appears, then, that the original term *nabi* was much more expressive of the truth, and we would thus not be far wrong in linguistically equating "prophet" with *buddha* ("enlightened, awakened") or *bodhisattva* ("enlightened being"), perhaps also rescuing its primal sense in the process. Since "Buddha" means "awakened" or "enlightened," in my opinion there is nothing wrong in calling the Prophet a Buddha (Muhammed Butsu, Ahmed-i Fo).

---

19. Julian Jaynes, *The Origin of Consciousness in the Breakdown of the Bicameral Mind,* Boston: Houghton Mifflin, 1977, pp. 299-300.

All these parallels suggest that East Asian philosophies/religions and Sufism draw their inspiration from the same wellspring of Truth. It becomes worthwhile, therefore, to investigate whether Sufism may in fact represent their natural culmination. I believe this is an unexpected situation, and we shall be concerned to see how this initially counterintuitive conclusion may be justified.

To be sure, there have always been followers of the separate paths of Taoism, Buddhism and Confucianism. Yet the great majority of East Asians have always recognized that each of these have their respective merits, and have even embraced the "Three Teachings" as one (or Four or even Five Teachings, if you also count Shinto and Zen separately).

This, however, is easier said than done. For all these teachings contain points that are not easily harmonized, and sometimes are even mutually contradictory. Here, Sufism can help show which parts in each fit together in what way, exactly. The result is a picture of breath-taking harmony, for it takes Absolute Reality (God) as its centerpiece, who is the source of all harmony and purity. Harmony requires two things: consistency and comprehensiveness. For if two things are inconsistent, they cannot be in harmony with each other. And a harmony that is partial (harmonious in some respects and not so in others) is only a mixture of harmony and discord. Ideally, all parts of a teaching should be in consonance with one another. When all the elements of a teaching are in "constructive interference" with each other, mutually supporting and completing other elements, then that teaching is truly harmonious. Sufism can show the way by lighting the path to the achievement of true harmony.

I have found that Sufism can also help to "fill in the blanks." Take Zen, for instance. Most people agree, of course, that it is highly oblique, perhaps to an extent even incomprehensible. When one looks at the sayings of Zen masters, one finds three categories: the first is quite normal, even ordinary, in accordance with everyday speech (at least in translation). Certainly the Zen masters were as entitled as anyone else to talk the talk of ordinary life; this does not necessarily mean that everything they uttered had to be profound, even when recorded. The second is suggestive, but only an enlightened person may understand what it suggests. The third expresses a deep and sublime truth, but even here the true meaning is not immediately apparent. What we can do is to use the insights of Sufism to discriminate between these categories, and to draw out the profound meaning where this exists.[20]

---

20. To give some examples:
   "I hold a sword with empty hands." Here, "sword" is symbolic of the spirit and its power, "held" within the body.
   "I run on foot on the back of an ox." The ox symbolizes the self (*nafs*), which has to be subdued if spiritual progress is to be possible. The bull in the famous "Ten Bulls" sequence also stands for the self.
   "The water does not flow, the bridge flows." The Way takes us ahead, across an ever-changing but actually static world ("static" in the sense that the same kinds of events are repeated incessantly). The bridge stands for the Master of Wisdom, who acts as an escalator for those wishing to progress spiritually.
   "What is the sound of one hand clapping?" It is the same as the sound of silence—not ordinary silence, but the silence from which all sound proceeds. As such, it is the equivalent of the "Uncarved Block" of the Taoists, called "unconditioned Brahman" in Hinduism and the stage of "indetermination" (*la taayyun*) in Sufism. The sound of one hand clapping is nothing less than the One (*Ahad*) in the act of creating the entire universe.
   There is something very much like Zen in Sufism—the terse answers, the enigmatic aspects.

Overview

The plan of the book is as follows. Chapter 1 introduces our subject by treating a time-honored Japanese institution, the Tea Ceremony, from a Sufic point of view. Although the Tea Ceremony is primarily a work of art, there is a symbolism hidden within it that can be teased out by applying a Sufic interpretation. Chapter 2 deals with matters of faith: faith in one's master, in the founder of the religion, and in God.

Chapter 3 is devoted to a ticklish subject—war. Although war is undesirable, yet humanity has not been able to escape it throughout its history. But now, the existence of unprecedentedly hideous weapons of mass destruction forces upon humanity a closure to war.

Chapter 4 deals with the concept of Unity, and the correlates that it brings in its train: truth, beauty, and goodness; peace, harmony, love, equality, and intimacy. The chapter ends with a description of the Pole of the Age. There is a Sufic pole (highest sage) in every age, and the qualities of such a person are described.

God and nature have often been set up against each other. Yet such an opposition is not only illogical, it is also untrue. This is the subject of Chapter 5, where it is found that the most sensitive and perceptive nature poets have never been in doubt that nature is the garment of God. Chapter 6 leads on to discuss the afterlife as a continuation of the present life. If one has purified oneself in this life, the reward cannot be anything except the Pure Land. Reincarnation is also treated in this chapter as an alternative scheme of recompense, and its incompatibility with the first is investigated.

Chapter 7 takes up the subject of God in East Asian culture. Although there has not been a strong trend of monotheism in

East Asia, yet the sages of various traditions have never been too far from the truth. It is only a slight rearrangement that will help us to discern this universal truth within East Asian wisdom as well. Especially important in this context is the concept of "*nirvana* in Brahman*," developed on the basis of an insight provided solely by Sufism. The chapter ends with the realization that "there is no deity but God."

Chapter 8 investigates a question of the utmost importance: why is there reference to emptiness rather than God in eastern mysticism? Here, a Sufic concept again comes to the rescue, allowing us to gain a deeper understanding of what is really meant by the Void. (This chapter is philosophically the most taxing, and may be skipped, but it is also one of the most important.) The investigation of selflessness brings us to the crucial realization that there can be no personal realization in the absence of ethics, and certain ethical points are mentioned in this context. In a nutshell, the esoteric cannot exist without the exoteric—the two are inseparably intertwined. This helps us to understand, in Chapter 9, why Confucian ethics, which may be treated as a subset of Islamic ethics, is so important.

Eastern mysticism reaches its highest peaks in a singular concept, Indra's Net. Chapter 10 deals with this both from the East Asian and Sufic points of view, leading to the conclusion that Indra's Net cannot even be considered apart from God.

The prime requirement of all East Asian thought, cultivation of the self, is also the requirement of Sufism. Chapter 11 discusses the stages of the self as outlined in Sufism, and the necessity of transcending the ground level, i.e. the Base Self, is emphasized. This chapter is also the heaviest in terms of teaching-stories, both Sufic and new. Finally, the culmination of self-cultivation is taken up in Chapter 12, by recourse to the points of contact between the most esoteric Eastern meditative techniques and Sufism.

cs   cs   cs

We have seen in this introduction that there is common ground, a vast area of intersection, between Sufism and East Asian thought. Some of these, mentioned above, were the original goodness of human nature, the importance of spiritual self-cultivation, human beings as the goal of creation, tolerance, love and respect for one's parents, sagehood or buddhahood, optimism, similar conceptions regarding good and evil, the Golden Rule, and the Golden Mean, and the use of teaching-stories. Sufic "Gnosis" is the equivalent of East Asian Enlightenment, and a prophet, or sage, may also be called a buddha.

All these parallels indicate that there is much to be gained by a study of Sufism in relation to the philosophies of East Asia. Of course, the latter diverge even among themselves, yet the framework provided by Sufism can lead to a higher synthesis of the compatible points in each of these philosophies within that framework.

The plan of the book has been outlined in an overview.

We are now ready to embark on our journey, and our first step will be the Tea Ceremony. Until now, of course, everyone has taken it at face value—there has been no reason to suspect the presence of anything deeper. Yet every aspect of the ceremony yields surprising insights when viewed under the ultraviolet light of Sufism. What secrets does it hold, and how may we decipher them?

I

SECRETS OF THE TEA CEREMONY

THE BUTTERFLY

A pang of sorrow
At its fleeting beauty
Even so are we
Here today
Gone tomorrow

January 1997 found me in Mecca. I was able to catch my first glimpse of the Kaaba ("the Cube") during that visit. Our guides had instructed us that, for maximum effect, one should not look at the Kaaba for the first time until one was up close. This we did, and my first sighting of it was almost from the border of the white marble platform surrounding it. I raised my head, and there it was—the Kaaba, draped in black, in all its radiant splendor!

I stood staring, then moved into a side aisle. Suddenly, I was suffused by an intense fragrance of tea, stronger than any I have felt before or since. This, I realized, was an experience granted only to me, for no one else remarked the occasion. I took this as a portent of wakefulness, of increased consciousness, and my thoughts were immediately drawn to China. For it was in China where tea was first discovered—its powers to awaken the mind were noticed, and its brew was first used by Zen monks during their long vigils of meditation. And, as Gustav Meyrink wrote,

"To be awake is *everything*." The very name of the Buddha means "the Awakened."

Tea and its accompanying ceremony traveled from China to Japan, and was there received so enthusiastically that the latter is known as the home of the Tea Ceremony (*cha-no-yu*, "hot-water of tea"). Of course, the Japanese have valued the Tea Ceremony as an aesthetic experience, where the beauty, humility, and tranquility of the attending souls are reflected in the arrangements in the environment, making of it an exquisite event. Nevertheless, it is possible to discern a spiritual symbolism as well in the elements of the Tea Ceremony.

The Tea Ceremony in its entirety is symbolic of the approach to higher consciousness, in keeping with its origin among the Zen masters. The host, or tea-master, is symbolic of the spiritual master who imparts to us the wisdom that leads to the Great Awakening, while the elixir of immortality is symbolized by tea. In Sufism, as in the tea ceremony, one approaches the house of the master with the highest courtesy, with sincerity and humility. The slightest frivolity would be inexcusable. It is for this reason that it is said in Sufism: "Enter the presence of the sages with courtesy, be showered in their bounty, and depart with wisdom." It is explained that discourteous behavior blocks the *baraka* (spiritual blessings) of the master, and distances its owner from the heart of the sage.

Since we have come upon the Sufi concept of courtesy (*adab*), perhaps I might dwell upon it for a moment. Courtesy combines gentleness, peacefulness, cheerfulness, accomodation, and consideration for others. Shuko, who formulated the basics of the Tea Ceremony, emphasized four qualities above all others in the participants: harmony, reverence, purity, and tranquility (*wa-kei-sei-jaku*). To these, the great tea-master Rikyu added a fifth: sincerity (*ch'eng*), nondeception. Closely allied with these is gentleness of spirit, softness of heart, or tender-mindedness (another reading of the character for "harmony"); simplicity, lack of ostentation, unpretentiousness (*sabi*); and spiritual poverty (*wabi*).

A Comparison between Japanese and Sufic Terms of Courtesy.

Elements of courtesy	Japanese	Sufism
Harmony, gentleness	*wa*	*hilm*
Reverence	*kei*	*hurmah*
Purity	*sei*	*safiyah*
Tranquility	*jaku*	*sukuun*
Sincerity	*ch'eng*	*ikhlas*
Modesty/solitude	*sabi*	*tawazu / halwat*
Spiritual poverty	*wabi*	*faqr*

Now as a matter of fact, these qualities exactly describe courtesy (*adab*) as it is required in Sufism. (Courtesy may be defined as good manners, exemplary conduct, gentleness, being a gentle(wo)man, to be well-behaved, politeness, elegance, refinement.) Only students who possess these qualities can benefit from an audience with their teacher. They constitute right action arising from right thinking. Spiritual progress means that these qualities should increase, become more enhanced, in the seeker. Even in combat, one must be respectful towards one's enemies—not only because today's enemy may become tomorrow's friend, but because, although circumstances may momentarily have cast both sides in opposition, the enemy is as much a human being as oneself. And the highest stage of courtesy is the highest destiny man can attain. According to a Sufi couplet:

> *Courtesy is a crown, made of the light of God*
> *Wear that crown, and be safe from all calamities.*

Put on the "force-field" of courtesy, in other words, and you can wander across the earth without fear. Sheikh Saadi of Shiraz, a Sufi of great renown, elaborates: "A person of bad habit is a prisoner of his own habit. No matter where he goes, he cannot escape the grip and worry of that habit. Even if such a person were to rise up into the sky in order to escape calamity, he will still be in calamity due to that bad habit."

An integral part of courtesy is that everything connected with religion should be shown proper respect. Dogen, for example, teaches: "If one is disrespectful of a priest because he is a hardened sinner, a statue because it is poorly done, a copy of the sutras because it is battered, then he certainly commits a sin. For...the statue, the scroll of scripture, and the priest contribute to the happiness of [human beings]. Therefore, one certainly profits by respecting them. One who treats them without faith is guilty of sin." It was in this spirit that the Zen monk Renyo, when he found a piece of paper passing through a corridor, raised it above his head, murmuring that one should not waste a thing of the Buddha's possession.

This is reminiscent of the story of the famed Sufi poet Hafiz (also of Shiraz):

> Earlier in his life, Hafiz was a drunkard having little to do with religion. One day, as he was staggering across the street, he saw a piece of paper in the gutter among the filth. Curious, he picked it up. The name of God was written on it.
>
> "Woe that I should see Your name fallen into such places!" Hafiz cried, brushed it off, and handled the paper with reverence. That night he had a dream. In the dream, a voice told him: "Hafiz, you have raised up My name from where it was, and I shall elevate your name among human beings." This is how Hafiz began his career as a Sufi saint.

The Tea Ceremony

The purpose of the tea ceremony is to cultivate beauty and harmony in the activities of everyday life. Every motion, performed with economy, must flow rhythmically into the next one. In seeing this silent symphony of motion, one is led to rapt adoration of the beautiful that can be manifested in performing the simplest chores.

Let us first describe the various aspects of the Tea Ceremony. One follows a winding garden path through the woods before catching sight of the Tea Room, or Tea Hut. An irregularly arranged series of flagstones leads up to an insignificant-looking, unpretentious hut. One may rinse one's mouth and wash one's hands in a stone water basin as a preparatory purification. These ablutions underline the second most essential fact about the ceremony—that the physical body, as well as the heart-mind (*kokoro*), should be cleansed. Bending over at this instant, one may catch a glimpse of the shimmering sea through the trees, an unexpected glimpse of infinity. Japanese people delight in doing kind deeds in secret, to be discovered only accidentally, if at all. It is the same refinement that leads them to conceal charming things in their garden which only a keen observer can discern.

There is a low aperture, not a door, that leads inside. One must leave all unnecessary trappings outside to crawl through the aperture into the tea-room. The purpose of this form of entrance is to inculcate humility and equality. This is a small bamboo or wooden hut with a low ceiling, sparely furnished, having a plain, unfinished appearance. Even in daytime, the light is subdued. The interior is spotlessly clean. Burning incense lends a soothing fragrance to the interior. In an alcove, there is a piece of calligraphy or a picture. A flower vase contains a single, humble flower. Every item in the room is arranged in harmony.

There is a square hole cut into the floor in which a fire burns. Over it, a heavy iron kettle contains boiling water, and emits a sound like a breeze sighing through a pine grove, adding serenity to the room. The hut does not muffle the sounds coming from the outside environment, but serves only to exclude the harsher elements. This gives a feeling as if one were in communion with nature, with the rustling trees and twittering birds, while being protected by the flimsy hut. The overall effect helps one to realize the beauty of simplicity and purity. The tea-room is the house of peace.

Both the tea ceremony and its host must be approached in a spirit of reverence. Every tea ceremony is a once-in-a-lifetime occurence: even if one participates in others, this unique occasion, in this moment with this host, will never be repeated again. So one must appreciate its worth.

The host first brings the tea utensils—such as the bowls and tea-whisk—into the room. A light meal may precede the serving of tea. The guests are offered sweets, and then tea is prepared and served. The tea is prepared by stirring pulverized tea leaf in hot water with the tea-whisk. It is usually thin and frothy with a mildly astringent flavor. Sometimes, a much thicker "dark tea" is made. After the tea is consumed, the guests may inquire about the various implements. These are then carried out of the room, and the tea ceremony is concluded.

The tea ceremony originated in the principles of Zen Buddhism and came to be considered a method of self-realization. The well-known wakeful effect of imbibing tea helped Zen priests to keep their minds alert during concentration. The myth that the first tea plants were formed from the eyelids of Bodhidharma, who cut them off and dropped them on the ground in his struggle to remain awake, underlines the awakening influence of tea. Monks would gather before an image of Bodhidharma and drink tea out of a single bowl as if it were a sacrament, a holy nectar. The tea-room design resulted from emulation of the Zen monastery. Zen itself originated as a synthesis of Taoism and Buddhism, and the Taoists claimed tea as an essential ingredient of the Elixir of Immortality.

As one sits sipping tea, one's mind goes back to the origin of things. One is reminded of the transience of this world, of the evanescence of life. The sharing of tea is not an end in itself but a means to an end—namely, the cultivation of the five essential qualities of courtesy: sincerity, harmony, respect, cleanliness, and tranquility.

Awakening to the One

To be awake, we have seen, is everything. And this awakening is what tea assists us in.

The most essential thing to wake up to is this:

All powers are one Power.

All spirits are ultimately one Spirit.

The 8 (or 80, or 800) million kami are One Kami.

All things are manifestations of one Great Unity who is all-pure, all-wise, all-powerful, and all-knowing. Without this Unity, harmony between things—and indeed, things themselves—could not exist. Everything is sacred, because they are all parts of the One Great Sacred. The material form or symbol does not represent some *other* and higher reality entirely unrelated to itself, but is a subset of that reality. We do not err, as long as we recognize that the signified is *more* than just the sign, as long as we do not confuse the finger that points to the moon with the moon itself.

But how can this be? How can all powers be one Power? We see boundless diversity wherever we look. Not even two plums are the same as each other, and this is far more true of a pine tree and a butterfly.

Think of electricity. We use it in our homes today without giving it a second thought. When we turn on a lamp, it gives light. When we turn on an electric stove, it gives heat. When we turn on the radio, it emits sound, voices and songs of every variety. When we turn on the TV, it gives us pictures of everything you can imagine. And when we turn on the computer, it gives us information from across the globe. *Yet it is all the same electricity.*

All these household articles have been designed for a specific purpose, or range of purposes. A television is very unlike a stove, and a lamp is very unlike a radio. Yet they all run on electricity, and the instant we cut off their power, they all fall mute and lifeless.

In the same way, all things are the works of the Great Spirit. He is within all things, within the trees, the grasses, the rivers, the mountains, within all the animals and birds.[21] But even more important, He is also above all these things and life-forms which He has designed and formed. As his father tells Svetaketu in the *Chandogya Upanishad*, if one strikes a tree in any of its parts, it will bleed, but live, because it is pervaded by the Great Self who is the Living. But if the Self were to depart from a branch, that branch would wither, and if the Self were to depart from the whole tree, the whole tree would wither. Likewise, the body dies when the Self leaves it—but the Self does not die.

---

21. The acupuncture points are the points at which the spiritual (subtle) body is coupled to the physical body, introducing the spiritual energy that infuses and animates matter. The Chinese landscape art/science of *feng shui* is an extension of this concept to the earth.

The universe of forms which we perceive is, according to Sufism, constituted of the Attributes and Actions of God; but God also has an Essence, which is beyond and prior to all form. It is this essence that Tao Sheng (a precursor of Ch'an/Zen) is referring to when he says: "Reality is not reflected in the images of what surrounds us here, but Real is what existed before this began to exist."[22]

Peace comes to the souls of men when they realize their oneness with the universe and all its powers, and that at the center of the universe dwells the Spirit of God. This center is really everywhere, in each one of us. Each natural form represents various aspects of the Great Spirit. But, says Sufism, only a human being has the potential to reflect *all* aspects, which is why human beings exist. The Unity of the Great Spirit is above all forms, because it is formless. This formless unity can be seen only with the Third Eye, the Eye of the Heart. This is the spiritual organ with which we know all that is good, true, and beautiful.

Human beings are many and varied. One person may like virtue. Another may love truth. A third may admire what is beautiful. But God in His bounty has provided a path for all. Because the organ of perception for all three is one, any of them can be led to God and are saved.

With this background information, we are now ready to look at the esoteric meaning of the Tea Ceremony.[23]

The Symbolism of the Tea Ceremony

We approach the "tea house" or tea hut through a grove or garden. The garden symbolizes the world of nature, the world of multiplicity we normally inhabit with all its kaleidoscopic phe-

---

22. Quoted in Edwin A. Burtt, *The Teachings of the Compassionate Buddha,* New York: New American Library (Mentor), 1955, p. 226.
23. Inspired in part by the writings of Joseph Epes Brown.

nomena. Passing through this world, we are approaching a momentous revelation: a state of higher wakefulness or higher consciousness.

Traveling along the winding path of life, one arrives at length at an unpretentious hut. Yet appearances can be deceptive. We should not be fooled by the humble appearance of the hut or of its host, because it symbolizes the Truth of the universe, and the tea master symbolizes the Master of Wisdom—the sage, or one who has already awakened—who will assist in our own awakening. The true meaning of life will then stand revealed. The hut is a microcosmos, at once the heart of the universe and the heart of man.

One washes using a basin in order to purify oneself physically. One must also purify one's heart/mind by doing good deeds and meditating on God. The Great Spirit, the spirit of all spirits, is all-purity. One must become pure and white as fresh snow in order to wake up to God's presence within oneself. To rinse one's mouth is to "speak no evil," and to wash one's hands is to "do no evil." This has the same meaning in the Ablution (*abdest/temizu*: literally, "hand-water") that precedes the Formal Prayer (*salat, namaz*). In order to approach God, one should be cleansed in heart and mind, and be clean physically from the top of the head to the tip of the toe. That which is impure cannot be united with that which is all purity.

The hut itself may be made of wood obtained from trees. In winter, trees shed their leaves and appear as if dead, yet in the spring they come to life again. Similarly, human beings die but live again in the real world of the Great Spirit. And we may know this true life even while here on earth, if we purify our bodies and minds.

Or the hut may be made of bamboo. Bamboo, because it is hollow, can also be used to make pipes for music. According to legend, the Chinese emperor Huang-ti wanted music to be played that would help establish his empire's harmony with the universe. Hence he sent a scholar, Ling Lun, to the western mountain to cut bamboo pipes that could emit sounds matching the call of the phoenix bird. The phoenix is a legendary bird that rises from its own ashes, and symbolizes the Perfect Human Being who "dies before s/he dies" to enter a different form of existence. The Complete Human then becomes a bridge between Heaven and Earth, harmonizing both. As for the bamboo pipe, it is a mode of the reed flute (*nay*) of Sufism, best known to us through its use in Rumi's poetry.

The sage, Rumi tells us, must make himself empty like a reed (or bamboo) pipe, so that the divine Spirit of God may be breathed into it. Emptiness, in other words, is not a goal but a precondition for the true goal. We must make ourselves empty, passive, receptive like the earth, in order that the Heavenly Lord, the Creative, the active, may enter into our hearts, may work His art within us—may turn us into awakened human beings. "The way of Yang is fullness and the way of Yin is emptiness."[24] Quiescence of the Base Self, humility, so that God's light may shine through: this is the true meaning of being a servant of God. It is to the reed pipe and this sublime inner meaning that Rumi refers below:

> *Hearken to this Reed forlorn,*
> *Breathing, ever since 'twas torn*
> *From its rushy bed, a strain*
> *Of impassioned love and pain.*
> *"The secret of my song, though near,*
> *none can see and none can hear...*

---

24. Ilza Veith (tr.), *The Yellow Emperor's Classic of Internal Medicine (Huang Ti Nei Ching Su Wen)*, p. 234.

'Tis the flame of Love that fired me,
'Tis the wine of Love that inspired me.
Wouldst thou know how lovers bleed,
Hearken, hearken to the Reed!" [25]

Not just the human being but all of nature, in fact, is animated by the Spirit of God. In a simile, Chuang Tzu describes how the wind makes all the hollows, the nooks and crannies of nature resound and sing. This is no ordinary wind but the Cosmic Wind, corresponding to the "Breath of the All-Compassionate" described by the great Sufi, Ibn Arabi. Though the wind is invisible, we feel its existence through its activity. Even so, we are able to perceive the existence of the Agent through His acts, which go on ceaselessly throughout the entire universe.

Leaving all unnecessary articles outside the entrance, one enters the hut. This is equivalent to leaving behind one's "excess baggage," one's preconceptions and impurities, but especially one's Base Self. One's crawl through the entrance signifies humility and is, in Sufic terms, symbolic of Prostration in Formal Prayer, which is the fitting attitude in confronting the Sacred. The natural branch-post at its center is at once identified as the "pillar of the universe," which supports the entire cosmos. One side of the branch-post is the area where the tea is prepared, the other side is where it is served. The pillar thus separates and unites the spiritual and physical worlds, and events that are decided in the spiritual world later find realization in the physical world, its projection.

The master serves us tea. Even so does the Sufi master impart his spiritual power and blessings (*baraka, fayz*) to the

---

25. These opening verses of the *Mathnawi* have been translated by Reynold A. Nicholson—*Rumi: Poet and Mystic,* London: Allen & Unwin, 1950, p. 31.

Hearts of those who visit him with the requisite courtesy. One's "tea bowl" must be empty; nothing can be poured into it unless there is room. This has been allegorized in Sufi literature as the "tavern" where the owner of the tavern, the Sufi master, serves "divine wine."

This is not ordinary wine. Rather, it symbolizes the intoxicating fire of love, the love of God, and by extension also the love of everything in the universe. How beautifully an old popular song captures this sense:

Everybody
Loves a lover
I'm a lover
Everybody loves me
And I love everybody
'cause I'm in love with You.

This is probably the most important treasure Sufism has to contribute to the rich traditions of the world: the message of all-embracing Love. Emptiness or poverty, self-effacement (*faqr, wabi*) is the first step. This leads to longing (*hasrah*). Longing leads to burning (trial by fire—purification by the fire of love). This is the "poverty of poverty" (*faqr* squared). And when one is emptied of even that (*faqr* cubed), when even the ashes are removed, when self-annihilation (*jakumetsu*: "death of tranquility," *fana, nirvana*) is complete, that—according to the great Sufi sage Geylani—yields God. Then, one is *sabi* with the *Sabi,* alone with the Alone.

As a Sufi poem puts it, in the state of Unity "There is no one who comes, none who goes." Rikyu the teamaster has aptly summarized this aloneness of the Absolute:

The snow-covered mountain path

Winding through the rocks
Has come to its end;
Here stands a hut,
The master is all alone;
No visitors he has, nor are any expected.

"When the Uncarved Block shatters, it becomes vessels."[26] When Spirit descends into Multiplicity, it finds its home in the hearts of human beings. As a Sacred Tradition states, "The heavens and the earth cannot contain Me, yet the Heart of My believing servant does." The tea bowl symbolizes the Heart, or sacred center. Hence, when the Zen Master Chao-chou tells a monk, "Go wash your bowl," he is, from the Sufic point of view, instructing him to clean out or purify his heart. The tea bowls also stand for man in his totality, or the universe of which man is a reflection.

Look closely into the cup. There are numberless tea grains at its bottom. These represent the infinite multiplicity we behold in the universe. Each grain of the powdered tea represents one of the myriad things in the universe. Taken together, they signify totality. But without the pure water, which represents the Great Spirit of God, they cannot be made into tea that leads to awakening, just as without the sacred, the universe is a great aggregate of dust particles—subject to the laws of statistical mechanics—with no further apparent significance. When the tea-whisk of one's invocation (*dhikr*) calls forth the presence of God, then the whole universe will be sacralized, it will be awash with the Divine. Thus the elixir of wakefulness is prepared. The calligraphy serves as an aid to meditation, and the flower points to its fruits.

---

26. *Tao Te Ching,* Chapter 28.

The sunken hearth is the abode of fire, not immediately visible to the senses. We know of its presence indirectly, through its action, the boiling of the tea kettle. The fire is a symbol for the power of God that energizes the universe. The heat that brings the water to the boil also represents the concentration and effort which will effect one's spiritual transmutation into a sage. Moreover, although each person drinks from a separate bowl, the kettle from which all the teas are poured is one. The Source is one. Even so does the spiritual power (*baraka*) of a Sufi sheikh fill the hearts of the disciples—hence the image of the mystical cupbearer, a tavern owner dispensing (spiritual) wine.

In drinking tea together, each person is aided in remembering his own center, which is also the center of every being and of the universe itself. The Divine Spirit is always flowing like water, giving His power and life to everything. The pervading influence of Spirit, like water, is everywhere. The water also reminds us of Lao Tzu: "The softest substance in the world vanquishes the hardest."[27] Water turns rock to sand. If one makes oneself humble and gentle like water, lower than all things, one will become stronger than rock.

Only in being nothing may one become everything, and only then does one realize one's essential brotherhood with all sentient beings. The person who drinks assists in the sacrifice of his own self, or ego, and is thus enabled to realize the Divine Presence in his own center. To wake up means to perceive that in reality, the little individual self does not exist, and that only the Great Self exists. Then, one can comprehend the true meaning of the following paraphrase from D.T. Suzuki: "when I am sipping tea in my tearoom I am swallowing the whole universe with

---

27. *Tao Te Ching,* Chapter 43.

it, and this very moment of lifting my bowl to my lips is eternity itself transcending time and space."[28]

 os   os   os

This chapter has discussed that beautiful Japanese tradition, the Tea Ceremony, from the standpoint of Sufism. We have seen that Sufic interpretation can help us to unpack the symbolism hidden in this ceremony. This also leads to the question: what other aspects of East Asian thought are amenable to treatment in terms of Sufism, and what additional insights may be gleaned from its study? As a preliminary, the next chapter will deal with the subject of faith, for faith is a main entry point into any religion or religious philosophy.

---

28. D.T. Suzuki, *Zen and Japanese Culture,* Princeton, NJ: Princeton University Press, 1971 [1959] (Bollingen Series 64), p. 314.

2

A SUFI'S WORSHIP

Everything begins with loving a human being.
—S. F. Abasiyanik[29]

Faith

Faith is an integral part of the human constitution. Even an atheist has faith, although his faith lies in different areas. Human beings have this ineradicable need to believe in *something*. Let me add immediately that the faith I have in mind is not *blind* faith, nor superstition. We are not being asked to believe in anything unreasonable, such as that the moon is made of green cheese, nor would it be right to ask others to do so. Faith without reason is naught, just as reason without faith is naught. This means that it is possible, after all, to have faith *with* reason, as in Sufism. "I believe because it is absurd," said Tertullian. No. On the contrary, one should believe what one believes precisely because it makes sense.

All cultures have emphasized the importance of faith in different ways. In Hinduism, the *Bhagavad Gita* states: "The faith of every man, O Arjuna, accords with his nature. Man is made up of faith; as is his faith, so is he...A man of faith, absorbed in faith, his senses controlled, attains knowledge, and, knowledge attained, quickly finds supreme peace. But the ignorant man,

---

29. Famous Turkish author. The quote is from his short story, "In Alemdag There is a Snake."

who is without faith, goes doubting to destruction. For the doubting self there is neither this world, nor the next, nor joy."[30] In Buddhism, the *Dhammapada* tells us right at the very start: "All that we are is the result of what we have thought: it is founded on our thoughts, it is made up of our thoughts."[31] Thoughts, which include beliefs, actively shape one's destiny, because they lead to concrete actions. And because human nature is originally good, the proper destiny of human beings takes them from the world and leads them to the Pure Land. It is for this reason that the following verses express a profound truth:

> *Sow a thought, reap an act;*
> *Sow an act, reap a habit;*
> *Sow a habit, reap a character;*
> *Sow a character, reap a destiny.*

In Buddhism, the role of faith has been emphasized especially in Japan. Thus, Shinran states: "To be reborn in the Pure Land, one must have faith above all and not concern himself with anything else. A matter of such magnitude as rebirth in the Pure Land cannot be arranged by the ordinary mortal." The founders of all Japanese Buddhist sects have made similar statements with regard to faith. Here, for example, is Nichiren: "He who understands the doctrines yet does not believe cannot become a buddha. He who believes, although he does not comprehend, can become a buddha."

In Sufism, too, faith is the beginning of all things. Out of many possible quotes, let me select just a single one. Muhammad said: "You cannot enter the Pure Land (Paradise) until you have faith, and you cannot (be said to) have faith until you love one another."

---

30. *Bhagavad Gita* 17.3, 4.39-40.
31. *Dhammapada,* Chapter 1 (The Twin Verses).

Faith in the Master

I should never have arrived at a proper appreciation of faith if it had not been for the Sufi master, Ahmet Kayhan.

A sage, a true buddha, a Perfect Human, is the most extraordinary being you have ever laid eyes on. Every action of such a person is infused with virtue (*te*). Every move of this person is worship, his every breath a blessing. His words are all pure knowledge and wisdom. His speech, clear as crystal, is a delight to listen to.

Mencius said: "The words of the Superior Man are not hidden, yet the Tao is contained in them." (7B:32) The words of a Friend of God are not hidden, yet God is contained in them. His sweet and impressive talk radiates peace, expands the heart, and is full of compassion. The Perfect Human incorporates all that is best in humankind, forcing a redefinition of what it means to be human. The *Doctrine of the Mean* states: "the people regard the movement of the Superior Man as the Way of the world. They regard his actions as the norm of the world. They regard his words as the pattern for the world. When they are away from him, they long for him. When they are near him, they never get tired of him." (29)

In the presence of such a sage, one's heart/mind is elevated with joy. It is inspired to contemplate the sublime. For, although we can't see it ourselves, this saint is face to face with divinity every instant, and is graced with the beauty of that dazzling presence. Like the moon that reflects the light of the sun, his wondrous state is in fact a reflection of that divine beauty. Endowed with such unmistakable indicators and miraculous qualities, the Perfect Human shines like the full moon and is recognized immediately.

A great artist is one who fashions a work of beauty. The sage is one who has perfected himself as a work of art. By purifying himself, he has allowed the divine light, potentially within us all, to shine out.

Those who visit a Perfect Human are engulfed in an aura of spiritual bliss. They can listen to his utterances for hours on end without ever noticing the passage of time. Their hearts are filled with sublime joy, their spirits bathed in divine light. The love of God is awakened in their souls, together with compassion for other beings, love for one another, and the desire to learn the ineffable Truth underlying all things.

Such a one was the Master. Without him I should not have known about Muhammad, and without Muhammad I should not have known about God. For, whereas originally I did have some general vague idea about religious matters, this was a miserable shadow compared to the vistas that were opened up before me subsequently.

Within each of us lies the possibility to become a sage, to wake up. Whoever is able to achieve this transmutation becomes a cosmic human being, and is no longer fettered by limitations of age, wealth, sex, or race. To the universal human being, all other human beings are one, equally worthy of love and respect. Hence, s/he treats them all with tenderness, care, and consideration, as if they were one's own children.

In more ways than one, the sage is like a magnet, who attracts human beings like iron filings. Not only that, but under the influence of that magnet, the iron filings themselves become magnetized, and are able to attract other pieces. Upon every human being, the saint superimposes an invisible envelope, a spiritual "force field." This impalpable, almost electromagnetic, field is nothing less than the form of a new self. It results in an exhilarating induction of love, an infusion of spiritual energy that accelerates our liberation.

For to be truly human is not just to minister to our animal needs. Man does not live by bread alone. Immediate needs such as food, clothing, and shelter are only the beginning. As soon as these are met, the need to approach the divine manifests itself—which is where faith comes in. Human beings were formed (created) with this express purpose. Otherwise, the dogs and apes had already been performing all other functions quite adequately. To condemn a human being simply to the most basic needs is like using a sophisticated computer only to add two and two, or like using a car as a bedroom to sleep in and nothing more. How wasteful to condemn a human being to the basement level of existence! How wasteful if we do this to ourselves!

By imitating the Perfect Human, those who follow him have the possibility to become what they pretend to be. By emulating such a praiseworthy personality, each follower affirms that personality within himself. In time, one's whole being begins to fill in those ideal outlines. One grows into that mold, until one is reborn in the image of the new personality. One must let the master who is in one come out.

The sage, however, is never an accidental occurrence. Awakening or spiritual rebirth requires long and sustained effort, doing specific things in a precise way, just like a chemistry experiment. Hence, both the faith and the daily practices of the Perfect Human need to be emulated faithfully. It is by seeing these beliefs and practices personified, and by admiring—even adoring—the person who embodies them, that we are motivated to follow in his footsteps, so that we may also eventually become endowed with similar wonderful traits. We have to tune ourselves to the right frequency of resonance. The sage lives the life, so that we may know the doctrine. He instructs us in the Divine

Law (*shariah* or *dharma*). And we must follow the doctrine or Way (*tao*), if we too want to live the life.

For having taught me who the Prophet is, I am indebted to my Master with something surpassing gratitude. And all people are indebted to their real teachers for their introduction to the founder of that teaching, not to mention the teaching itself.

Let me illustrate this by a Sufi story. But first, I have to explain two points. One: Kissing an elder's hand is a gesture of respect in the Middle East. And two: In Sufi lore, Khidr (Khezr) is an earthly immortal who roams the world until the end of time, rushing to the rescue of those in distress who call upon his name. For an ordinary mortal to see him is a very rare event.

> A master had a devoted student. One day, when the student arrived, he found that his master had a visitor. The master told him: "That's Khidr sitting over there. Go ahead and kiss his hand." The student replied, "Yes, Master," but instead of going over to Khidr and kissing his hand, he took his master's hand and kissed it. At this, the master smiled and said: "My child, you should be kissing Khidr's hand. Go to him and do so." The disciple said, "Yes, Master," but again he kissed his master's hand, instead of doing what he was told. The master then asked: "What is it that makes you kiss my hand instead of Khidr's?" The disciple replied: "If it had not been for my master, I would never have seen Khidr. It is to my master that I owe gratitude, for having shown Khidr to me."

Faith in the Prophet

If God can be compared to the sun, the founder of Islam/ Sufism is like the full moon (a reflection of the sun's light), and a saint is like a reflection of the moon in a clear, still pool. The less ruffled the surface of the water, the more perfectly the image of the moon appears. If the waters of the mind are troubled, that mental agitation can entirely prevent a reflection from coming through. In my case, I was blessed with the incredible good fortune of meeting a person who is called "the Pole" (*qutb*) in Sufism. His reflection of the moon never wavered, to the extent that one might be tempted to think he was the full moon itself. Not everyone can be like this, of course, but it should give us pause before we dismiss a religion on the basis of faint echoes ricocheting from perturbed minds.

But how to "unruffle the mind"? How to calm it so that no stray thoughts appear that are at variance with the teaching? If there is too much static, reception on the radio or TV will be poor or even impossible.

Turbulence of the self is the cause of turbulence in the mind. Hence, before the mind is stilled, the self must be brought to quiescence. And in Islamic Sufism, this is done by sparse eating and drinking, sleeping sparely, performing the Formal Prayer, and all the other practices and worship that constitute Sufism.

A Heart polished in this way becomes the "Spotless Mirror" of Chuang Tzu or the "Mysterious Mirror" of Lao Tzu. In Sufism, it is called "the Mirror of Alexander" or the "Wineglass of Jam." Looking into such a Heart, one sees the entire universe revealed within, which is why Chuang Tzu said: "Without going out the door, one can know everything under Heaven." And the Master explained, "Without leaving your chair, you can be in Europe, in America."

If the sages are reflections of the full moon, it follows that the Prophet, who is the master of them all, must possess qualities superior to any single saint. This casts matters in an entirely new light.

Herewith, a Sufi quatrain:

This cosmos is a mirror
Everything stands with the Real
From the mirror of Muhammad
God always is seen.

Thus we study his teachings, his every word, with utmost care, and then ourselves apply them in our lives. It is true that God revealed the Divine Law through him. But if it weren't for the Prophet's example, who embodied that Law in flesh and blood, it would not be so beneficial to us human beings. Then we would not be able to properly interpret the Koran, the Heavenly Classic. That is why the Radiant Way of the Prophet—his conduct and sayings in various concrete instances—is so important.

Only when the Divine Law is embodied in a person of flesh and blood can it be beneficial to us human beings. Otherwise, it is too abstract, and needs to be translated into concrete action that we can emulate in practice.

One of the things that we thus come to comprehend is that the Prophet cannot speak an untruth, and when he speaks about God, what he says must be true. Thus, it is through Muhammad that we learn about God. How could we—mere mortals—come to know of God, the most sublime secret of the universe, if it had not been for the one who informed us of Him?

The Prophet combined *sageliness within and kingliness without*—he was a sage-king. The highest achievement of a sage is identification with the universe through spiritual cultivation. (According to a Chinese sage, Tseng Lao-weng: "The mind of one who returns to the Source thereby becomes the Source. Your own mind, for example, is destined to become the universe itself." It was in this sense, perhaps, that Maharishi once remarked to a friend of mine: "Muhammad is the universe.")

But the ideal sage should not be a recluse; s/he should function within society. Now one of these possible functions is political. "Kingliness without" here means that only the noblest person should be king, and the Prophet was indeed the ruler of the Islamic community during his lifetime (called the "Age of

Bliss"). He was humble toward God, yet human beings saw him as majestic. He united spiritual power and political power in his person, although a prophet should never be regarded in the same light as ordinary politicians or statesmen. He was perhaps the best example of Plato's "philosopher king"—but of course, it stands to reason that a prophet king is spiritually superior to even a philosopher king.

After him, the spiritual and political offices in Islam were segregated, never to be combined again. The caliphs became his political successors, whereas the saints inherited his spiritual legacy. Indeed, the two offices do not mix well at all; only in the Prophet could their ideal fusion have taken place. And a fusion of much more besides—as Alphonse de Lamartine observed:

> Philosopher, orator, apostle, legislator, warrior, conqueror of ideas, restorer of rational dogmas; the founder of twenty terrestrial empires and of one spiritual empire, that is Muhammad. As regards all standards by which human greatness may be measured, we may ask, is there any man greater than he?[32]

We see, in his example, the full flowering of all aspects of the human personality—the archetype, in other words, of the ideal human being.

Faith in God

Now we have said that only by virtue of the master do we come to know the Prophet, and only by virtue of the Prophet do we come to know God. Just as we are indebted to our master or

---

32. Lamartine, *Histoire de la Turquie,* Paris, 1854, Vol. 11, p. 277.

teacher, so also should we be grateful to the Prophet for this knowledge.

But what, or who, is God?

To answer this question, let me quote from the great thirteenth-century Zen master Daio:

"There is a reality even prior to heaven and earth. Indeed it has no form, much less a name."

To my mind, this is as good a definition of God as any other. This Reality has no name because it was/is prior to everything else, including names, and the reason I call it "God" is in order to be able to refer to it in shorthand. God Himself is without form, but He is the One who gave form to everything.

The great Sufi sage Ibn Arabi compared the world to a waking dream, and claimed that events in this world are comparable to dream events. In this, he was supported by the saying of the Prophet: "Human beings are asleep. They wake up when they die." The essential point here is that the world we live in is an illusion, heaven and earth are a dream, and the Reality prior to them is the only true reality. Or, if we accept that the world of our senses, the world of phenomena, is real, then Absolute Reality (i.e. God) is the most real. And indeed, one of the names for God in Sufism is the Real or the Truth (al-Haqq).

Now that Reality, which some call Buddha-nature, is within all human beings, and indeed within all things. (Although it is a little confusing to say: "All things possess Buddha-nature." We say it, but do we really understand what it means?) And, conversely, all things are within It. In other words, the essence of all things is One. It is that Reality. Everything in the universe is a manifestation of that Essence.

Islam, and hence Sufism which is based on it, combines naturalism with transcendence. The Absolute and the phenomenal world are one. But this does not mean they are identical. The

Sufis have long used the simile of invisible (and formless) water vapor becoming visible by assuming form as rain and snow. Nature is a condensation of the Absolute, but the Absolute—or sacredness—would exist even without nature (because it is prior to heaven and earth). It is boundless grace for us that the Real manifests itself from every corner in heaven and earth. The Sufis have a famous motto: "Be in the world but not of the world." To the extent that we live in nature, we are in the world, which is an inevitable part of our existence. To the extent that our spirits are with God, we are not of the world. And it is this part that requires self-cultivation.

We have already seen that the Prophet referred to God as "the Beautiful." In fact, everything that we regard as beautiful is none other than a manifestation of some aspect of the Most Beautiful (*al-Jamil,* one of the many names of God). In the beauty of the transient, we behold breath-taking intimations of immortality. Consider a butterfly, which we may with justification call a "flying flower." Its wonderful colors, its delicate texture, fill us with a joy tempered by sorrow for its brief existence. But after it, there will be another butterfly, and after this year's cherry blossoms there will be next year's cherry blossoms, for the Beautiful never ceases to manifest beauty ever anew.

In what follows, I shall bypass all the intermediate levels of Ibn Arabi's elaborate cosmology, and concentrate on the beginning and the end: the Source and the phenomenal world, the Formless and the final form.

The formless Essence manifests the world by assuming form. The Real is beyond form, and is able to manifest all forms. When it gives rise to a form, all other forms are negated in that particular form. To take an example, a cat is not a mouse, it is not a mountain, it is not a flower, it is nothing else but a cat. Out of the possibility of all forms, only the form of a cat has become manifest. The reality of catness has been affirmed, and all other realities (which we know to be possible because they exist) have been negated. Hence, any specific form is *less real* than the Real. Western philosophers might call a cat an *ontological subset* of the Real, and might designate it as $Real_{cat}$. And similarly for $Real_{mountain}$, $Real_{flower}$, $Real_{universe}$, etc. To the Japanese mind, everything is Buddha. Or, as Niyazi Misri put it,

From every atom comes the call: "I am the Real."[33]

Order and Harmony

If the reader is patient enough, I would like to take this discussion a step further. Otherwise, this section can be skipped. The point is subtle, but it is an important one to make.

We now say that the Real is the source of all order and harmony in the universe. Of course, the trivial argument is that since the Real is the source of everything, it is also the source of order and harmony. But suppose we try to understand *how* this occurs.

Take biology. In cell differentiation, every cell "knows" what it is supposed to do. It has the same DNA as all other cells, yet somehow, only that part of the DNA is expressed which will make it the right component with respect to its neighbors. You do not find a liver cell in the midst of bone cells.

Or take quantum physics. In the famous Young double-slit experiment, the electron seems to "know" whether the second slit is covered or not. If it is covered, it manifests itself as a particle. If it is not, the electron manifests itself as a wave.

And the same applies to all the remaining examples of order and harmony in the universe. Now, how is such a thing possible?

---

33. The famous utterance of Mansur al-Hallaj.

How do the cell, the electron, etc., "know" their rightful place, the function appropriate to their specific situation? They do not possess intelligence, so it is not right to speak of knowledge in their case.

Recall that everything is a subset of the Real. This means that the Real is *potentially present* in everything, within even the tiniest particle. Here is how we can understand this: my finger is a part of me; it is neither me nor not-me. In any case, it is connected to me and not separate from me.

Because it comprises infinite intelligence, infinite consciousness, and infinite knowledge, the Real knows what the adjacent cells and the second slit are doing, since it is potentially present within them also. Each form, because its essence is the Real, potentially contains all other forms as well. The selection of the appropriate response is thus made by the Real itself, and out of any number of possibilities, the suitable form is manifested. The laws by which the formless Real manifests itself as myriad forms, and can be discovered by observations in the phenomenal world, are called the laws of science. Therefore, you do not see plums growing out of cherry blossoms, or the sun rising from the west.

The Importance of God for Human Beings

Further, that Reality, which is also within human beings, is not only more real than the phenomenal world, it is also more perfect (because more complete). In fact, it is Absolute Perfection. In that case, the closer one approaches that Reality, the more perfect must one become. And the person who has fully realized Absolute Reality, fully awakened to it, becomes a Perfect Human Being. What a magnificent destiny this is!

So faith leads us to human improvement and perfection, because this is the purpose of human existence—to become a sage, a buddha, a Perfect Human Being. Once you have realized that God is your true essence, you find true peace, a peace that passes understanding, a tranquility that is supreme. Then, your concerns and troubles fall away like dry leaves, and you devote yourself with humility to the task of improving the lot of human beings.

The Sufi would agree, then, with Daisetz T. Suzuki when he says: "To realize my original nature and to do good is my religion." For one's original nature is the Real, and doing good, serving humanity, is a morality that can only be called divine.

Realizing one's true, original nature entails the perception that there is no distinction between oneself and others. Of course, one may feel this as a vague emotion, which is nice, but actually *knowing* and *seeing* this to be true is as different from that feeling as a mountain is different from a molehill.

We owe thanks to God for being allowed to live. We owe God thanks because He formed us as human beings, rather than as a rock, a tree, or an animal. We owe Him thanks because we have been fortunate enough to survive until this moment. And we owe Him gratitude because He has given us the opportunity to perfect ourselves by approaching Him.

Empiricism

All this talk of faith is a waste of time unless it leads to concrete improvements in our lives. And for this, we have to do or not-do (*wu-wei*) certain things. Of course, the requirements of Sufism are many and varied, but the Master boiled them down to three points. We must refrain from doing (not-do) two things, and we must do one thing. The two things we must not do is to engage in (1) illicit gain and (2) extramarital sex. This is for everyone, whether or not one is a Sufi or a Moslem. The thing we must do, in order to attain Sufi sainthood, is to (3) perform the Formal Prayer. (In the last chapter, we shall see the full mystical benefits offered by Formal Prayer.) By (not-)doing these, we shall contribute immeasurably to the well-being of others and to our own. Of course, there are many other things, but these three requirements are essential. They are the foundation on which everything else rests.

In the final weeks of his life, the Master threw down the following challenge to all empiricists. "For one week," he said, "start everything you do by repeating the formula *Bismillahir Rahmanir Rahim* ("In the Name of God, the Compassionate, the Merciful"). Then, during the next week, do not repeat it. And then compare how things fare during those two weeks."

Try it and see.

Such, in brief, is the faith of a Sufi.

ଔ   ଔ   ଔ

We have investigated the subject of faith in this chapter. The faith of a person is the key to everything he does, and we can infer his faith from his actions. If a person says one thing but does another, it is his actions and not his claims that count.

The true beginning of faith comes when one finds a living model whom one can fully trust, love, and adore. In Sufism, such a person is the Sufi sage. He, in turn, introduces the Prophet, the founder of Islamic Sufism. But the Prophet himself never called anyone to anything other than God, and it is he who originally introduced God as the proper object of worship. Hence God, who is intangible, can be approached by what is tangible—a human being who shows us the methods by which this approach is made possible.

The next chapter will now be devoted to the subject of war.

3

ON WAR

If you want peace, prepare for war.
—Vegetius

Two great armies stood arrayed face to face. All the most lethal weapons, the most invincible warriors of both sides were in the forefront. As the implacable foes regarded each other with hostility, in the brief silence that precedes the storm, Arjuna, the commander of one side, told his charioteer, the great Krishna, to drive his chariot between the narrow divide that separated the two walls. On both sides—soon to be locked in mortal combat—Arjuna could recognize fathers, teachers, uncles, sons, and brothers. He was filled with deep compassion, and in his despair he turned to Krishna, in search of an answer as to why this war must be fought out. "What can we hope from this killing of kinsmen?" he cried.

The core of the *Bhagavad Gita* is devoted to answering this single question: "Why war?" Krishna, whom we have the choice of regarding either as God incarnate or as a sage, begins by saying: "The truly wise mourn neither for the living, nor for the dead," and continues:

The Unreal never is;
The Real never is not.
This truth indeed has been known
By those who have known the Truth.

Leave attachment behind. Surrender to the inevitable. What is destroyed is only outward form. As for the indestructible essence of human beings, which is the Godhead, there is no way that can ever be destroyed. All phenomenal things are transient; they enter and exit the realm of being in some way or other, and *war is one of the ways in which they do this*. The duty of those who have come face to face with this inevitability is to carry out this task selflessly, without desires or attachment to results.

> *Who sees his Lord within every creature,*
> *Deathlessly dwelling amidst the mortal:*
> *That man sees truly.*

> *One to me are fame and shame;*
> *One to me are joy and pain;*
> *One alike are loss and gain.*

Perhaps the following Zen *waka* (poem) explains it more clearly:

> *He who strikes and he who is struck—*
> *They are both no more than a dream that*
> *Has no reality.*[34]

Such, in brief, is Krishna's advice. Deplorable as war is, there may come a time when it becomes inescapable. When circumstances force it upon one, there is nothing to do but to carry it out with a sense of duty. This is what Krishna, as a sage or mouthpiece of God, is in effect saying. And it is in this light that we should understand the wars of the Prophet. Just think: where would we be, in what kind of world would we be living, if the

---

34. D.T. Suzuki, *Zen and Japanese Culture*, p. 123.

war against Hitler had not been fought? Even Einstein, a great pacifist, drew the line when it came to that.

In recent years we have seen efforts to define a "just war," and to conduct war in the light of higher moral principles. War is manslaughter, except when waged in self-defense or in defense of a weak side against a belligerent, powerful enemy. In recognition of the latter, international peacekeeping efforts have had to resort to the use of force since 1990. In other words, while it is to be deplored, there are cases under which war simply cannot be avoided. "Though you dislike it, combat is prescribed for you" (the Koran, 2:216).

I tend to regard *The Art of War*, written by Sun Tzu thousands of years ago, as an extended commentary on the wars of the Prophet. Paramount among its concerns is to obtain the maximum effect by inflicting the minimum amount of damage. We have it on the authority of Muhammad Hamidullah that the total number of casualties on all sides in the wars of the Prophet—virtually all of which were conducted in self-defense—did not exceed 500. Measured against the vastness of his accomplishment, this is indeed a small sum, especially when compared with war casualties before or since. The greatest victory, according to Sun Tzu, is that which is won without firing a shot, without waging war at all—the less wasteful war is in terms of human beings, weapons, and economic resources on both sides, the better. This is diametrically opposite to the doctrine of total war, first discussed by Karl von Clausewitz in the nineteenth century and practiced indiscriminately in the twentieth, where the entire assets of nations were pitted against each other in a "war to the death." The actual exercise of brute force is seldom a wise substitute for strength combined with intelligence. To engage in combat only when it could no longer be avoided, to obtain results diplomatically and by peaceful means whenever possible—these were the hallmarks of the Prophet's policy as regards warfare.

God's Attributes, and the Names which are expressions of those Attributes, can be classified under two headings: those of Beauty or Bliss (*jamal*), and those of Majesty or Wrath (*jalal*). This is in accordance with the *yin/yang* Principle of Complementarity. War, as the hallmark of discord, is the epitome of hellish states. Antoine de Saint-Exupéry observed that in times of old, war fulfilled youth's need for gallantry, bravery, and adventure, but that it had become, in our age, much too terrible to serve such a purpose. The Master taught that with the advent of weapons of mass destruction (WMDs), bloodshed had ceased to be a viable option for humanity. It was his opinion that in our age, the pen had taken the place of the sword, and that true conquest was no longer that of lands, but of hearts and minds. This is not *blitzkrieg* any more. It is bliss*krieg,* a struggle for the happiness of human beings, to be won between the covers of a book.

Kendo and the "Sword of No-Abode"

Kendo (*ken-tao*, or "the way of the sword") occupies an exalted place among the martial arts of the East. It has been closely associated with Zen throughout its history, and Daisetz T. Suzuki has pointed to the ways in which the swordsman must have a grasp of basic Zen principles. Swordsmanship, in this higher view, is not an "art of killing," but first and foremost a path of spiritual self-discipline.

Suzuki describes the concept of "the sword of no-abode," due to the swordmaster Ichiun.[35] The sword, of course, is a symbol of the spirit—it stands for spirituality and spiritual power. The sword of "no-abode" (*apratistha, wu-chu*), perhaps the most

---

35. Suzuki, *Zen and Japanese Culture,* pp. 170-182.

esoteric concept of swordsmanship, has its ready explanation in Sufism. We are enabled to understand what it is by looking at the Sufic term for "no-abode"—*la makaan*, Nonspace.

Recall that space is that in which distances can be defined. This presupposes separation. However, when everything is One, or united by a Unity that is indivisible, then there are no more distances or intervals, and space itself ceases to exist. This is what is meant by the Sufic term "Nonspace." Ever since Einstein, we also know that nonspace also means nontime, or in short, "nonspacetime."

Nonspace is the abode of Divinity. It denotes the pure Essence of God. It is also the root of all spaces—all spaces emerge from it, it is the space of spaces. And it is also what is meant when we speak of "the Emptiness of Emptiness."

Now, to return to the "sword of no-abode" or the "sword of Nonspace," this is the sword (weapon or instrument) wielded by the Perfect Human, who has firmly established himself (or his mind) in Nonspace. As Rumi says,

My place is the placeless,
My trace is the traceless.

Such a person has transcended the subject-object dichotomy; he is in a state which can no longer be described as either subject or object. He cannot even be called a swordmaster in the ordinary sense. Thus established, the Perfect Human becomes not unlike a force of nature: irresistible and invincible. He can no more be withstood than a flash of lightning or an earthquake.

When the Battle of Badr was raging, and the enemy seemed to be winning, the Prophet of God picked up a stone and hurled it at the enemy. Suddenly a storm arose, blowing against the enemy and incapacitating its army. God later informed the

Prophet and posterity: "When you threw the stone, it was not you who threw it, but I." It is in such unexpected ways that God comes to the rescue of the Perfect Human, even when there is no consciousness of how it is done. It is also an instance of "Nothing exists except God."

Chuang Tzu claimed that the Perfect Human "cannot be drowned in water nor burned in fire." Indeed, when Abraham was cast into a blazing bonfire, it turned into a bed of roses, for God commanded the fire to "be cool and safe." This is the reason why the adept swordsman, having put the fear of death behind him and having surrendered to God (although this might not be the way he would consciously describe the situation), cannot be vanquished. In fact, a confrontation is more than likely not to occur at all in such a nonconfrontational state of mind.

Which reminds me of a true story.

Ali, the Prophet's cousin and later the fourth Caliph, was engaged in combat with an enemy warrior during a battle. He felled the enemy, and just as he was about to strike the final blow, the soldier spat in his face. Ali immediately got up, and released the fellow.

The warrior was astonished. "Why did you release me when you were in such a superior position?" he asked.

Ali replied: "Before, I was battling you in an entirely impartial way, for the sake of God alone and without any personal involvement. You and I were one. But once you spat in my face, my self reared up. After that, I could no longer combat you, because I would then be doing it for my Base Self and not for God. We must now do battle again." At this, his opponent let down his sword and joined Ali's side.

War Against Oneself

Sufism asserts that a shameful situation should be remedied if it cannot be avoided. But, it says, the way to do this is not to die, but to "die before you die." This is the more honorable thing to do. Because it is the Base Self that lands us in dire straits. The Base Self wants to destroy us, and driving us to suicide may be one of the methods it uses. We should, instead, vanquish the Base Self, and once we have achieved this, we shall see that we have "no self" (no little, local, individual self) left. We shall, in effect, have done away with the cause of our disgrace. This is the victory in spiritual warfare (*jihad al-manawi*).

One way out provided by Sufism for the atonement of one's errors, intentional or unintentional, is repentance (*tawba*). If one repents to God with all the sincerity of one's heart, one will find God merciful. God says, "My mercy precedes my wrath," and will forgive all sins except the denial of His Unity. Once the slate has been wiped clean by sincere repentance, one is freed of all earlier burdens and can proceed afresh with one's life.

Sufism rules out suicide. "Do not kill/destroy yourselves" (4:29) and "Do not ruin yourselves with your own hands" (2:195), says the Koran. A human being is the acme of existence, and to take any human life when we have no right to do so is to run counter to the purposes of the universe, of God. The Koran states: "Whoever kills a human being, it is as if s/he has killed all humankind, and whoever saves a human being, it is as if s/he saves all humanity." (5:32) *This includes oneself.* Since you too are a human being, the same rule applies. Suicide is also an act of supreme ingratitude, since even being born human is such a great gift to us. So, to anyone contemplating suicide, Sufism would say: "Do yourself a favor! Save all humanity!"

ଓ ଓ ଓ

We have investigated war in this chapter—something that has accompanied humanity throughout its history. Sometimes, war is inevitable. Yet the weapons of mass destruction made possible by modern science and technology are so terrible that humanity must now forsake war, and finally begin to build a durable peace. For peace is the true meaning of "Islam," and of the all-encompassing Unity (*Ahad*) that we call God. This Unity, and the associated concepts that it entails, will now be taken up in the chapter that follows.

4

UNITY AND ITS FAMILY

Wherever you turn, there is the face/truth/essence of God.
—The Koran (2:115)

Heaven arms with love
Those it would not see destroyed.
—*Tao Te Ching*[36]

Unity

Lift the veil of Multiplicity, and you will find Unity beneath. The One transcends the object-subject distinction. The "Greatest Sheikh" Ibn Arabi postulated what has been called the "Unity of Being" (*wahdah al-wujud*—unity of things, bodies, objects). And Ahmed Sirhindi (Imam Rabbani) set down his doctrine of "Unity of Observers" (*wahdah al-shuhud*—unity of selves, spirits, subjects). Finally, the unity of objects and the unity of subjects are combined in a single, all-embracing Unity in a saying attributed to the Prophet: "Bodies are spirits, spirits are bodies" (*ashbahuqum arwahuqum, arwahuqum ashbahuqum*).

One of the basic conclusions of Mahayana Buddhism has likewise been the unity of all beings. Enlightenment (*bodhi*) is awakening to the unity of existence, the spiritual communion that pervades the entire universe. From this principle, several

---

36. Ch. 67 (Lin Yutang translation).

results follow. This subject is so important that it needs to be dealt with in greater detail.

In the beginning is the One, and only the One is Real. The "Suchness" is nondual, undivided. All things are manifestations, parts of a single, unmanifest, Ultimate Reality. This Reality is, at the same time, supreme Enlightenment. Consequently, all things are informed by this Enlightenment, though It is owned by none of them. It alone is Real.

"Our Essence of Mind is intrinsically pure," said the Patriarch Hui-neng. "All things are only its manifestations..." All things are One and have no existence apart from It. Similarly, the One is in all things. Thus one is enabled to speak of the "entrance" of all into One and One into all. But each part still retains its individuality, and the One is no less One for being manifested in uncountable individual parts. This has led to the doctrine of *jijimuge* in Japanese Kegon (Hua-yen) Buddhism. *Jijimuge* means "unimpeded interdiffusion" or "mutual interpenetration" of all things.[37] In the words of Li T'ung-hsüan,

> Where in each mote of dust whole multitudes of worlds are contained, with all spaces pervaded and all worlds enclosed; where domains of unflagging recompense abound without limit, where truth pervades and principle penetrates—this is called the Dharma Realm.
>
> And when in a single subtle sound one hears oceans of worlds, when a single filament of hair spans the infinite; when views of great and small vanish; when self and others are seen to be of the same substance; when consciousness gives way,

---

37. Summarized from Christmas Humphreys, *Buddhism,* Harmondsworth: Pelican, 1969 [1951], pp. 16-17. See also Dusan Pajin, "One is All: Translation and Analysis of the *Hsin-hsin ming,*" *J. Chinese Phil.,* vol. 19 (1992), p. 81-108.

emotions cease, and insight pervades without obstruction—this is called Entering the Dharma Realm.[38]

"All is One, One is all"[39]—or, as it is called in Sufism, Unity in Diversity, Diversity in Unity (*kesrette vahdet, vahdette kesret*). Not only are the cherry blossom and the moon united by virtue of the fact that their Essence is One, but—inconceivable as this may appear—the cherry blossom and the moon, the doorknob and the orange, the little bird and the mountain, ceaselessly flow into each other. In fact, they *are* each other—something that is not obvious at all in our Multiplicity-consciousness. As physicist David Bohm once expressed it, they are all "knots being knotted and unknotted" throughout the fabric of the universe. They are local "standing waves" in a field of incessant flux, themselves to be replaced by other, similar "standing waves" when their term is over.

Let me try to explain this further by referring to a personal experience. Years ago, I visited the Duden waterfall in the south of Turkey. It was a beautiful sight; the air was so pregnant with moisture that you could almost squeeze the water out of it. Downstream, there was a small bridge, and I stood on it, looking toward the waterfall. Beneath me I could see a large rock, over which the water was hurtling with tremendous speed.

Now here is the interesting part. The water was moving so fast, and yet without any turbulence or bubbles, over the rock that the water covering the rock appeared stationary. I watched,

---

38. Li Tongxuan, *Exposition of the New Avatamsaka Sutra,* Chapter 39: "Entering the Dharma Realm." I have altered the wording slightly. (www.courses.fas.harvard.edu/~eabs212/assignments/LiTongxuan.pdf, accessed Feb. 21, 2001.)

39. Seng-ts'an, *Hsin Hsin Ming,* stanza 35. Although this work is normally considered to be a Zen text, Dusan Pajin has pointed out the affinity with Hua-yen: "Dumoulin was among the first to recognise that in many passages the composition of *Hsin-hsin ming* is akin to the *Avatamsaka sutra...*" D. Pajin, *J. Chinese Phil.,* vol. 19 (1992), p. 81.

fascinated. It was as if the scene were frozen, and yet I knew that the water was moving at amazing speed, enough to carry me away if I were to step into it. Even so, everything that we see as stationary or having definite form is exchanging its very substance with all the rest of existence. Perhaps this is why the "probability wave" describing a particle is spread out across the universe, and it has a finite, though inifinitesimal, chance of existing at the other end of the cosmos. The wave function may actually be describing "mutual interpenetration" in mathematical terms.

What is described theoretically above for Kegon Buddhism is an actual perception in Sufism, obtained in mystical states of consciousness. The One (*Ahad*) and the Real (*Haqq*) are two names of God, the Essence of whom is called *zat*. Enlightenment (*mushahada*: Observation) *is* God-realization, and God is basically realized (*tahqiq*) in and through Himself. In the unfolding of Ultimate Reality into the universe (the "arc of descent") and its return to the Source (the "arc of ascent"), various levels of being are spawned until the level of this world (the physical universe) is reached. The Sufic picture differs from *jijimuge* in that it takes "mutual interpenetration" to its ultimate limit: not only all things in the physical world, but *all* things in *all* the worlds, are inseparably interlinked from top to bottom.

Truth, Beauty, Goodness

The wise people of humankind—including the Sufis—have agreed that the pursuit of happiness entails the search for the good, the true, and the beautiful. The Greeks had already observed that "Truth is Beauty, Beauty Truth"—to which John Keats added the rejoinder: "That is all you know on earth, and all you need to know." Truth and Beauty are intimately related. Art is a pathway to higher consciousness, which here means the

perception of Absolute Reality, who is the Beautiful: "The ultimate aesthetic value is closely connected with the notion of a
higher experience to create beautiful things, but ultimately to
reach this higher state of mind. The skills and techniques of the
arts are...nothing more than the means to reach this deeper aesthetic value...[R]eligious enlightenment and aesthetic enlightenment are the same thing..."[40]

Just as three points define a plane, and a table needs at least
three legs in order to stand, Truth and Beauty, a student of
Sufism would say, need Goodness to complete and complement
them. To choose Truth over untruth and to prefer Beauty to its
opposite is, at the same time, a moral attitude. Hence, religious/
philosophical values and aesthetic values cannot be divorced
from moral values.

In Sufism, it is beautiful morals that will escalate us towards
the truth. The Arabic term *hasan* simultaneously means good
and beautiful—a single word combines both aesthetics and ethics ("aesthethics"). When one's conduct is beautiful, when one's
every action and movement are full of grace, then Truth cannot
stay away, because Goodness and Beauty are Truth's very nature.

Aesthetics is the adoration of the beautiful. We are dazzled
by the breath-taking beauty of a work of art. As Kakuzo
Okakura explains:

Nothing is more hallowing than the union of kindred spirits in
art. At the moment of meeting, the art lover transcends himself. At once he is and is not. He catches a glimpse of Infinity,
but words cannot voice his delight, for the eye has no tongue.
Freed from the fetters of matter, his spirit moves in the
rhythm of things. It is thus that art becomes akin to religion

---

40. Hideo Kishmoto, "Mahayana Buddhism and Japanese Thought,"
Philosophy East and West, vol. 4, no. 3 (Oct. 1954), p. 221.

and ennobles mankind. It is this which makes a masterpiece something sacred.[41]

For the lover of beauty, nature has a place all its own. In Sufism, nature—in fact, the entire universe—is a self-expression of God. If nature is beautiful, therefore, this must be telling us something very profound about God. The Prophet said: "God is Beautiful, He loves beauty," and indeed, the beauty we find in nature is a reflection—as in a mirror—of the Beautiful (*Jamil*), who is also the Supreme Artist (*Sani*).

Beauty is a subtle combination of symmetry and assymetry, of perfection and imperfection. Pure symmetry is static; it is the element of assymetry that infuses dynamism into the world. The same is true in physics, where time becomes comprehensible as irreversible change, or where there is more matter in existence than antimatter. And similarly in biology, where the molecules of life are always left-handed. Asymmetry, in other words, is an indispensable part of the world, of nature. A work of art therefore becomes a more faithful reflection of nature when it incorporates imperfection, like the pinch of salt that makes a cake more delicious, or the spice that adds tang to a meal. Moreover, absolute beauty belongs only to the Most Beautiful. In recognition of this, a Persian rug always includes a built-in flaw, enhancing its beauty at the same time that it acknowledges the limits of human art, by leaving the domain of perfect beauty to the Beautiful alone. In testimony of this fact, every creature of beauty has an imperfection in nature, too. One has only to remember the feet of a peacock or the thorns of a rose. Thus, art that incorporates imperfection is more "natural," because it imitates nature more closely.

---

41. K. Okakura, *The Book of Tea,* Tokyo: Kodansha International, 1991 [1906], p. 100.

Just as we speak of the beauty of forms, we are also able to speak of beautiful actions. In the human sphere, courtesy (*adab*) is the epitome of virtuous and beautiful conduct (*akhlaq al-hasana*). The Taoists thought of living in the world as a form of art. The Sufis likewise endeavor to turn their entire lives into an art masterpiece, through nobility of spirit and behavior. To cultivate one's self until one reaches perfection, until one is oneself a work of art, is the aspiration of all sages. When the person at length achieves sagehood, all his actions reflect the graceful flow of movements observable in the Tea Ceremony.

As an example, take charity or alms-giving. This must be done, not in ostentation, but as covertly as possible. The Sufi saying applicable here is: "The left hand should not know what the right hand is doing." If possible, one must do a good deed without its recipient ever finding out who the helper is. It was in this spirit that "charity stones" were erected in the Ottoman empire (some still stand in Istanbul today). A wealthy person wishing to make a donation would leave a sum on top of a stone pillar. Later, a poor and needy person would come by, reach up, and take what he needed from the deposit, without having to suffer the shame of being recognized by the donor. Yes, what sounds like a fairy tale today was a daily reality back then. Kind deeds should be done in secret as far as possible. This is only one example of beauteous—and hence praiseworthy—conduct.

As we have just seen, the Arabic word *hasan* is both an aesthetic and an ethical term. It describes both the beauty of form and beauty of conduct. Here, we have an aesthetic definition of ethics: the good is that which is beautiful, that which is harmonious. One who has a true appreciation for beauty will not fail to recognize what is beautiful in virtue. Gentleness, for example, is both good and beautiful—it is both aesthetic and ethical.

Starting from this, we are able to postulate a whole range of beautiful morals—cleanliness, purity, simplicity, humility, modesty, pity, compassion, respect, reverence, tranquility, self-composure—all of which were among the character traits of the Prophet, and which must indeed be possessed by all refined human beings. Ultimate Reality will disclose Himself to all those who approach Him with purity and courtesy. When it is seen that Truth, Beauty, and Goodness mutually reinforce each other, the circle is closed, it is completed, and the way lies open to elevation in an ever-ascending spiral.

Our human condition, however, is such that one is not always able to distinguish good from bad and right from wrong. How is one to choose the correct way?

It is here that a written book and a human example come to the rescue. In the Koran, Truth Himself declares what is Good and what is Beautiful, i.e., the things that will lead us towards Him. And just in case there is room for error, the precedents set by the Messenger of Truth serve as a guiding light on this path.

Peace

All strife results from the illusion of separateness—from the mistaken conception that the universe is composed of irreconcilable opposites. But when one sees that the opposites do not contradict, but rather complete and complement each other, that they are all parts of an all-comprising unity and indeed are inseparably interfused, strife falls away and one is left with true peace (*anjin, salaam*). In Sufism, the way that leads to the One (*Ahad*) is called "Unification" or "making One" (*tawhid*). As a long poem dealing with the Messenger's birth states,

If you once say "God" with love
All sins drop away like autumn [leaves].

47

The root letters of Islam, SLM, give rise to a family of words that are "relatives" of Islam and without which the meaning of the latter cannot be fully understood.. In particular, the word *salama* means liberation, security, improvement, and perfection. *Salam* means peace, as well as comfort and friendship. In the Koran, Paradise (the Pure Land) is called "the abode of peace." *Sullam* means a ladder, and thus has the same meaning as Ascension (*meeraj*: "ladder"). The Ascension is a shaft of divine white light that "beams one up" towards the summit of Unity. Hence, the higher one climbs towards that summit, the greater the peace and tranquility one shall experience.

Harmony

Since all phenomena are manifestations of the Blessed One, they are in perfect harmony (*tanasub*) with one another. They all fit together like the pieces of a stupendous jigsaw puzzle and therefore contribute to Totality. According to the *Book of Changes*, the highest achievement of Heaven is the Supreme Harmony that permeates all things. As Chang Tsai observes, "The Great Harmony is known as the *Tao*," by which he means the Supreme Ultimate (*tai chi*). And the highest achievement of humanity is harmony with one's self and with human society.[42] This is none other than *musalama*, which means being at peace, good-natured, gentle, and kind. Here we also find the character traits that will lead to harmony. According to D.T. Suzuki, the character for "harmony" (*wa*) also reads "gentleness of spirit" (*yawaragi*),[43] which he thinks better describes the art of tea. We have the direct counterpart of this concept in the Arabic *hilm*, "gentleness," which was one of the prime characteristics of the Prophet.

---

42. Laurence C. Wu, *Fundamentals of Chinese Philosophy*, pp. 164, 279.
43. D.T. Suzuki, *Zen and Japanese Culture*, p. 274.

As he said: "God is mild and is fond of mildness, and He gives to the mild what He does not give to the harsh." If all human beings were to be adorned with this courtesy (*adab*), can there be any doubt that harmony and peace would soon be achieved?

Love

Love, like gravitation, holds the universe together. Not only that, but love is also what holds the universe in existence. If all things are One, if I am you and you are me, love becomes the only proper response to the universe, since at bottom nothing is separated from each other. The Sacred Tradition (Saying) on the "Hidden Treasure" states: "I was a Hidden Treasure, and I loved to be known. Hence, I formed (created) all beings in order that I may be known." The Sufis have freely interpreted this as: "I formed all beings with love." Another saying of the Messenger states that God's love for each is a hundred times greater than the love of a mother for her child. Our whole existence, from beginning to end, unfolds in that love, and could not be sustained for an instant without it. All the good things that are our lot, all the love we ever receive from anyone, are coming indirectly from God. We are being allowed to live, to enjoy this wonderful universe. If this is true, thankfulness or gratitude is the only proper response.

Of all creatures, God has lavished His love most on human beings. Because all things were created for Man. And God created human beings for Himself. According to the Master:

God says, "I love them, but I wish them to love Me, too. I created you, I love you very much, and I wish you to love me to a very high degree."

Closely related with love are compassion and charity. This is the basis for the compassion of the Buddha. This is where *Avalo-*

49

kitesvara, "the Lord looking down in pity," and Kuan Yin, the archetype of compassion, both take their origin.

One of the basic formulas in Islamic Sufism is *Bismillah ar-Rahman ar-Rahim,* "In the name of God, the Compassionate, the Merciful." We might pause for a moment to savor the meaning of these words. Both *Rahman* and *Rahim* derive from *rahm,* meaning "womb." An unborn baby is nourished in the body of its mother; the mother cares only for the proper growth of her baby, and freely gives it life and nourishment without expecting anything in return—indeed, with no thought of recompense. In the same way, the entire universe is a womb to us, fine-tuned—as the Anthropic Principle recognizes—to precisely the right conditions that assure our survival.

Rahman, the Compassionate, is the expression of God's infinite love for His formations (creatures); he sustains them all, without drawing any distinction between members of His family. But there is an even higher level for the expression of love, and that is *Rahim,* the Merciful. Mercy is a more enhanced and concentrated form of compassion, which God reserves for those who draw close to him through the Way He has prescribed. Just as a parent loves all his or her children, but holds the most obedient child closest and will shower that child with greater love and leniency, God holds His most obedient servants in higher esteem.

Charity, too, is a direct consequence of love. The fundamental oneness of all beings means that by saving others, one is actually saving oneself. The Master used to say, "If you see a fly struggling in water, save it." If this is the case for a fly, how much more so for a human being! In a world where many people have truly understood the meaning of the Unity of Existence (*wahdah al-wujud*), everyone would reach out with charity to everyone else, and there would be immeasurably fewer poor, needy, suffering, and sick people. Charity is the gate to Paradise, and if everybody could practice it, this world itself would become a Pure Land. Charity is not just giving money. "Smiling at another is charity," said the Prophet, "saying Hello to someone is charity." To please another person is, at the same time, to please God.

Equality

"All things are One" brings with it the corollary that in some fundamental sense, all things are also equal. "In non-duality all is equal—Very small and large are equal" (and *vice versa*).[44] If God has placed a divine spark in me, He has done the same with all things. If any one thing is a mirror reflecting God's light, the same applies to the rest of existence. Thus, although differentiation without number or reckoning is the rule of Multiplicity, all things share the same Essence at the level of Unity.

The same applies to human beings. Although no two human beings are alike, yet in some sense they are equal, and equally worthy of love and respect. If in saving others one saves oneself, it does not matter who the "other" is—one should not discriminate.

After a certain battle was over, the Messenger of God—the Prophet—asked his Companions: "Suppose you have some water with you, and wandering around the battlefield after the fighting is over, you see two wounded, thirsty soldiers, both crying out for water. One is on your side, the other is an enemy soldier. Which one would you give water to?"

The Companions replied that surely they would give water to the friendly party. "No," said the Messenger. "The battle is over. In that instant, that wounded soldier is no longer an enemy, but a human being in need." And he explained that the water should be shared between the two soldiers.

---

44. *Hsin Hsin Ming*, stanzas 31, 33.

Intimacy

If all things are One and manifestations of the One, everyday reality is itself sacred. Every single thing directly manifests the highest sacred reality. For the enlightened Sufi, God is present everywhere and in all things. Likewise, the Prophet, as the direct recipient of Universal Mind (*aql al-kull*) and of Enlightenment, is present spiritually in all parts of the universe.

But many human beings are not aware of this intimate unity of all things—far from it. They have fallen into the error of believing that the universe is a shattered, disconnected wasteland, rather than the stupendous Unity that it is in reality. They inhabit a dark world in the nether regions of existence, and treat each other according to the dictates of their delusion.

The thing to do, then, is this: human beings must re-establish intimate connection with all things. This is done by carrying out the advice of God and following the guidance of the Messenger. One should act with courtesy towards all things. One should strive to attain purity of heart. And, along with many other things, one should perform the Formal Prayer.

Why should one do this last, though?

When the Prophet made his Ascension to God, Formal Prayer was prescribed for all human beings. "Formal Prayer," said the Messenger, "is the Ascension of the believer." The Ascension leading to Enlightenment, in other words, is available to all human beings, and is potentially present at every point in the universe. (All points can be "mapped" to that higher state.) It is the prime activity of the Messenger. And Formal Prayer is what allows human beings to participate in that activity. In fact, if one considers, the Formal Prayer itself can be called the activity of God and His Messenger, since both participate in it. This participation is relived through the postures and recitation that specifically access the Ascension every time the Formal Prayer is performed (correctly). This is the true meaning of the Master's saying, "There is no Prayer without Ascension and no Ascension without Prayer."

The Ascension, *meeraj,* literally means "stairway." The name of a chapter in the Koran, "Stairways" (*maarij*), suggests that there are many Ascensions, many stairways to God. In general, Ascension is the process that elevates one to God. And the Formal Prayer is the action of climbing that stairway.

The Master said: "Every prophet came with Formal Prayer." He said this on the strength of the Islamic notion that other religions also originally had "Formal Prayers" of their own, similar—though not identical—to the Formal Prayer as we know it today. Also, Formal Prayer is a treasure—of worship, of meditation. If we define Formal Prayer as "the means to reach Ultimate Reality," it becomes clear that no human being can be barred from it, for Enlightenment is the birthright of every human being. The Master also said: "Formal Prayer [in the form as we know it from the Prophet] belongs to everyone."

The result of Formal Prayer is an increase in intimacy with God, who is the Origin, the One at the heart of all things. One can re-establish intimacy with anything—with God, with one's Beloved, with the world—only by completely relinquishing even the slightest sense of self.[45] A Japanese word, *jocho,* describes a state of emotion where there is no distinction between oneself and others. Here we glimpse a dimension of the *anatman* (selflessness) doctrine, provided we understand this in the sense that one has to lose one's selfhood in order to be able to establish intimacy. As a stanza of Ibrahim Hakki's Sufi poem states,

---

45. Cf. Thomas P. Kasulis, "Intimacy: A general orientation in Japanese religious values," *Philosophy East and West,* vol. 4, no. 4 (Oct. 1990), p. 445.

Forget yourself and find Him.

This sense of the *anatman* concept is expressed in Sufism as self-lessness, lack or forgetfulness of self (*la ana*: "no-I," *la nafs, bi-khudi*: "no-self"). One cannot realize God before one loses one's sense of individual selfhood. The unreality of separation, of diversity, does not mean that the self does not exist, but that it is One Self. *Atman* is *Brahman*—to use an expression from the *Upanishads*, "Thou art That," or as Ibn Arabi put it, "Thou art He." But this is realized only when the little local self is transcended. Only when individual selfhood is obliterated, only when *atman/nafs* reaches *anatman*, can one be united with *Brahman*. Selflessness also brings us back to compassion, because selflessness implies that there is in fact no difference between oneself and others. In Buddhism, too, compassion (*karuna*) is one of the noblest qualities. The *bodhisattva*, like the Sufi sage, "embraces all others as 'we,' which includes not just 'me' and 'you,' but also 'them.'"[46]

Now such selflessness leading to intimacy—and ultimately, to Unity (*wahdah*)—is known by another name in Sufism. It is called Love (*ashq, hubb*). So intimacy brings us back to love. There is no escaping love, no way to avoid either its joys or its duties. For one can truly love another only if one thinks everything of the other and nothing of oneself. Sufi psychology ("self-knowledge") tells us that this ultimately leads to a sense of identity with the beloved. In the famous Middle-Eastern love story, *Leila and Majnun,* Majnun is so infatuated with Leila and suffers so many trials trying to reach her that he finally comes to a point where he is able to say,

---

46. Sungtaek Cho, "Selflessness: Toward a Buddhist Vision of Social Justice," *Journal of Buddhist Ethics, 7* (2000), pp. 76–85.

"I am Leila."

He looks inside himself, and can find no trace whatsoever of Majnun. This is the pinnacle of love, of selflessness. One has become so intimate with the beloved that only consciousness of the beloved remains. (Another famous Middle-Eastern love story, *Ferhad and Shereen,* relates how Ferhad bores a hole in the mountain of his self to reach his beloved.)

Even intimacy in its ordinary sense, and even love, still imply separation. For in ordinary love there are two: the lover and the beloved, and a relationship that connects them, namely love. In the state of Consummation or Attainment (*wuslat*), the lover, the beloved, and love itself are totally fused. This is why God addresses the great Sufi sheikh, Abdulqader Geylani, as follows:

"Love Me, love for My sake, because I am that Love.[47] And keep your heart and your every state away from everything but Me.

"When you find and know the exterior of Love, you should annihilate yourself from Love, for Love is a veil between the lover and the Beloved. The lover meets his Beloved only when annihilated from Love. And you should also be annihilated from everything other than Love, for things other than Love are also veils between the lover and the Beloved."[48]

Love demands that there should be no existence outside the beloved. So it is love that leads us to intimacy and, finally, to Unity.

This is no easy task, and cannot be performed in one step. Sufism has therefore instituted a program that carries one

47. A variant reading of the "Hidden Treasure" holy tradition is: "I was a hidden treasure, and wished to be known. From Myself to Myself, I created the universe through Love."
48. From Geylani, *Treatise on Divine Aid (The Holy Bestowal).*

through various stages. The first step is to establish "connection" or "binding" (*rabita*) with one's master. During meditation (*tafakkur*), one should clothe oneself in the master's spirituality. That is, one should imagine[49] that one is clothed in the master's appearance and attributes, which is intimacy with the master. This is to say that one should don the master's morality/courtesy, almost like a garment. Otherwise the Binding will not hold, it will not have lasting effect—the spiritual transplant will be rejected. *The Base Self will repel the higher state.* Here, Sufism provides the connective tissue between ethics and mysticism, between the exoteric (outward behavior) and the esoteric (inner state). By this means, together with Formal Prayer, one eventually reaches a point where only the self-consciousness of one's master remains (*fana fi-sheikh*). After this, other steps follow that lead one to ever higher degrees of intimacy.

Shin, the Japanese character for intimacy, also means "parents." To be intimate with all things means to be gentle and tender towards them, even inanimate objects, in the same way that a parent is towards his or her child. Kindness is the morality of intimacy. The Messenger excelled in loving kindness towards all things, and his example should inspire us all, as it has inspired so many Sufi saints and sages down the ages, in our endeavor to re-establish intimacy with the universe and with God.

---

49. One should never underestimate the power of the imagination. "Imagination can not only cause that-which-was-not, to be; it can cause that-which-was, not to be." Harold C. Goddard ("Transcendence," in Theodore Roszak (ed.), *Sources,* New York: Harper Colophon, 1972, p. 514). It is this kind of Active or Creative Imagination (as Henry Corbin translates Ibn Arabi's term, *quwwat al-khayal*) that is used in *tulpa* creation in Tibet (according to Alexandra David-Neel).

The Tree Metaphor

Unity can be metaphorically described by comparing it to a tree. A tree has a root which is underground, a trunk or stem above ground, then branches that become thinner and thinner from which sprout leaves and flowers. Our world of Multiplicity, the visible universe, is represented by these thin branches, leaves, and flowers, but as one descends to "deeper levels of existence" these are all seen to combine and eventually become merged into One Great Unity. The stem represents this unity, which is a metaphor for the Revealed God—i.e., God in His capacity which manifests itself in the phenomenal world. But the tree does not end there. It continues underground, in the "unseen world," which stands for both the spiritual world and the Hidden God— God in His invisible, unobservable aspect. The root may not be visible, but it is as real as the visible part. The fruit on the topmost branch is nourished by the root, to the extent that it receives sap—life-giving nutriment—from the root. And the fruit of this tree is the human being.

Which calls to mind a Sufi story.

A sage walking along a road one day happened to sit under a walnut tree. As he was relaxing in its shade, a walnut dropped in front of him from one of the higher branches.

The sage was lost in thought for a moment. Then he asked the tree: "This walnut that you have just dropped in front of me — did it come from you, or did you come from it?"

At this, the tree began to speak, and said:

"O sage, at first glance it may appear as if this walnut has come from me. My branches are laden with hundreds of its kind. In reality, however, I came from it. Many years ago, an honorable sage such as yourself was good enough to plant a walnut just like this one in the ground. Years passed, and from that humble walnut I emerged, as you now behold. I now bear *tons* of walnuts."

This Sufi story suggests that nature can teach us something about the divine, for "there is a lesson in everything." The story also tells us that a human being is like a seed, and when the pinnacle of self-cultivation is reached, all things will bloom from the heart of the Perfect Human.

Let us conclude this chapter with the following selection[50] from the Sufic literature of Ahmet Kayhan that describes the Perfect Human Being.

The Divine Helper

He is the matchless pearl in the ocean of bliss. He is the one who is perfect in the Divine Law, in the Ways, in Gnosis, and in Reality. He is known by many names: Sheikh, Leader, Guide, Savior. He is called Sage, Wise, Perfect. He is called the Imam, the Pole, the Pole of Poles, the Master of the Age. He is designated as the goblet that shows the world, the mirror that reflects the universe, the greatest elixir.[51] They call him the one who raises the dead, the Master of the Elixir of Life.

All beings are parts of his being. The totality of Being is a single person. The heart of all Being is that single Heart. The cosmos cannot be without a Heart. The invocation of God in that Heart, singular in the universe, is what upholds the world. Nothing in the realms of existence is hidden from that Heart; it knows and sees all things and the reality of all things as they

50. Translated from Haci Ahmet Kayhan (comp.), *Abdulkadir-i Geylani*, Ankara: Gimat, 1998, p. 1.
51. The references are to the mythical Wineglass of Jamshid and the Mirror of Alexander, which were capable of reflecting the entire universe. Both are symbols of the Perfect Human. The elixir is the Elixir of Immortality which, if imbibed, makes one a Perfect Human. One then becomes the Elixir oneself. That is, one becomes the Philosopher's Stone, turning every human being one touches into gold (metaphorically speaking, of course). For details, see H. Bayman, "The Case of the Cryptic Wineglass," in *Science, Knowledge, and Sufism* and *The Secret of Islam*.

actually are. All Being is under his gaze, both in appearance and in meaning. The events of the world unfold within his joy.

The helper never ceases, not even for a moment, to order the world, to dispel the bad habits and customs of the people and to spread the good, the true, and the beautiful in their place, to invite humanity to God and proclaim His greatness and oneness, to open the material and spiritual paths of humankind, to declare the value and eternity of the afterworld, and to explain that this world is transient, finite, and empty of value. His service to the people in the name of Truth is incessant. He does not have in himself a strength or power special to himself, any desire of his own. He is always with God and for God. He is in ceaseless servanthood in the palace of the Emperor. Still, he is completely free. Human tendencies and needs cannot bind him. He is Spirit and the Spirit of the spirit of Being. He is the fortress of existence. He is the one to whom the angels bow down. When "Human" is mentioned, he is the one who comes to mind. He is the possessor of honor and of the Trust. He is the Messenger of God, and the Messenger's inheritors in every age who bear his Light.

വ‌ദ   വ‌ദ   വ‌ദ

We have dealt with Unity and its correlates in this chapter. When we look around us, we behold a dizzying display of multiplicity. Yet the world's religions and philosophies have been insistent in telling us that this multiplicity is a side effect, even illusory, and that it is Unity that holds in actual fact. If this is true, a radically different way of ordering our relationship with the world lies before us—a way based on the appreciation of truth, beauty and virtue, on peace, love, and harmony, on equality and intimacy. A person who begins to tread on this way is like a walnut, and if he travels far enough, he will blossom into a tree.

In every age, there is one who is the most accomplished, the highest tree of all. Such a person is either the Prophet, or—in later times—an inheritor of his spiritual legacy. Such a person is the Sage of the Age, whose characteristics have been outlined above.

We now proceed to the next chapter, in order to investigate the relationship between nature and God.

5

FROM NATURE TO GOD

Nature is…the art of God.
—Henry David Thoreau

When the Eye of the Heart does not see,
the eye of the head cannot see at all.
—Yunus Emre

It is only with the heart that one can see rightly;
what is essential is invisible to the eye.
—Antoine de Saint-Exupéry

Look deeply into nature, and you will not fail to observe the signature of the Divine written all over it. The great poets of nature were able to discern this sublime truth. Here, for example, is William Wordsworth:

There was a time when meadow, grove, and stream,
The earth, and every common sight,
*   To me did seem*
Apparelled in celestial light,
The glory and the freshness of a dream.[52]

---

52. Wordsworth, *Intimations of Immortality*.

...And I have felt
A presence that disturbs me with the joy
Of elevated thoughts; a sense sublime
Of something far more deeply interfused,
Whose dwelling is the light of setting suns,
And the round ocean and the living air,
And the blue sky, and in the mind of man:
A motion and a spirit, that impels
All thinking things, all objects of all thought,
And rolls through all things. Therefore am I still
A lover of the meadows and the woods,
And mountains; and of all that we behold
From this green earth... [53]

Today, astrophysics tells us that all the heavier elements out of which nature is constituted were forged in the interiors of long-dead stars. Those stars, in other words, gave their lives so we may live. In that case, can Walt Whitman's insight in the first line below be described as anything less than prescient?

I believe a leaf of grass is no less than the journey-work of the stars,
And the pismire is equally perfect, and a grain of sand, and the egg of
the wren,
And the tree-toad is a chef-d'oeuvre *for the highest,*
And the running blackberry would adorn the parlors of heaven,
And the narrowest hinge in my hand puts to scorn all machinery,
And the cow crunching with depress'd head surpasses any statue,
And a mouse
is miracle enough
to stagger sextillions of infidels. [54]

---

53. Wordsworth, *Lines Composed a Few Miles Above Tintern Abbey.*
54. Whitman, *Song Of Myself (Leaves of Grass).*

Another person who was not a poet, but who wrote such prose that he deserves to be called a nature poet, was Henry David Thoreau. With an eye that took in all of nature, seeing that it was alive and alight with the divine, Thoreau saw what others, who wish to reduce life to death and joy to despair, cannot or will not see:

> Beside this I got a rare mess of golden and silver and bright cupreous fishes, which looked like a string of jewels. Ah! I have penetrated to those meadows on the morning of many a first spring day, jumping from hummock to hummock, from willow root to willow root, when the wild river valley and the woods were bathed in so pure and bright a light as would have waked the dead... There needs no stronger proof of immortality. All things must live in such a light.[55]

> Early in May, the oaks, hickories, maples, and other trees, just putting out amidst the pine woods around the pond, imparted a brightness like sunshine to the landscape, especially in cloudy days, as if the sun were breaking through mists and shining faintly on the hillsides here and there.[56]

The beauty, the intelligence we behold in nature is breathtaking. Only those who have an appreciation for beauty can recognize it, only those who are themselves highly intelligent can recognize the fingerprint of an intelligence superior to their own. How can this work of art be ascribed to anything other than an infinite intelligence?

Years ago, this writer had a discussion with a Turkish parapsychologist. The man could not believe that God worked as a sculptor, shaping a statue from without. But that is not the way God works. He gives form to everything *from within*. He is like

---

55. Thoreau, *Walden,* Chapter 17: "Spring."
56. Ibid.

a hand in a glove that makes the glove move. And He is also the one who designs the glove and manufactures it. He is the one in a plant making the plant grow, the one in each of its cells, the one in its DNA. The very fact that the laws of science, which are also the laws of nature, are the same everywhere, is proof enough that the Tao is all-pervasive. Do not seek for miracles beyond nature, even if these are possible. As the Zen poet P'ang-yun put it:

> *Miraculous power and marvelous activity—*
> *Drawing water and hewing wood!*

For nature itself is so miraculous that our indifference to it can only be explained by the adage: "Familiarity breeds boredom." Those who cannot understand the One Sacred are lost children, misguided babes in the woods. As the Sufi poet Misri sang:

> *Nothing is more visible than the Real*
> *He is hidden only to the eyeless.*

Another Sufi poet, Sheikh Ibrahim, adds:

> *The effusion of the Real on the cosmos*
> *Is uniform—if you understand*
> *All these things that are visible*
> *Are One Face—if you understand…*

> *To see the Face of the Real*
> *The sight[57] of Man is required*
> *On this mirror, the cosmos*
> *Is a speck of dust—if you understand*

And another, Ghaybi:

---

57. The Eye of the Heart.

What appears to you as the world
Is, in reality, God
God is One, to this I swear
Do not think He is several.

This is not pantheism. As Ghaybi explains,

Love is the Essence of the Real
The cosmos is His Attributes

Nature is not God. It is the *manifestation* of God, neither Him nor wholly separate from Him. As the Master explained: "God is in each particle, but each particle is not God." Nature is the garment of God, woven by Him with infinite love, and human beings are the crown jewel of that beautiful costume—not because many of them wallow in the mud, but because of what they have the capacity to *become*.

In designing nature, God has put everything into it. Wherever you look, you find unmistakable signs that this is all the handiwork of a Great Artist, a Great Mathematician, a Great Scientist, a Great Architect, and a Great Engineer. Thoreau discusses the case of snow:

Nature is full of genius, full of divinity; so that not a snowflake escapes its fashioning hand...The same law that shapes the earth-star shapes the snow-star. As surely as the petals of a flower are fixed, each of these countless snow-stars comes whirling to earth...these glorious spangles, the sweeping of heaven's floor.[58]

With a knowledge, a science that is infinite, God fashions the ten zillion things down to the smallest quark. He is within the smallest, yet He is greater than the greatest. It is easy to see

---

58. Thoreau, *Journal [1906]*, January 5, 1906.

how the Limitless cannot be encompassed by any finite thing. If we said that He is in this tree and not in that bird, or vice versa, we would be limiting Him. By extension, this applies to the entire universe, which—though vast—is still finite. Therefore, there must be a component of the Transfinite that extends beyond the physical cosmos. This is where the transcendence comes from.

At the same time, God is present everywhere and sees all things. God fills the universe in the same way that the void which forms the cavity of a lake is filled to the brim by the lake's water, or every nook and cranny of the seabed is filled by the sea. Just as the heart is the center of the circulatory system which is comprised of arteries, veins, and capillaries, the Self of God is at the core of all selves. And just as all the neurons of the nervous sytem are connected to the brain, all spirits are ultimately connected to the Spirit of God. Rumi rejects all duality, and by inference all multiplicity:

Say not two, know not two, call not on two!...
One I seek, One I know, One I see, One I call. [59]

⚃   ⚃   ⚃

God is the Artist (*Sani*), nature is His artwork (*su'n*). Every beauty we behold in nature is a reflection of an aspect of His beauty. Yet it is not as if God were entirely outside nature, for He is within it also. God is both transcendent and immanent, both incomparable to all other things and similar to them in His qualities. The naked eye beholds nature. It requires the inner eye, the Eye of the Heart (*ayn al-basira*), to discern the presence of the Divine within, behind, and beyond nature.

---

59. The first line is from the *Mathnawi*, the second from the *Diwan*.

A time comes when one inevitably dies. What, if anything, lies on the other side? The fact that there already exists something invisible—God—behind the nature exposed to our senses, leads us to suspect that there may be other components to Unobservability as well. In fact, we know these already exist, since another person's thoughts and memories—which we know exist because we have them too—are invisible to us. These are all parts of the Invisible Realm (*alam al-ghayb*). As Chuang Tzu remarked, "The frog in the well can see only a little sky, and so thinks that the sky is only so big."

So what else does the "sky" harbor? Is death the end, or is the human spirit immortal, to continue living in a different sector of the Unobservable? This we shall be dealing with in the next chapter.

6

LIFE AFTER DEATH

*God has rewarded them [with] Gardens underneath which rivers flow,
wherein they will abide forever. That is the reward of the good.*

—*The Koran* (5:85)

The Metaphor of the Garden

Istanbul used to be—and, despite all the desecration it has undergone, still remains—one of the most beautiful cities in the world. It is probably the only city that bridges two continents. From one side, one can see Asia from across a body of water not much wider than a river, while sitting on the opposite side, one beholds Europe. That water is called the Bosphorous, a wonderful azure blue on which everything from small fishing boats to gigantic oil tankers may be seen to be making their way. The city welds beauty and history together, for a rich Ottoman heritage is visible in the palaces and villas that decorate both shores like pearls on a necklace.

One of the ports on the Asian—Anatolian—side is called Beylerbeyi, which may be translated as "Prince of Princes." One disembarks at the port and wends one's way up numerous narrow roads set upon a slope lined with one- or two-story houses. It was on a lovely day of late spring or early summer that a child went to visit his relatives there in the late 1950s. Their house was set upon a hill, which had a main entrance on the road below. The child climbed an extended, rather steep stone stairway lined with fig trees and other trees bearing fruit. At the top, one came upon a flat area where the two-story mansion was situated. In the upper rooms of that mansion, one could still inhale the deep peace that once pervaded the Ottoman past, now gone forever. In front of the house there was a beautiful, well-kept garden with pink magnolias, a small fountain in which goldfish swam, and, behind both the mansion and garden, a much vaster but untended garden where nature was in full bloom. It is written in *The Aesthetics of Love:* "desiring to be close to nature [to the greatest extent], Muslims have interfered with nature as little as possible in the gardens they made...Clashing with nature, damaging it, interfering with its balances, appeared to Muslims to violate its sacredness. They knew that the sacredness in nature is perennial, while they themselves were mortal."[60] The same applied to this garden.

The child walked into the back yard. Because he was small, the tall grass, now slowly turning yellow in the heat, rose to the level of his eyes. Butterflies, ladybugs, and insects of every assortment danced among the wild flowers, while birds could be heard singing in the relatively few trees. The fragrance of a hundred flowers wafted through the air. It was the closest thing to Paradise the child had laid eyes on. Slowly walking through this splendor of nature, the child's attention was by and by attracted to the big, double-winged door on the high rear wall that enclosed the back yard.

The door became an object of fascination arousing intense curiosity. In the child's mind, it became a mysterious portal. Who knew what lay behind it? It was only natural that this inquisitive child should slowly approach this door dwarfing him, reach up,

---

60. Beshir Ayvazoghlu, *Ashk Estetighi,* Istanbul, Turkey: Otuken, 1993 [1982], p. 138. This is a study on Islamic aesthetics by a Turkish art critic. As he points out, the aesthetics of Islam is deeply informed by Sufism.

and unhitch the latch. The movable wing creaked inward, and the child stepped out.

What he saw was this:

A narrow, level road, paved with cobblestones just like the other roads. On the other side, a low wall. And beyond that wall, easily visible, a vast expanse of nature that reached out to infinity as it were, from which the tombstones of a cemetery could be spied from afar, under the graceful cypress trees which are customary in Turkish cemeteries. In Istanbul as in many other Turkish locations, the graveyard is situated within nature in just this manner, and it is a place not to be feared, but an abode of calm tranquility, where the dead may be presumed to indeed rest in peace. Life and death exist side by side here, each as natural and peaceful as the other, both part of the grand design of the universe.

After gazing at the scenery and the distant, rolling hills for a while, the child turned back, crossed the road, and entered the back yard again, respectfully closing the big door behind him. Again he found himself in the wonderful display of sounds, colors, and smells described earlier. It was a memorable day, to be cherished many years hence.

As he grew older, however, the description above would slowly change in the child's mind into a metaphor of the afterlife. Suppose, he would think, that he had not turned back, and the second time around, the great doorway had been, not behind him, but on the other side of the cemetery? In his imagination he placed the doorway on the other side. In that case, the graveyard would be an isthmus, a brief intermission, between two beautiful gardens—this world and the next. If this metaphor is true, then, as the Turkish poet Yahya Kemal expressed it,

Death is a tranquil land of spring

—an abode that separates, but also joins, two gardens for those who have lived a pure life, who have been careful not to sully themselves with impurities. For to the pure, all things are pure. Both this world and the next world will be, for them, two Pure Lands. As one lives, so one will die, and what one has forwarded with one's own hands will be there to meet one on the other side. If one has done wicked deeds, one will find them rising up to face him over there, for the two worlds are symmetric. Do as you would be done by, for as you do, so you *will* be done by (17:7, 99:7-8). But if one has lived with love and respect, that same love and respect will envelope one when s/he has crossed the bridge, a bridge that both unites and divides two continents, two worlds.

Reincarnation

All religions have an ethical aspect. Moreover, all religions have a schema by which ethical action is reinforced. Actions defined as good will be rewarded, whereas actions falling under the category of bad will be met with retribution.

Thus far, all—or at any rate, most—religions are in agreement. When it comes to the exact form this recompense takes, however, we find that conceptions diverge. There are two major paths.

One is the approach taken by the later monotheistic religions. At the risk of repeating the obvious, one is born, dies, enters an after-death spiritual realm where one is judged for one's actions, and is consigned to heaven (a space of positive states) or hell (a space of negative states). One is not reborn into this world. When these traditions speak of "rebirth," this is always in the context of spiritual—not physical—rebirth. What is meant is the total transformation of the human personality during one's lifetime, or else the rebirth is in the afterworld.

The second approach is that of Eastern philosophies. Here the notion of *karma* assumes importance. *Karma* is one's accumulation of merit or demerit based on one's good or bad deeds. Up to this point, it is not much different from the monotheistic conception. It is in how *karma* operates that the real divergence occurs. The scene of recompense is conceived to be this world. One is reborn into this world many times, and the total karmic accumulation of past lives each time determines the conditions of one's rebirth into this world. (Transmigration allows for rebirth even as an animal or a plant.) If one has done dastardly deeds in a previous life, one may be reborn in conditions of extreme deprivation and undergo suffering in a later life. For example, if one has put out someone's eyes in a past life, one may be reborn blind the next time around. The cycle of deaths and rebirths is ended only when one dissolves into *nirvana*.

Sufism, of course, sides with the monotheistic scheme. The Koran states quite clearly that "there is a barrier" which prevents deceased spirits from being reborn into this world until the resurrection (23:100). Unfortunately, there is no "second chance" to relive one's life, let alone endless chances.

It is not my purpose here to argue whether reincarnation is true or untrue. This is a matter for private belief. I can only point out that the two schemes do not mix: like water and oil, they are mutually incompatible. There are two important reasons for this.

The first is that according to reincarnation, there is no "other world" where payback occurs. Even though human beings possess spirits and these spirits reincarnate or transmigrate, it would appear that spirits have no abode, no spiritual world to which they, as spirits, ought to belong. Upon death they rise towards the Light, but cannot sustain that presence and fall back into rebirth almost instantaneously. In this conception, heaven is the positive states in this world and hell is the negative states in the same world. We know, however, that this world is a mixed blessing, that even in the most charmed life there is no continuous purely blissful state. So whereas single-incarnation allows for the existence of a separate spirit world and much-enhanced blissful or wrathful states, reincarnation is set wholly in this world and the only escape from *samsara* one can hope for is extinction in *nirvana*. One may perhaps call reincarnation "materialistic spiritualism" or half-hearted spiritualism—although the existence of the human spirit is acknowledged, its drama is played out entirely within the confines of this world.

The second reason why the two theories don't mix is that in single-incarnation, the subject is well-defined, while in reincarnation this is not the case. A person is born, grows up, lives a life of predominantly good or bad deeds, and dies. When judgment takes place in the afterworld, there is no confusion as to who is being judged for what deeds. But now suppose that a person were to live several lives before going on to a last judgment in the spiritual world. Which of these lives is to be judged? The first? The second? All of them? If a person were a saint in one life and a sinner in the other, should he go to heaven or hell? In other words, trying to mix the two approaches lands us in extreme logical difficulties, and one is forced to a choice between alternatives.

If people reincarnate into this world, there must be some this-worldly method of investigation by which claims of reincarnation can be verified. Ever since his seminal *Twenty Cases Suggestive of Reincarnation* (1974), Professor Ian Stevenson, a psychiatrist at the University of Virginia, has conducted the most meticulous research into cases taken to indicate reincarnation.[61] He is care-

---

61. For a recent review of Prof. Stevenson's work, see Tom Shroder, *Old Souls: The Scientific Evidence for Reincarnation,* New York: Simon & Schuster, 1999, and check out the site www.childpastlives.org.

ful to point out that, after thousands of cases, there still exists no conclusive proof. Memories recalled under hypnosis, a state of high suggestibility, are dismissed by Stevenson himself. His most compelling cases are those involving birthmarks or birth defects supposed to carry on from an earlier life. I myself have become convinced that once fraud is ruled out, there could still be other explanations for phenomena that suggest reincarnation.

In his *New Dimensions of Deep Analysis,*[62] a thoughtful book which few people probably remember today, psychiatrist Jan Ehrenwald suggested, on the basis of the therapist-patient experience, that one had to entertain the possibility of the *multiple location of psychic contents.* The therapist could effectively cure a patient only if "transference" occurred, i.e., the patient deeply trusted the therapist, accepted him as a sort of father-figure, and even identified with the therapist to a certain extent. Under such cases, it sometimes happened that certain contents of the therapist's psyche emerged spontaneously in the patient's mind, and were communicated back to the therapist as though they belonged to the patient's own self. In terms of mystical/unitive states, this is a quite understandable—if rare—event. (Not only thoughts but even physical attributes can be shared in these states, e.g. through psychosomatic "imprinting," especially where highly traumatic incidents are involved.) Such "psychic bleed-through" or "osmosis" may also explain telepathy. All this is in accordance with the conception of the Sufi sage Ahmed Sirhindi (Imam Rabbani)—in his "unity of subjects" (*wahdah al-shuhud*: unity of observers), he postulated that all perceivers are ultimately one. Indeed, in Sufism a dream that you see as happening to yourself may actually be a telepathic or precognitive dream pertaining to someone else, and the Master himself explained

---

62. Jan Ehrenwald, *New Dimensions of Deep Analysis,* New York: Grune & Stratton, 1954.

some dreams in this way. (Perhaps such dreams could be called "osmotic.") Suppose, then, that these dreams were complemented by osmotic retrocognitive recall in waking life?

Think of a computer network. A shared file on any one of the computers can be accessed from any other (depending, of course, on permissions). For example, a setup program on the main server can be accessed from a client as if it were the client's own file, it can even be used to install the program for the client, but all the while the installation program is sitting on the server and does not belong to the client.

If the contents of one psyche can be distributed across different locations, not only in space but in spacetime, this could also serve to explain many phenomena attributed to reincarnation. In the same way that the thoughts of the therapist emerge in the patient's consciousness, the psychic contents of a dead person come to be shared with a living person.. The living person becomes flushed, even swamped, with the mental contents and recollections of the dead person, a situation closely linked with mediumship and channeling. One case of Stevenson's, that of the Indian boy Jasbir, illustrates this possibility. When he was two-and-a-half years old, he started claiming he was Sobha Ram, a man who had just died and stumbled into Jasbir's body, at that time weakened by smallpox. He began to exhibit striking differences in behavior and personality. It has been suggested that "spirit possession" is a more plausible explanation in this case.[63] Thus, phenomena that appear to suggest reincarnation may actually have other—quite different—explanations.

One final point remains to be made: the belief in reincarnation helps to support the rigid caste system of India, and hardens one's heart against the misfortunes of others. Suppose you pass

---

63. "Reincarnation, its meaning and consequences," www.comparativer-eligion.com/reincarnation1.html, accessed March 30, 2001.

by a blind beggar, for instance. "Serves him right," you may reflect, "he probably put out someone's eyes in a past life." Insensitivity to injustice has been explained on the basis that with karmic rebirth, a system of justice is already in place.[64] As such, its effects on ethics and human mentality run counter even to Buddhism, which lays emphasis on compassion. (Another noted contradiction with Buddhism is found in the *anatman* doctrine, where it is not clear what, if anything, reincarnates.)

This is as far as evidence in the physical world will take us. Beyond this, it is a question of belief, and each person must make a choice based on one's own disposition.

ଔ   ଔ   ଔ

All the world's religions have found that man's soul is immortal, and that for every action there is a payback, a recompense. It is in their scheme as to how this retribution occurs that they diverge. In one scheme, one is reborn in a Pure Land or an Impure one, depending on one's actions in this life. In the other, one is reborn into this world, into good or bad conditions also dependent on one's previous life. Notice that the basic plan does not change. However, the evidence for rebirth into this world can be explained by other means. A fully convincing proof of reincarnation has not yet been found, and after thousands of years is unlikely to be found in the future. Rebirth, not into this world but into a Pure Land, is the likeliest result in the after-death state. No matter what scheme one adopts, one must not forget that we pay for our deeds, and that crime does not pay.

We are now ready to investigate the concept of God as this occurs in East Asia. Scholars know about it, of course, yet there

---

64. Winston L. King, "Judeo-Christian and Buddhist Justice," *Journal of Buddhist Ethics,* 2 (1995), p. 75.

is a widespread conception, even in today's East Asians, that God is unknown in the East. We shall see whether, or to what extent, this is true—in the next chapter.

7

GOD IN EAST ASIAN CULTURE

The greatest has nothing beyond itself and is called the Great One.
—Hui Shih

Even those who worship other deities, and sacrifice to them with faith in their hearts, are really worshiping Me, though with a mistaken approach.
—Bhagavad Gita

Tao, T'ien, Ti, Kami

The earliest ancestors of the Chinese believed in One God (called *Shang Ti* or *T'ien Ti*). It is impossible to overemphasize the fact that Chinese culture and Chinese history begins with the concept of One God. Although today, God is not recognized explicitly in East Asian thought, yet His recognition is just around the corner. The Chinese terms Tao, T'ien, Ti, and the Japanese term Kami all refer to sacredness or the Absolute. Since there cannot be more than one Absolute, at bottom they all must refer to the same thing

At first, a person may find the identification of Tao, T'ien, Ti, and Kami in this way unusual, even objectionable. They appear to be referring to different concepts. But in reality it is correct, for Truth is only One. It is called "Heavenly Oneness" (*ch'ien i*) in the *Book of Changes,* "the All-pervading One" (*i kuan*) in the Confucian classics, "Holding onto the One" (*shou i*) in Taoist scriptures, and "One" (*Ahad*) in the Koran. The goal of human beings, the end result of all self-cultivation, is to realize this Oneness. As the Zen master Hui-neng remarks in the *T'an Ching* (Platform Sermons), "When One is realized, nothing remains to be done."[65]

In what follows, we shall first investigate the emergence of God in East Asian culture, and then go on to draw out the meaning of the profession of faith in Islam, "There is no god but God."

God in the *I Ching*

Great was the wisdom of the ancients. Among their heritage is the *I Ching* or Book of Changes, perhaps the most sophisticated book of divination ever produced by any civilization. Although the *I Ching* is, naturally, focused on giving practical advice, God is briefly mentioned in it.[66] Itself already ancient, the *I Ching* states (in the hexagram Y_j - Harmony, Joy, Enthusiasm) that "the ancient kings" made music and offered it to *Ti* (God, Supreme Deity). According to Chu Hsi, "by Ti is intended the Lord and Governor of heaven," and Wang Pi, who lived much earlier, states that "Ti is the lord who produces (all) things, the author of prosperity and increase." Wan Ch'ung-tsung, a collector of explanations on the *I Ching,* adds: "God (Himself cannot be seen); we see Him in the things (which He produces)."

The commentaries to the *I Ching* add more details. The *Shuo Kua* states: "God comes forth in the sign of the Arousing [Thunder, Exciting Power]; he brings all things to completion in the

---

65. Lu Kuan Yü, *Taoist Yoga: Alchemy and Immortality,* New York: Samuel Weiser, 1973, p. 70.

66. The following discussion is based mainly on *The I Ching or Book of Changes,* tr. Richard Wilhelm/Cary F. Baynes, Princeton, NJ: Princeton University Press (Bollingen Series 19), 1973 [1950], pp. 68, 268, 272, 298, 370, 468, and *I Ching,* tr. James Legge, Raymond Van Over (ed.), New York: Mentor (New American Library), 1971 [1882], pp. 365-366.

sign of the Gentle [Gentle Penetration];...he brings them to perfection in the sign of Keeping Still [Mountain, Arresting Movement]." A little further on, we find: "The spirit is mysterious in all things and works through them" (Wilhelm). Or, to use a different translation: "When we speak of Spirit, we mean the subtle presence (and operation of God) with[in] all things" (Legge).

The *Ta Chuan* (Great Commentary), in discussing the Tao, states: "As continuer, it is good. As completer, it is the essence." This definition of the Tao accords with the term "Lord" (*Rabb*) in Sufism, which is explained as "He who gently guides things to their completion and perfection." And in the *T'uan Chuan,* attributed to Confucius, the commentary on the first hexagram (the Creative) is: "Great indeed is the sublimity [generating power] of the Creative, to which all beings owe their beginning and which permeates all heaven." The Creative is the primal cause of all that exists. (In the *Chuang Tzu,* the Creator is referred to as *chao-wu,* "He who creates things.")

It will not escape notice that Ti, Tao, the Spirit, and the Creative are being explained in substantially the same terms. This is what the ancient Chinese philosopher Hui Shih called "the Great One" (*Ahad* in Sufism), "that which has nothing beyond." According to the commentary by K'ung Ying-ta, the Great Ultimate mentioned in the *I Ching* is the undifferentiated One, before Heaven and Earth were differentiated. Apparently, then, the ancients were speaking about the same thing, but qualifying it by different names. Perhaps they thought that the connection was so obvious that the point needed no laboring. As the *Hsün Tzu* explains, "These different views are single aspects of the Tao...Those...who see only a single aspect of the Tao will not be able to comprehend its totality..." (Ch. 21) Now in Sufism, too, we find that different aspects ("modes") of God are given different names, of which 99 are known as the "Most Beautiful

Names of God." And, even more interesting, many of the hexagrams in the *I Ching* are described in exactly the same terms.

The Creative (*Ch'ien*), to begin with, is God in His capacity of creativity (*Haliq*). The Receptive (*K'un*), the second hexagram, corresponds to all of creation (*mahluq*). Nourishment (*Hsü*) and Providing Nourishment (*I*) would resonate with God in His aspect of Provider (*Razzaq*), while Peace (*T'ai*) is another Beautiful Name of God (*Salaam*). Among other such correspondences are Possession in Great Measure (*Ta Yu - Ghani*), The Power of the Great (*Ta Chuang - Qaadir*), Oppression (*K'un - Kahhar*), Obstruction (*Chien - Maani*), the Gentle (*Sun - Halim*), and Inner Truth (*Chung Fu - Baatin*).

Other hexagrams bear titles corresponding to names of God that are not among the 99, but are His Names nevertheless. Examples are Splitting Apart (*Po - Faatir*) and Deliverance (*Hsieh - Naaji*). And of course, the *yin/yang* (active/passive, male/female, etc.) complementarity, which is essential to the *I Ching,* is echoed in such complementary attributes and names of God as Beauty/Majesty (*Jamal/Jalal,* which also means Bliss/Wrath and is referred to as "the two hands of God"), Exalter/Debaser (*Muizz/Muzill*), Life-giver/Death-giver (*Muhyi/Mumit*), First/Last (*Awwal/Aakhir*), etc.

Naturally enough, not all hexagrams are associated with a name of God. This is only to be expected. It was never the intention of the anonymous compilers of the *I Ching*—nor could it have been—to construct an edifice in complete accord with Sufism, since the latter did not even exist as such at that time. Nevertheless, the interesting correspondence above does help to shed light on a curious phenomenon. In later times, we find, the trigrams and hexagrams of the *I Ching* came to be "invested with *operational power.* They no longer stood for specific changes, they actually brought about these changes."[67] Likewise, Shao Yung "maintained that before the trigrams were first drawn by their discoverer, the *Book of Changes* already ideally existed."[68]

This kind of "emanationism," which we find most famously in Plato's Ideas/Archetypes, is totally incomprehensible if we confine our thinking to the hexagrams themselves, and smacks of magic and unreason. If, however, we concentrate instead on the concepts that the hexagrams are held to represent, everything falls into place. For in Sufic cosmology, especially as expounded by Ibn Arabi, the Essence of God gives rise to His Attributes and Names, which in turn combine or "intersect" to bring about the various objects/processes of the phenomenal world. Since we have already discovered that a number of hexagrams are named after the Names of God, a Sufic approach yields a happy solution. In this process, "the Primordial Breath" (*yuan-ch'i*) of the *I Ching* is called "Breath of the Compassionate" (*nafas al-Rahman*) by Ibn Arabi, where exhalation refers to differentiation into myriad things (the Primordial Breath producing Heaven and Earth) and inhalation refers to the return or gathering back of all things to God.

The Yin and Yang of God

"Make a hairbreadth difference," says Seng Ts'an in "Faith in the Heart-mind" (*Hsin Hsin Ming*), "and Heaven and Earth are set apart." Draw a line, and in geometrical terms, an infinite plane is at once divided into right and left half-planes. As soon as we draw a distinction, which in the ordinary world is all the time, yin and yang spring into existence. But who drew the line at the Great Beginning? This question is answered in the Classic. "God

---

67. Laurence G. Thompson, *Chinese Religion: An Introduction,* 4th ed., Belmont, CA: Wadsworth, 1989 [1979], p. 22.
68. Fung Yu-lan, *Short History…,* p. 285.

said to Heaven and Earth: 'Come into existence, willingly or unwillingly.'" (the Koran, 41:11) As Niyazi Misri explains, "Wherever you see a rose garden, beside it arises a briar patch." There can be no *yin* without *yang,* no Earth without Heaven, no emptiness without fullness, no Form without the Formless, no cosmos without God. (The "Two Truths," Multiplicity and Unity, thus complement each other.) When, however, one makes the myriad and the three and the two One, then yin and yang no longer exist—only God exists. Such is the "Uncarved Block" of the Taoists.

The *yin/yang* concept can be fruitfully applied in order to gain a proper appreciation of God. *Yin* and *yang* are always opposite, like night and day, passive and active, female and male. Yet they are both necessary to the ecology of the universe, and complement one another. Out of their combination follows the propagation of the universe, as well as great virtue and right understanding. Below, we shall see two examples of this in relation to Sufism. The first pertains to Beauty and Majesty, the second to Similarity and Incomparability.

Take Beauty and Majesty first. Another way of classifying God's attributes is to consider them in their blissful and wrathful aspects. God is the Exalter as well as the Abaser, the Benevolent as well as the Wrathful; the Generous as well as the Avenger. Thus, two categories suggest themselves: "Beauty/Bliss" (*jamal*) and "Majesty/Wrath" (*jalal*). The Sufis, however, have always claimed that taking either one of these alone is insufficient, and that taking the two together (*jamal* plus *jalal*) leads to "perfection" (*kamal*). It is only when we recognize that both wrathful and blissful attributes/activities belong to One Source that we approach Truth.

Similarity and Incomparability

God possesses attributes similar to those of existence, including human beings. This means that God sees, listens, and knows just like a human being (only to an infinitely greater extent). Whatever things are, that God is also. This is called "similarity" (*tashbih*) in Sufism. Similarity involves those Attributes of God which are similar to attributes of beings He has formed. Thus God is the Living, in which respect He is similar to living beings (or rather, the latter get this attribute from God's Attribute of Life). He is the Seeing, the Hearing, similar to all living things that see and hear. He is the possessor of Knowledge, similar to human beings. (Here, one should make the distinction that God possesses infinite life, that He is the All-seeing, the All-hearing, and the Omniscient.) Similarity combines immanence and the positive approach, by asserting that God's Attributes are shared by the world of form and affirming positive qualities for Him.

At the same time, God possesses attributes which belong only to Him and set Him apart from all things that were formed subsequently. Whatever things are, that God is not. This is called "incomparability" (*tanzih*) in Sufism, and is a prime example of *via negativa,* the "way of negation." Thus, God is *in*-finite, *im*-mortal, limit-*less,* eternal, self-existing, etc. Incomparability combines transcendence and the negative approach (*via negativa*), because we declare God's transcendence by negating every positive assertion for Him.

Now true Islam—and hence, true Sufism—consists in taking these two together. Accepting either one without the other results in imbalance and, taken to its extreme, is apt to lead one astray. To declare the Similarity of God to existing things can lead, for example, to collapsing God onto the universe, which is pantheism, or if the similarity with human qualities is emphasized, it can lead to the notion that a certain much-revered human being is God. Emphasizing the attributes of Incomparability, on the other hand, leads to the notion of a remote God, a God so totally different and "other" that human concerns mean nothing to Him. At the extreme, negating all attributes from God can lead to arguing Him out of existence. Thus, leaving Similarity can lead to atheism, while leaving out Incomparability can lead to pantheism. It is only the happy balance of these two that can help us to cross the river of life. Thus one follows the Straight Path without straying right or left.

The right way is to combine Similarity with Incomparability. The Sufi sage Ibn Arabi often drew attention to a verse from the Koran which does exactly this: "Nothing is like Him. He is the Seeing, the Hearing." (42:11)

At first glance, it would appear that the first part of the verse negates the second. But this is not the case. As Ibn Arabi astutely points out, there is a profound meaning buried here. Similarity and Incomparability are not mutually destructive, but *complementary*. For if we said that God is only similar to things, this would be to limit Him, who is Limitless. And if we said that God is only incomparable to anything, this would also be to limit Him, too. Proper courtesy, as well as right understanding, requires that we acknowledge the combination of Similarity and Incomparability. Leave out either Similarity or Incomparability, and you leave out the yin or the yang.

God and the Taoists

The concept of the Tao, Dao, or Way, is at first glance quite similar to the God concept. Further reflection may lead one away from such a notion. The Tao, one finds, is the ultimate metaphysical principle, is impersonal, and is never conceived of as Deity.[69]

On the other hand, further study may also reveal deeper affinities between the Tao and God. In metaphysical terms, Taoism claims that the Tao both is everything and created everything. Only the Tao exists. It has no parts or divisions and nothing inside or outside It. It transcends both time and space.[70] These are all equally valid descriptions of the Real from the standpoint of Sufism.

Probably the work that delves most deeply into the relationship between the concepts of God and Tao is Toshihiko Izutsu's seminal study, *Sufism and Taoism*.[71] We shall make use of the insights of this study to reach a conclusion.

According to Izutsu, the Absolute is called *Haqq* (the Real) by Ibn Arabi and *Tao* (the Way) by Lao Tzu and Chuang Tzu. Since Chuang Tzu wrote in greater detail than Lao Tzu, it is to the work of the former that we must turn to find references to God, if indeed there are any.

According to the *Tao Te Ching*, "the Tao produces, or makes grow, the ten thousand things." So when Chuang Tzu says that the sage "reaches the primordial Purity, and stands side by side with the Great Beginning," he is saying that the sage is made an eyewitness to the creation ("production") of the universe (*shêng*: produce, bring into existence). This he calls the "Great Awakening" (*ta chüeh*), which he contrasts with the "Big Dream," our

---

69. Laurence G. Thompson, *Chinese Religion*, p. 6-7.
70. Chad Hansen, "The Status of Lao-Zhuang Daoism," hkusuc.hku.hk/philodep/ch/Status_LZ.htm (accessed Nov. 16, 2000).
71. Toshihiko Izutsu, *Sufism and Taoism: A Comparative Study of Key Philosophical Concepts*, Berkeley, CA: University of California Press, 1984 [1967], Part II: Lao-Tzu & Chuang-Tzu. Rather than inflate the number of footnotes by indicating the page in each case, Part Two is what I have generally used as a source in what follows.

mundane experience of the world in ordinary waking consciousness. Ibn Arabi concurs: "The world is an illusion; it has no real
existence."

According to Chuang Tzu, all things freely transform themselves into one another, which he calls the "Transmutation—or
Transformation—of things" (*wu hua*). This is the Taoist version
of "mutual interpenetration" or *jijimuge,* and is called "the flow-
ing/spreading of Existence" (*sarayan al-wujud*) by the Sufi sage
Ibn Arabi. This suggests that boundaries are real-yet-unreal (a
situation highlighted by the phrase "No Boundary"), and that
ultimately, all things are merged together into an absolute Unity.

If the Tao "produced" the ten thousand things, then the Tao
is in some sense the "creator" of things. Do we find anywhere
within the *Chuang Tzu* (the name of his work) explicit reference
to a Creator? The answer is: Yes, we do.

In Section 6, in particular (and also in Section 7), we find
repeated references to both the True Man (*chen jen* or *sheng jen*)—
called the Perfect Man (*insan al-kamil*) in Sufism—and to the
Creator or "maker-of-things" (*chao-wu* or *tsao wu chê*). This name,
Izutsu explains, represents the Way in its personal aspect, and is
also sometimes referred to as the Great Lord (*ta shih*) or Heaven
(*t'ien*). In Sufism, Creator (*Haliq*) is just one of the Attributes and
Names of God (*Allah*), called the "Infinite One" by Chuang
Tzu. God is all-comprehensive and, as such, comprises both personal and impersonal aspects, but whom we always address as a
person: "You." The title of one chapter in the *Chuang Tzu* is
"The Great Lordly Master."

(While "Heaven" is usually considered impersonal, the Chinese *did* traditionally conceive of Heaven in what we would call
personal terms. The *Book of Songs,* which is one of the Five Classics, states: "Heaven is now displaying its anger," "Great Heaven
is intelligent," "Great Heaven is clear-seeing" (*Book of Songs,* Ode

10). The same book also speaks of "the will of Heaven" and "the blessing of Heaven," and goes on to say: "Heaven created people and gave all creatures suitable law, so following this law people can reach their moral perfection." Confucianism accepts this understanding.[72] At the end of the *Analects,* Confucius says: "Without recognising the Ordinances [decrees] of Heaven, it is impossible to be a superior man.")

God is both hidden as spirit, and manifest as the universe. *Allah* is the all-comprehensive "Uncarved Block" out of which all His other Names/Attributes are "cut out," and each phenomenon in the universe is a locus of manifestation for a set of specific Names/Attributes. According to Sufism, indeed, when God taught the first human being (Adam) the "names of things" (2:31—the original reads "all the names"), it was not as if one instructs a child: "This is a bird, that is a tree," etc. Instead, Adam learned which of God's Names are active in which things, giving immediate insight into every thing's essential function. Adam wasn't the first prophet (sage, buddha) for nothing.

Chuang Tzu concludes that "there is some real Ruler (*chên tsai*)":

It is impossible for us to see Him in a concrete form. He is acting—there can be no doubt about it…He does show His activity, but He has no sensible form.

The way Chuang Tzu uses another term, Virtue (*tê*), reminds us of another Name, Lord (*Rabb*), in its Arabic sense. Etymologically linked to the terms "trainer, teacher" (*murabbi*) and "governess" (*murabbiya*), *rabb* describes one who oversees something from beginning to end, who fosters it, nurtures it and brings it to completion. Chuang Tzu says: "The Way gives birth to the ten

---

72. www.blesok.com.mk/tekst.asp?lang=eng&tekst=474&str=2 , accessed March 17, 2005.

thousand things. The Virtue fosters them, makes them grow, feeds them, perfects them, crystallizes them, stabilizes, rears, and shelters them."

Other affinities between Sufism and Taoism abound. Chuang Tzu's expression, "sitting in oblivion" (*tso wang*) is the equivalent of the Sufic "Annihilation" (*fana*). In this connection, Chuang Tzu makes a master say: "I have now lost myself," which means that the sage is ego-less. This points to the annihilation of the subject/object boundary. As Izutsu explains, where there is no "I," there are no "objects." It is one of the most difficult things, however, to nullify one's own self. Once this is achieved, says Chuang Tzu, "the ten thousand things are exactly the same as my own self." Chuang Tzu's "illumination" (*ming*) is another name for Gnosis (*marifah*). The "sacred man," he says, "illuminates everything in the light of Heaven," and according to the Koran, "God is the Light of the heavens and the earth" (24:35). The Ultimate Man (*chi jen*) and God are inseparable. Chuang Tzu speaks of "those who, being completely unified with the Creator Himself, take delight in the realm of the original Unity before it is divided into Heaven and Earth." A sage, according to him, is "the Helper of Heaven," in parallel with Abdulqader Geylani, who was called the divine Helper (*gaws*). Chuang Tzu's "Mystery of Mysteries" (*hsüan chih yu hsüan*), the ultimate metaphysical state of the Absolute, also happens to be the name of a book by Geylani, "The Mystery of Mysteries" (*Sirr al-asrar*). This, Izutsu explains, is none other than the Essence of the Absolute (*zat al-mutlaq*). According to Ibn Arabi, the world is the shadow of the Absolute: "He exists in every particular thing...as the very essence of that particular thing."[73]

---

73. Izutsu, p. 492.

All this points to a further confirmation of a central thesis of this book: God is non-explicit in the East, but this does not mean He is non-existent. Just below the threshold of consciousness, and ready to bloom at the earliest convenience, is the full acknowledgment that God exists.

Shinto

Shinto has long been thought of as polytheistic or pantheistic. The number of kami are conceived of as 8 million, or even 800 million, which is perhaps another way of saying that "There is no place where a god does not reside." (And how true this sentence is, but with one small revision: "There is no place where God does not reside." For God is everywhere and within everything.) Interestingly, these deities are not conceived of as immortal or infinite, but are subject to some of the same trials and tribulations as ordinary mortals. Izanagi's loss of his wife Izanami in the Japanese origin myth exemplifies both cases. Evidently, these *kami* are not conceived of as the infinite and immortal God who is One. Similarly, for the Chinese, the many deities they later invented can be concretized by an image, i.e. are finite, but the Supreme Ruler (*Ti*) in Heaven (*T'ien*) (Superior Emperor: *Shang Ti*) is formless and imageless. The most ancient ancestors of the Chinese believed in One God, also called the Heavenly Emperor (*T'ien Ti*), but *ti* (the Sovereign) was later pluralized into other deities to approximate a heavenly counterpart of the imperial bureaucracy. These would correspond to angels and the souls of saints in monotheism.

In the Chinese world view, there was an unseen but completely real dimension to the world: that of spiritual beings (the "other world" of early Shinto). The gods, who existed in this spirit-world, were alive because they manifested themselves through their effects. Much the same, I think, can be said regarding the *kami*. For both the Chinese and the Japanese, the souls of dead people could easily be "deified" (exalted) if they had accomplished some outstanding feat during their lifetime.

Contrary to initial expectations, however, the concept of One God occurs in Shintoism as well. In Restoration Shinto, the creator of the entire universe is Amenominakanushi, the chief ruling *kami*. "Ame-no-Minakanushi-no-kami" means "God Ruling the Center of Heaven." Many Shinto scholars have held that all the gods of Shinto are merely manifestations of this one deity.[74] The Konko sect of Shintoism worships "the Golden God of the Universe" as its principal god—gold is, as we know, a universal symbol of purity and high worth. In the case of Buddhism, if we consider Kukai's Shingon esotericism, the central buddha is *Dainichi Nyorai* (Sanskrit: *Mahavairocana*), who is not an anthropomorphic figure but an abstract deity embracing all the phenomena of the universe. All nature is a manifestation of *Dainichi*, who exists in each one of us.

Some of the "new religions," too, acknowledge One God. Kurozomi-kyo, for example, teaches: "One kami is embodied in a million kami, and a million kami are found in one kami." It holds that the solar deity, Amaterasu Omikami, created the universe and was the *kami* who nurtured all things, that all human beings are spiritual emanations of this *kami*. Amaterasu alone is the absolute god and creator of the universe. Tenri-kyo, likewise, teaches that: "The true and real God of this universe is Tsukihi. The others are all instruments." (Miki Nakayama, *Ofudesaki*.)

---

74. At times, this kami was worshiped together with the two *musubi* kamis as a trinity, or with the addition of Amaterasu, as a quaternity (Joseph M. Kitagawa, *Religion in Japanese History*, New York: Columbia University Press, 1990 [1966], pp. 216-17). *Musubi* denotes creation and development in harmony, or harmonious growth, and the principal *musubi* deities were Takamimusubi-no-kami (Exalted Musubi Deity, male) and Kamimusubi-no-kami (Sacred Musubi Deity, female).

And according to the teachings of Seicho-No-Ie, man is a child of God, he is created in the image of God in the world of truth, and already has the divine quality within himself. (Hence, if we manifest this perfect quality in the phenomenal world, we can enjoy true happiness.)

The unity of the myriad kami is implicit in their equation with the Buddha. After Buddhism was introduced in Japan, it came to be accepted that the kami's original nature, *Honji*, is Buddhahood. It has been said that "God [kami] and Buddha differ in name, but their meaning is one."[75] Kami are regarded as temporary manifestations or temporary incarnations of the Buddha. Since there is only one Buddha-nature, the various kami are but manifestations of a single essence.

It is not clear, however, just why kami and Buddhahood should be the same, on the basis of either Shinto or Buddhism. Here, Sufism can provide a bridge. Buddhahood means awakening or enlightenment, the attainment of *nirvana*. But according to Sufism, *nirvana* can only be *nirvana in* God, and awakening is waking up to the sacredness of all that is. If kami denotes the sacred, Buddhahood denotes awareness of the sacred. And it is obvious that God is both sacred and self-aware. He is also the one who bestows God-realization, or awakening to the sacred, on the Perfect Human Being (the sage or *Butsu*). This connection explains the otherwise abstruse relationship between kami and the Buddha.[76] Ultimately, there is no kami but Kami, the One, the Cosmic Deity, the Lord of the Universe and of all the worlds. And Buddhahood is (or should be) God-realization.

---

75. Kitagawa, p. 162.
76. Another connection of the Japanese *kami* (godly spirit) may be through the Uighur *cham, kami* (spirit, holy) and the Mongolian *kami* (shaman) to the Turkic *kam* (*kaman*), which means shaman or holy person. This provides a more direct link with a human *buddha*.

The Sun Behind the Sun

As an aside, I can't resist drawing a comparison between Ameno-minakanushi-no-kami and the Egyptian deity Amen on the one hand, and between Amaterasu Omikami and the Egyptian Ra on the other. Amen, "the Hidden One," represented the Hidden God, whereas Ra, like Amaterasu a solar deity, represented God in His revealed aspect. The Egyptians later achieved a combination of the two in Amen-Ra (or Amon-Re). The problem, of course, was that they never did succeed in unifying the many. They were unable wholeheartedly to say that Amen-Ra was One and not two. Akhenaton declared monotheism long before the Hebrew prophets, but even his attempt was flawed, because his deity, Aton, was another representation of the sun disk, and also because he was unsuccessful in winning over the priesthood or the Egyptian masses to his cause.

Here I would like to dwell upon the significance of Ameno-minakanushi-no-kami, the "God of Central Heaven." We may surmise that this kami is, in parallel with Amen, a concealed divinity, "the Sun behind the Sun." It is the Deity in its unmanifest aspect. As for Amaterasu, she is *a symbol for* both the manifest aspect of God (*Zahir* in Sufism), a symbol for the universe, and for the Sun behind the Sun, the Hidden God (*Batin* in Sufism), the spiritual cause behind the physical. (This also reminds us of God's Essence or *Zat* in Sufism, often referred to as *Hu.*)

The Knowledge of No Knowledge

The Taoist sages were well aware that the cognition of Unity entails an entirely different order of knowledge. Chuang Tzu asked: "Who knows this knowledge-without-knowledge?" Fung Yu-lan explains: "In order to be one with the Great One, the sage has to transcend and forget the distinctions between things. The way to do this is to discard knowledge...to discard knowledge means to forget these distinctions. Once all distinctions are forgotten, there remains only the undifferentiable one, which is the great whole. By achieving this condition, the sage may be said to have knowledge of another and higher level, which is called by the Taoists 'knowledge which is not knowledge.'"[77]

The Sufi sages agree. According to the famous Sufi Sahl Tustari: "Gnosis (*marifa*) is the knowledge of no-knowledge." Mahmud Shabistari explains:

Everything emerges with its opposite.
But God has neither an opposite, nor anything similar!
And when He has no opposite, I don't know:
How can one who follows reason know Him, how?[78]

God informs the Grand Sheikh Abdulqader Geylani, "My Way for the Learned is in abandoning knowledge. The knowledge of knowledge is ignorance of knowledge."[79] In other words, all differentiation and distinctions have to be "unlearned." The Yogic term *samadhi* (synthesis, integration) and the Vedantic *advaita* (nonduality) point to this un-differentiation, as do the Sufic terms *tawhid* (Unification) and *jam* (Fusion). By "unknowing" the Many (Multiplicity), one comes to know the One (Unity). As Rumi says, "Where should we seek knowledge? In the abandonment of knowledge."[80] These views have found expression in the Sufi saying: "Forget all you know, transform your knowledge into ignorance." The Hindu tradition also rec-

---

77. Fung Yu-lan, *Short History...*, pp. 115-116.
78. Shabistari, *The Secret Rose Garden*, couplets 92-94.
79. *Treatise on Divine Aid* (*Risala al-Gawsiyya*).
80. *Mathnawi*, 6/823, quoted in Chittick, *The Sufi Path of Love*, p. 175.

ognized this truth: as the *Kena Upanishad* puts it, "To know is not to know, not to know is to know."

Let us conclude this section by statements to this effect by respective luminaries from the two teachings. Says Lao Tzu: "The further one travels along the Way, the less one knows." And Abu Bakr, the foremost Companion of the Prophet: "O God, the pinnacle of knowing Whom is unknowing." Can there be any doubt that both are speaking of the same thing, of "Knowledge of the One"?

Hollow Chestnut, Delicious Walnut

We shall now look at two metaphors of Chinese Buddhism. Both are due to Seng Ch'üan. The first of these is the "meatless chestnut," the second is the "bobbing melon."

The meatless chestnut is a chestnut whose innards have been gnawed out by rodents. It is used as a metaphor for the emptiness of form. Externally, the shell of the chestnut gives the appearance of being substantial. But when one looks inside, one discovers that the chestnut is, after all, empty.

Sufis, too, consider that forms are, *in and of themselves,* empty, hollow. They also hold the view that all forms are pointers to something beyond themselves. One of the greatest Sufi sages, Abdulqader Geylani, has this to say about the world of appearances:[81]

"What I emphasize is the essence, the principle. I don't care about the shell, the sediment. This exterior [form] is just sediment, it's just a rind, a shell."

From the Sufic perspective, all things are manifestations of the Absolute. The Absolute is immanent in the sense that He is

---

81. The quotations are from Geylani, "The Sublime Revelation" (*Fath ar-Rabbani*). Translated from the Turkish by the author.

the Manifest One. But the Absolute is also transcendent, i.e., beyond all manifestation, and this is called the Essence.

There are other contexts where Geylani talks about a "shell." One of these is being sincere in one's words and deeds. "Both words and actions," he says, "become a shell, mere sediment, if they are lacking in sincerity...Every insincere deed is an empty walnut, a husk without a core, a dried-up tree, a corpse without a spirit, a form without meaning."

The Grand Sheikh Geylani views theoretical knowledge in a similar way. "Knowledge (science)," he says, "is a rind, a husk. Deeds [practice] are the essence, the life-juice. The shell is preserved to protect the essence. And the essence, the seed, is protected for extracting oil. If there is no essence in the shell, what use is it? And what use is the essence if it doesn't contain oil? Knowledge is gone, wasted. Because if one does not act on one's knowledge, that is, when action is gone, knowledge departs too, no doubt about it. This is why the Prophet said: 'Knowledge calls for action which uses that knowledge. If this is done, all is well. If not, knowledge passes away.'"

The Sufis use the metaphor of a delicious walnut for the process of attaining Enlightenment or Gnosis (*marifa*). A walnut has two shells, not one. Covering the better-known hard, brown shell is a green coating that has a bitter taste. This, the Sufis compare to the Divine Law (*shariah*), which contains injunctions that are not always to one's liking. The hard shell corresponds to the Spiritual Paths (*tariqah*), which contribute an added measure of spiritual discipline. Once these obstacles are overcome, one reaches the delicious core, the Essence, which is Truth or Reality (*haqiqah*) and the whole point of the walnut.

The Bobbing Melon and the New Creation

Seng Ch'üan explains the "Two Truths" theory (i.e., there is a lower, conventional, relative truth and the highest, absolute truth) by means of an ingenious metaphor: "This is comparable to sinking a melon in water. Raise your hand and the melon *in toto* appears; this is the mundane truth (reality). Push it down and the melon disappears; this is the highest truth (reality)." As Whalen Lai explains, "The 'bobbing melon' conveys this: that the same reality, from two perspectives, can be *in toto* being or nonbeing. When the melon bobs out of the water, there is only being. When it is submerged, there is only nonbeing."[82] Note, however, that even when the melon is submerged, it is merely hidden from view, not nonexistent. The Void is a Pregnant Void, not an empty one. Again, we are faced with the necessity of using the terms "manifest" and "nonmanifest" rather than "emptiness" and "void." In Sufism, nevertheless, the heart must be emptied if it is to become capable of accepting the spiritual power and effusion (*baraka, te*) of the Master, and the self and spirit must be emptied to make way for the divine light of God, which can then manifest itself without hindrance.

The "bobbing melon" metaphor, however, makes wonderful sense if it is applied to one of the most abstruse concepts of Sufism, namely Ibn Arabi's "new creation" (*halq al-jadid,* 50:15). According to Ibn Arabi, the entire universe ceases to exist and is formed anew at each instant. Every instant, the world of forms and appearances returns to the Nonmanifest Essence of God, and is instantaneously restored to existence in a slightly different form. The bobbing melon is ceaselessly submerging and surfac-

---

82. Whalen W. Lai, "Further developments of the two truths theory in China," *Philosophy East and West,* Vol. 30, no. 2 (April 1980), pp. 148-49.

ing, but displaying a different spot of its surface area each time it emerges. The bobbing melon thus provides a beautiful metaphor for this Sufic conception. It also raises the question as to who the "bobber" is. Who is it that pushes the melon down (dissolves the universe), and who is it that pushes it back up? God, naturally.

The Homecoming

The reason why the Tao/T'ien/Ti/Arch-Kami formed heaven and earth was to form human beings, and the reason He gave form to human beings was that they become sages by following the straight path back to Him. Parents send their beloved children far away to study at a university, and when they return after accomplishing this task, they rejoice. God has said: "I was a hidden treasure, and desired to be known." At this far-away school that is the world, man's purpose is to learn about God (*marifat Allah*: Gnosis or God-knowledge), return to Him, and find (*kashf*: discovery or Unveiling) the Hidden Treasure, thus becoming a sage. As one Sufi sage (Osman Bedreddin of Erzurum) has put it, "The purpose of existence is re-uniting with God."

The first thing Tao/T'ien/Ti/Arch-Kami formed was the Buddha-nature of the Prophet, the Reality of Muhammad (*haqiqa al-muhammediyya*). This is also called the Light or Spirit of Muhammad, and the Pen (because it is an immense shaft of light, inscribing on the receptive tablet of the universe). From this initial light and spirit, the Ten Thousand Things were formed. This is why "The Messenger is nearer to believers than their selves." (33:6)

The Prophet received Enlightenment (in one sense, *fath*: conquest—of darkness) in a process called Ascension (*meeraj*), where he was elevated to Absolute Reality. As a token of that journey, the Formal Prayer was bestowed as a gift on all followers of the Prophet. The Formal Prayer is the royal way that leads to Enlightenment. It is the Ascension of the believer. In the Ascension of the Prophet, a pathway—Formal Prayer—was opened by which all his followers could reach the Truth and the Light.

Although becoming a sage represents the greatest accomplishment for a human being, there are no losers in Sufism. Even a follower of lesser accomplishment is assured of reaching the Pure Land when he dies. Here, a person will also be able to witness Absolute Reality from time to time.

A human being has a soul that is immortal. This is true whether he knows it or not. There is only one death: "Who dies once, does not die again." This also means there is only one birth. While Sufis do speak of a second birth, this is meant in the spiritual and not the physical sense. Rebirth does not mean coming into this world a number of times, as in reincarnation, but to be reborn either in the afterworld, or in God after entering *nirvana.*

Sufis, like all Muslims, believe that since God has sent the most universal form of the Law via the Prophet, one has the greatest chance of achieving the highest success if one follows the precepts he has brought. This does not mean that other paths are wrong, because all truth has come from the Truth. But because they are less complete than the teachings of the Prophet, a follower of another path is not able to avail himself of all the merit that one could if one followed this Way. Inevitably, certain things are left missing. Other paths also suffer loss with the passage of time. Human error creeps in.

Here, the role of the Prophet must be emphasized. The world, the conditioned reality, that human beings live in appears far removed—even though it is not—from Ultimate Reality. The

Hidden Treasure has been extremely successful in hiding Himself—so successful, in fact, that without the path He has charted and the clues He supplies, it would be impossible to find one's way back to Him. The Prophet represents the link between humanity and God. Not only is he the chosen means by which God has conveyed information to humanity, but he is the perfect example to be emulated in acting on that information in everyday life, in putting it into practice. And in every age there are sages who are his followers, so that his model may be renewed for successive generations. Without the Prophet and his foremost followers through time, we could not know the Path in its completeness, and without their example we could not practice the Law correctly. This is why the first part of the Formula of Faith—"There is no deity but God"—asserts the existence of the One Reality, but it is completed by the second part: "Muhammad is His Messenger," where "messenger" means a conveyor of information between God and human beings.

Nirvana in Brahman

The Sufic term, *fana,* means "extinction" or "annihilation." It denotes the transcendence of the individual ego, and is the direct equivalent in Sufism of *nirvana,* "extinguishing" (literally, the snuffing out of a candle). Some Sufis have equated *nirvana* with *nur-u fana*—the Light of Extinction, known as the Clear Light of the Void in Buddhism.[83]

However, *fana* is used only infrequently as a single word. Most of the time, it is used in the form *fana fi-Allah,* "annihilation in God." Now if we were to try to express this phrase in

---

83. Another connection: the highest heaven in Buddhism is Nirvana (the ninth heaven), in Sufism it is the Paradise of the Essence (*jannat al-zat*).

Indic terms, the only way we can do this is to call it *nirvana in Brahman.*

This opens a whole new vista of comprehension. For traditionally, higher Hinduism has been regarded as monotheistic, while Buddhism has been considered nontheistic. Here we face an entirely new concept. For if we ask: what is *nirvana* a *nirvana* "in"? then the answer has to be, *nirvana* in Brahman.

Nirvana is thus seen to denote *a state of consciousness,* the spiritual state of the seeker. And in that state, what is perceived is Ultimate Reality, Brahman. The Buddha lived at a time when there were millions of gods in Hinduism, literally a hyperinflation of deities, and it is thus quite understandable that he did not want to phrase his Eightfold Way in theistic terms. But the connection between the two concepts (and religions) is already made in the *Bhagavad Gita,* which speaks of "the *nirvana* that is Brahman."[84]

Moreover, here is how the *Mundaka Upanishad* describes Brahman:

"In the highest golden sheath is Brahman, stainless, without parts; pure is it, the light of lights. This is what the knowers of the Self know. The sun shines not there, nor the moon and stars, these lightnings shine not, where then could this fire be? His shining illumines all this world. Brahman, verily, is this Deathless."

And here is how the Buddha describes Emptiness in the *Udana*:

"Where water, earth, heat and wind find no footing, there no stars gleam, no sun is made visible, there shines no moon, there the darkness is not found; when the sage, the brahmin,

84. *Bhagavad Gita,* V, 24, quoted in Mircea Eliade, *Yoga: Immortality and Freedom,* Willard Trask (tr.), Princeton: Princeton University Press (Bollingen Series), 1971 [1954], p. 166.

himself in wisdom knows this place, he is freed from the form and formless realms, from happiness and suffering."[85]

If we are able to talk about "*nirvana* in Brahman" in the Indian tradition, then the equivalent term in the Chinese tradition would be "*nirvana* in Tao," because Tao is the Chinese term for Ultimate Reality. This is where the meaning of Chinese Buddhism and Zen (*Ch'an*, direct enlightenment, the combination of Buddhism and Taoism) is to be sought. As a matter of fact, *nirvana* in Tao may be a more sanitary term for the squeamish, a more neutral and acceptable phrase for the faint of heart.

Of course, there are differences between the conceptions of Brahman and Tao, but basically they are the same. This is only to be expected, since Ultimate Reality is only One (not-two), and descriptions of it have to be in agreement, at least up to a certain point. Now there is still a further stage in Sufism, *baqa bi-Allah*, "subsistence in God." But I am unable to find an equivalent term for it in Hinduism, Vedanta, or Buddhism, perhaps because Eastern thought stops at *sunyata*.

Scholars such as Fung Yu-lan have seen a difference, even a contradiction, between Taoism as a philosophy (*chia*: school) and Taoism as a religion (*chiao*). In this view, Taoist philosophy aims to work *with* nature—as exemplified in the works of Lao Tzu and Chuang Tzu, its goal is harmony with nature. Taoist religion, on the other hand, is basically focused on how to avoid death, which is to work *against* nature. Other scholars, notably Nathan Sivin and Russell Kirkland, have disputed such a division of Taoism, maintaining that the Taoists aimed at "spiritual perfection through moral purification."

The early religious Taoists were known for their quest for immortality. Even if they could not immortalize physical life,

---

85. Quoted in "Is the Buddha's Emptiness the Brahmin's Brahman?" *What is Enlightenment,* No. 14 (1998).

they thought they could at least prolong it by certain methods. Two approaches developed out of the quest for the "elixir of eternal life." Some sought for the "outer elixir" (*wai-tan*), the "pill" of immortality or the philosopher's stone. This was closely linked with the effort to transmute base metals into gold, and led to various early scientific discoveries in China. The other approach sought for the "inner elixir" (*nei-tan*), or liberation of the spiritual essence from finitude and the body using techniques of Taoist Yoga.

Now, whatever the result of these methods, *nirvana* in Tao *is that immortality.* Your soul is immortal, but you may not have direct perception of this prior to death. If you attain *nirvana* in Tao, however, *that* is immortality. And here we have the link between Taoism as a philosophy and Taoism as a religion, if indeed they were at all separate. For you arrive at the unmediated discovery that your spirit/self will survive bodily death. Your mind becomes mapped onto the Universal Mind (*aql al-kull*). Although it requires great effort, there is a way in nature that leads out of nature, to the Source of nature. It is a terribly difficult climb for salmon to reach their original breeding grounds, a bitter struggle against gravitation, yet nevertheless some salmon do succeed.

Fana or *nirvana* is, in the Prophet's words, to "Die before you die," and having died once, you cannot be destroyed, death cannot harm you. "Who dies before he dies, does not die when he dies." Once you die from the physical world, you continue to exist in the spiritual world. And you come to realize this directly. What, for others, is merely unproven conjecture, becomes for you an incontrovertible truth that you have experienced yourself.

No god but God

The Word of Unity, "No god but God, " is like a coin. It is single, but it has two sides. One side is negation, the other is affirmation. One face is *yin,* the other, which complements it, is *yang.* One side says there is no self, no essence, no being, no deity. The other side says, *except* Self, except Essence, Being, God—who is only One.

The Buddha, who took the negating approach, effectively said the first (an*atman,* nih*svabhava, sunyata, nirvana*). He did a good job of negating 3 or 30 or 330 or 8 or 80 million gods. For this we must forever be in his debt. He did not deny the second side, nor did he say it explicitly. But in order to achieve completeness, we need to do both.

Can you have a coin with only one face? You can. But it will be half a coin.

The highest reaches of Hua-yen Buddhism have come within an inch of actually saying this. An orange (or anything else) is in reality not an orange, but a "sign" that points to something beyond itself. In fact, it is a direct manifestation of Ultimate Reality. However, we cannot reduce Ultimate Reality to an orange, nor can we reduce it to the "ten thousand things," for we must avoid pantheism—vast as the universe is, it is still finite.

Symbolic form is negated (*min*) in order to point beyond itself to the ultimate truth that it symbolizes. The symbolic object is revealed as being empty in itself so that it is evident that its true significance is not itself but rather its referent, ultimate truth...*The object itself is conditioned and empty. It is not itself ultimate truth but rather the locus for the manifestation of that truth.*[86]

---

86. Dale S. Wright, "The significance of paradoxical language in Hua-yen Buddhism," *Philosophy East and West,* vol. 32, no.3 (July 1982), p. 329 (italics added).

The Orange and the Sage

A sage is sitting under an orange tree, when suddenly a big orange drops in front of him. The sage gazes at the orange. "Are you an orange," he asks, "or not?"

Energized by the spiritual power (*baraka*) of the sage, the orange begins to speak—in the language of states (*lisan al-hal*), of course—and says: "You think I am an orange, and indeed I am, from the point of view of conventional truth. But from the standpoint of absolute truth, I am something quite different. Where oranges and trees and the ten thousand things do not exist, I am not an orange at all. In fact, I don't even exist. Even where we do exist, we are all interwoven together, so we have no individual existence apart from the rest. We are only signposts, and what we signify is Absolute Reality."

Emptiness symbolizes the relativity of symbols as such, including itself. In its self-negation, the symbol['s] emptiness denies its own ultimacy (*svabhava*) as a symbol, and precisely in that activity refers beyond itself to the ultimate truth. In the self-denial of the symbol, its referent may be evoked.

The…symbol['s] emptiness (k'ung/sunyata) *is inherently paradoxical; it is a negation that is simultaneously an affirmation. Ultimate truth becomes manifest only to the extent that the symbol in which it becomes manifest negates itself…*Fa-tsang says, "One cannot grasp emptiness by means of emptiness"…*Emptiness (the concept/symbol) is* [generated by] *not[-]emptiness (the referent, that is, ultimate truth).*[87]

The orange continues: "I cannot explain myself. Finitude, dependence, relativity, cannot explain itself. It can be explained only by reference to the Absolute. The Absolute and the relative are complementary: the one necessitates the other."

---

87. Ibid.

None-self but One Self

The *Mahaparinirvana Sutra* speaks of *nirvana* as eternal, blissful, personal (the Self), and pure, but furthermore as "nonemptiness,"[88] and we have already seen that *nirvana* is *nirvana* in God. Form may be empty, but the Buddha-nature (that which is realized in Enlightenment) is nonempty (*asunya*), the "embryo of the Buddha" (*tathagatagarbha*)[89] is nonempty.[90] Nonemptiness can be read either directly as fullness, or as being beyond both emptiness and fullness. Ultimate Reality (i.e., God) is not emptiness but beyond it, and if we understand emptiness in the Buddhist sense of mutual interdependence (dependent co-origination), God is independent of all things. (Some Buddhist sutra passages portray *nirvana* as the cessation of dependent arising.) God is only shorthand for the Ultimate Reality (which is sometimes called *dharmadatu* in Zen).

The Chinese *Secret of the Golden Flower* begins with the words: "That which exists through itself is called the Way (Tao). Tao has neither name nor shape. It is the one essence, the one primal spirit." In Sufism, self-existence (*qiyam bi-nafsihi, svabhava*) is one of the Attributes belonging to God's Essence. The Sufic term translates literally as "standing by His own self," and means "dependent on nothing and no one else for His existence." It is one of the Attributes by which the Essence differs from all other things. All things which the Essence gives rise to, on the other hand, are other-dependent and non-self-existent (*qiyam bi-ghayrihi, nihsvabhava, pratityasamutpada*). That "other" is the rest of

88. Ming-Wood Liu, "The Yogacara and Madhyamika interpretation of the Buddha-nature concept in Chinese Buddhism," *Philosophy East and West,* Volume 35, no. 2 (April 1985), p. 178.
89. Equivalent to the "Child of the Heart" (*walad al-qalb, tifl al-maani*) in Sufism, but this is not the place for a digression on this subject.
90. Whalen Lai, "The Defeat of Vijnaptimatrata In China," *Journal of Chinese Philosophy,* Vol.13 (1986), pp. 11-12.

existence and—since the rest of manifestation is equally depen-
dent and powerless—in the final analysis, the Other is the
Essence. If Nagarjuna had not equated Emptiness with depen-
dent origination, thus introducing a different ontological cate-
gory (*sunyata, adam*), it would have been much easier to see this.
Yet even this statement needs to be qualified by the fact that
Nagarjuna was originally referring to the "void of self" that the
Buddha spoke of, which is technically not at all inaccurate.

To cut a long story short: we *deny* that anything has an existence of its own, and we *affirm* that its existence is due only to
Ultimate Reality, which is independent of anything else. There,
we just said it: "No god (or anything else) but God" (*La ilaha/
mawjuda ill'Allah*).

If in reality there exists nothing other than God, it follows
that there also exists nothing more adorable, more wonderful
and worthy of worship, other than God.

If, however, we commit the fallacy of identifying Ultimate
Reality also with emptiness, we will have made a form out of the
Formless, a dependent out of the Independent—the Far-Eastern
version of pantheism. Just as a person's shadow is not that person, this world, which is a shadow (manifestation, lesser-dimen-
sional projection) of God, does not exhaust God.

One can also discover other possibilities if one looks deep
enough: e.g., there is no-mind (*wu-hsin*) except One Mind (*i-hsin*),
nonself but One Self, no-atman but Brahman (*mahatman*: Great
Self). All little, local selves are fictitious, invented by the One Self
for the grand No play that is the universe.

This also tells us that the East Asian traditions are *almost* saying God, *implicitly* affirming God, though not doing so explicitly.
Thus, when they use such terms as the real nature of things
(*dharma*), suchness, thusness (*tathata*), and Buddha-nature, they
are actually trying to say God, but stopping just short of it,

because theistic affirmations are not traditionally part of Buddhism.

The Mouse that Bit the Balloon

A mouse once came upon a cheery-colored balloon. Thinking it was a different kind of melon and good to eat, it tried to take a bite out of it. But as soon as it did so, the balloon exploded. The mouse was knocked senseless with a *bang!* When it came to, there was no balloon to be found, only a torn sheet of thin rubber.

"Everything is connected to everything else." Any single thing is dependent on the rest of existence. This means that it is powerless on its own. But the opposite is also true. The rest of existence is equally dependent on that single thing. This means that, despite its immeasurably greater size, it is equally powerless. This last is a surprising result. Without the one, you cannot have the all. It is like cutting a small hole in a balloon, like taking a small bite out of it. So the all is as weak as the one. Ontologically, they are on the same level. Nor does their combination yield an attribute that they both lack individually.

No matter how you carve up the universe, the parts will be equally interdependent and not relevant—indeed, not even existent—by themselves. This means that the phenomenal world, the world of forms and processes, ultimately must rely on an outside agency, better known as "God." By Occam's Razor, we need only postulate *one* such agency, and it is enough.

This universe is like a balloon. Who made it, who blew it up? One answer is enough.

Once a person has uttered: "There is no god but God, and Muhammad is His Prophet" with sincere belief, one becomes a recipient of divine mercy, and from then on must observe the precepts in order to purify one's self further. (The repetition of

this formula is an essential part of Sufi training, as it helps concentration in the proper direction.) But there is hope even on the
deathbed. If one utters the same formula before one's last
breath, just once, one is again accepted. In the afterworld, one
can hope for the intercession of the Prophet, who will show
mercy with regard to spiritual defilements.[91]

Ɔ Ɔ Ɔ

We have seen that the concept of God occurs under different names in the *I Ching,* in Taoism, and even in Shinto. The
prime referent of complementary opposites in the East, *yin* and
yang, is applicable to the way God is conceived in Islam and
Sufism. God-knowledge is the "knowledge of no knowledge."
Two East Asian metaphors, the "hollow chestnut" and the "bobbing melon," have allowed us to gain insights into the relationship between God and the universe.

The purpose of the universe—and man's—is to take the
return trip to God. (This is not a purely philosophical issue but a
matter for concrete experience, and will be dealt with later in the
book.) This results in "extinction in God" (*fana fi-Allah*) as it is
called in Sufism, for which the Indic/Sinic equivalents are *nirvana* in Brahman/Tao. At one stroke, Buddhism is united with
Brahmanism and Taoism, thanks to this Sufic concept.

God, or Absolute Reality, is nonempty and dependent on
nothing outside Himself. Our investigation has shown that no
deity—indeed, nothing else—exists other than God. We now

---

91. There is an especially effective formula, involving unceasing contem-
plation of the Prophet and chanting his name, which is bound to
improve one's station in both worlds. The Prophet himself has prom-
ised that one is elevated by ten degrees at each invocation. For the
sake of those who are interested, this is: *Allahumma salli ala Muhamme-
dun wa ala aali Muhammed.*

turn to the toughest nut to crack in the East Asian armory—
Emptiness. Why is there so much mention of Emptiness rather
than God in the East? And what new insights does Sufism possess which may be used to shed light on this matter?

8.

EMPTINESS OR GOD?

*The Supreme Principle is one and not two. It is unreasonable,
therefore, that two types of truth should exist.*

—Tsung-mi

Nirvana and Nihilism

The relative absence of the God concept in certain Eastern philosophies and religions has long been a source of perplexity to those who are able to recognize the sublime mysticism that does exist in these traditions. On one hand, we have all the trappings of full-fledged mystical experience in these Eastern doctrines. On the other hand, the concept of God is de-emphasized at the least, and practically almost nonexistent in general. The Tao, to the extent that it points to the Divine, refers to an impersonal divinity. How is this situation to be explained?

This is indeed the million-dollar question. If we were merely dealing with the Buddhist concept of *nirvana*, the answer would be relatively straightforward. For we have seen that *nirvana*, literally "the snuffing out of a candle," has its direct correlate in the Sufic concept of *fana* (extinction or annihilation). This term refers to the spiritual/perceptual state or station of the seeker. As we saw in the last chapter, the term *fana fi-Allah* naturally corresponds to "Nirvana in Brahman," thus uniting Buddhism and higher Hinduism at a single stroke.

But there is a further complication. For one encounters, again and again, the concept of *sunyata* (Void) in texts dealing with Buddhism, almost as frequently as mystics in the West and the Middle East speak about God. This is a fascinating issue to discuss, especially since the same concept also occurs in Sufism, where it is called *adam*, and means Nonbeing (absence) as well as non-self-existence. Its opposite is *wujud*, Being (presence). According to Sufism, when one transcends the individual, finite self, one reaches a "place" or "stage" where no form and nothing finite remain—which is the same as saying that what remains is the formless, the Transfinite. Hence there is a covert positive implication about *adam*.

Not-being. Non-Being. Void. Emptiness. Nonexistence. All these terms are implied by *adam* to a greater or lesser extent. Annemarie Schimmel explains: "Nonexistence, *adam,* is the ineffable divine essence, which has been seen in this way by some of the mystics, and particularly by Rumi, because it is beyond every possible mode of expression or imagination—it is like the *neti neti* ["not this, not that"] of the Upanishads."[92] In this sense, *adam* means "nonmanifest," hidden (*ghayb*), and the stage of non-delimitation (*la taayyun*), for the divine essence is ontologically prior to existence. But in another sense, it refers to the world at large. As William Chittick rightly indicates, although the world appears to be full of a myriad existents, in reality only God exists. "Hence what outwardly appears existent is really nonexistent, and what seems to be nonexistent is really Existence."[93]

Seng Chao's "On the Unreal as the Empty" (*Pu-chen k'ung-lun*) says, "Though it is, it is not. Though it is not, it is."[94] This is

---

92. Annemarie Schimmel, *Mystical Dimensions of Islam,* Chapel Hill, NC: University of North Carolina Press, 1975, p. 322.
93. William C. Chittick, *The Sufi Path of Love: The Spiritual Teachings of Rumi,* Albany, NY: State University of New York Press, 1983, p. 175.

reminiscent of the Sufic formula: "is, yet is not; is not, yet is" (*mawjudan madum, maduman mawjud*), by which it is meant that God exists, yet is not manifest; whereas the world does not exist, yet is manifest to the senses. Conventional reality can be described as "unreal, yet apparently existing." As Mahmud Shabistari elaborates,

> *Know the cosmos to be light of God's light*
> *God is hidden in the world because He is [so] evident,*
> *His obviousness has caused Him to remain hidden.*[95]

On the basis of all this, Rumi says:

> *Where should we seek existence? In the abandonment of existence.*
> *Felicity lies totally in nonexistence, but the fool seeks it from existence.*
> *There is no place of rest but the Desert of Nonexistence, for existence has no faithfulness.*
> *When I exist I am nonexistent, and when I am nonexistent I exist!*[96]

With *fana* in Sufism corresponding to the Buddhistic *nirvana* and *adam* to *sunyata*, one may at first suppose that in Sufism, the culmination of *fana* should be *adam*. Yet it is not. As a matter of fact, *adam* is not a concept that is greatly emphasized in Sufism.[97] Annihilation (*fana*) is an extinction not in nothingness, but in God (*Allah*). Why?

This must be due to the fact that Not-Being itself is *preliminary* to a further, more exalted goal.

It is due to Buddhism's emphasis on Emptiness that the West has tended to equate it with the closest conceptual equiva-

94. Whalen W. Lai, "Further developments of the two truths theory in China," *Philosophy East and West,* Vol. 30, no. 2 (April 1980), pp. 150.
95. Shabistari, *The Secret Rose Garden,* couplet 98.
96. Whalen W. Lai, "Further developments of the two truths...," pp. 176-78.
97. In fact, one may think of *fana/ifna* as the *act* of extinction and *adam* as the *state* of extinction.

lents in Western culture—nihilism, pessimism, and atheism. To be sure, as the Japanese scholars Nishida and Nishitani pointed out, *sunyata* is not the same as nihilism or nihility, especially as encountered in the existential philosophies of Nietzsche and Heidegger. But the confusion is an easy one to fall into. In particular, it is futile to expect that anyone who approaches the matter from an abstract philosophical rather than an empirical/experiential angle will be able to distinguish between *sunyata* and nihility. Form arises from Formlessness, Form is Emptiness and Emptiness is Form—these are Eastern teachings that are not confined to Buddhism alone. It seems clear that the mystics of the East have transcended the phenomenal world. At the same time, they apparently have not quite arrived at the point where God manifests Himself to a human being in His full glory, otherwise they too would be speaking in the same terms as the Sufis.

Evolution of the *Sunyata* Concept

Historically, the concept of *sunyata* has undergone an interesting evolution.

1. In the earliest Buddhist writings, it was used to denote *anatman*, the absence of selfhood. In this sense, it stands closest to spiritual poverty or "emptying the self" which occurs in other traditions. (In this respect, one even encounters the composite term *atma-sunya*, "self-void" or "empty self." This view still has adherents among Buddhists today.) It implied the state of non-attachment, the cessation of desire. Buddhism was originally a religion of non-ego.

As the *Tao Te Ching* states: "Empty yourself of everything. Let the mind become still. The ten thousand things rise and fall while the Self watches their return. They grow and flourish and then return to the Source. Returning to the Source is stillness…though the body dies, the Tao will never pass away."

(Chapter 16) This reminds us of the passage: "We are from God, and to Him we shall return." (2:156)

2. Nagarjuna later used the concept, not in a "psychological," but in a philosophical sense: he demolished all concepts and viewpoints used to describe reality, declaring them all "empty." (His equation of Emptiness with dependent origination will be dealt with later.) This is quite in accord with the ineffability of *nirvana* and the futility of theorizing about it. Nagarjuna explicitly points out that one should properly call Reality neither *sunya* (void) nor *asunya* (nonvoid). The Buddha is supposed to have held similar views: "I call him incurable," he told Kasyapa, "who clings to *sunyata* itself as a theory. ... *sunyata* is an antidote to all dogmatic views, but if a man were to cling to it forever as a view in itself, he is doomed."[98]

And that's what we are today, doomed. Because the term has stuck. Furthermore, it has stuck in the wrong sense, for:

3. It was only later that—in the next step of the term's evolution—Chinese thinkers elevated *sunyata* to the status of an ontological absolute, claiming that it was the reality underlying all things. They were right, but only partially. The "emptiness" of the phenomenal world is not the same as the "emptiness" intended for the noumenal world. But who shall distinguish between the two? For we have, on one hand, the comparatively very few enlightened sages throughout history who have lived the experience and consequently know what they are talking about, and on the other hand a vast majority of interested parties who have not and do not. For the latter, the otherwise quite valid doctrine of *sunyata* thus quite naturally collapses to nihilism.

This is the great danger of the term "Emptiness." Having evolved from the psychological to the philosophical to the onto-

98. G. C. Nayak, "The Maadhyamika attack on essentialism: A critical appraisal," *Philosophy East and West, 29*, no. 4 (October 1979), p. 478.

logical contexts, it is used in—not even the last sense, but only the shadow thereof (its reduction into a lesser dimension). And indeed, this has occurred in the Chinese tradition, for the Neo-Taoist rationalists Hsiang Hsiu and Kuo Hsiang reached the conclusion, around the third century A.D., that the Tao was non-existent: "the *Tao* is nothing. Since it is nothing, how can it be prior to things? ... there is no Creator of things. ... there is no Creator, and everything produces itself."[99] Here we see, in almost graphic terms, how *sunyata* is used to argue God out of existence. The materialistic ideology that came to dominate China in the twentieth century was actually prefigured right there and then.

Yet had they merely said "the Tao is no thing" instead of "nothing," they would have been exactly right, for God is "no thing" (*la shay*), not a "thing" among other things. What a tiny nuance, and yet what a world of difference!

Because the forces of modernization tend toward secularity and away from traditional religion, the religious experience has all but vanished today, resulting in a spiritual emptiness almost as great as the realm of *sunyata* itself. This spiritual vacuum leaves the spirit starved, and the "God-shaped hole" (Sartre) that is left behind can only be filled by God again. What secularity and modernization have done, in other words, is to bring about a crisis, actualizing a danger that was potentially always there, but thankfully avoided until the modern age.

God is like oxygen. How can one live in a vacuum without oxygen?

So from here, we cannot move back to *sunyata*, for this is where we came from originally. In our age, there is nothing left to prevent *sunyata* from collapsing immediately onto nihility. We

99. Quoted from the *Commentary on the Chuang-tzu*, chapters 22 and 2, in Fung Yu-lan, *Short History...*, p. 221.

have reached a dead-end. The only place we can go in this spiritual desert is forward, by filling the hole with its proper content.

What is meant by the ontological sense of *sunya* or *sunyata* (void) is not nothingness as we ordinarily understand it, but something that ontologically precedes and transcends both being and nothingness. In the words of the *Rig Veda*, the Absolute is a state of "neither existence nor nonexistence." (X, 129.) In his "Examination of Nirvana," Nagarjuna himself states that Nirvana is neither Being nor non-Being.[100]

It cannot be called void or not void,
Or both or neither;
But in order to point it out,
It is called "the Void." [101]

(Here we also have a small problem, because the Essence is incomprehensible, which is why the Prophet said: "Do not speculate about the Essence of God." Yet the very act of naming constitutes or leads to speculation in the above case.)

According to Huang-po: "the Void is not really void, but the realm of the Real." One of the earliest Chinese Buddhist texts states: "The Tao is formless, that is why it is described as Void."[102] For this reason, "formlessness" or "nondifferentiation" would be a less misleading term. As Nagarjuna says, "diversity...is terminated in the state of Voidness." *Sunyata*, being absolute negation, permits nothing differentiated. It is

100. Edwin A. Burtt, *The Teachings of the Compassionate Buddha,* New York: New American Library (Mentor), 1955, p. 172-73.
101. *Madhyamika Shastra,* XV, 3, quoted in Alan W. Watts, *The Way of Zen,* Harmondsworth, England: Penguin (Pelican), 1970 [1957], p. 83.
102. Tang Yi-Jie, *Confucianism, Buddhism, Taoism, Christianity and Chinese Culture,* The University of Peking, the Council for Research in Values and Philosophy, Cultural Heritage and Contemporary Life Series III. Asia, vol. 3. www.crvp.org/book/Series03/III-3/chapter_ix.htm, accessed September 2, 2004.

devoid of all qualifications, like the Essence (*zat*) of Sufism, and no conceptual determination can be formed about it. Hence the term itself, however appropriate it may be, is also misleading.

To be sure, the greatest Eastern thinkers and mystics never fell into the mistake of equating the Void with ordinary nothingness. When Chuang Tzu says: "At the great beginning there was Nonbeing (*wu*)" or "All things come from Nonbeing," for example, he does not mean ordinary nonbeing as opposed to being which we experience in the phenomenal world, but a Nonbeing that is ontologically prior to both being and nonbeing. (When they became informed of Buddhism, the Chinese would later equate *wu* with *k'ung*, "emptiness.")

But if we are talking about a Reality that is beyond both being and nonbeing, why should we call it "Nonbeing"? What, for example, is there to prevent us from calling it "Being"? Listen to the *Chandogya Upanihad*: "Some say that in the beginning there was non-existence only, and that out of that the universe was born. But how could such a thing be? How could existence be born of non-existence? No, my son, in the beginning there was Existence alone—One only, without a second."[103] The Zen master Dogen likewise called the Absolute "All-being."

This emptiness, in other words, is also a fullness; it is a Plenum-Void or "Pregnant Void." Perhaps we should steer clear from both the terms "Being" and "Nonbeing," because some other term, such as Nondifferentiation, Nonduality, or Unity, seems called for.

The problem, of course, arises when Chuang Tzu elects to call the Tao "Nonbeing." Whereas Lao Tzu cautions: "The Tao that can be named is not the absolute Tao... The Nameless is the origin of heaven and earth." There it is, right at the beginning

---

103. *The Upanishads* (Swami Prabhavananda and Frederick Manchester, tr.), New York: New American Library (Mentor), 1957 [1948], p. 68.

of the *Tao Te Ching*. And to the extent that Tao means "the Way," even that is already a name.

The reason that Lao Tzu wants the Absolute to remain nameless is because it is ontologically prior to all things, and there have to be things—and human beings to name them—before names can come into existence. But the Tao is different from them all. Nevertheless, we have to be able to refer to the Absolute in some way in order to be able to talk about it at all. The Taoists called Ultimate Reality the Tao. The Chinese Buddhists called Buddha-nature "the Principle" (*li*), the One absolute, a word closely associated with the Tao. It has been called God in the West, and *Allah* in Islam. The *Rig Veda* expressed an age-old truth: "Reality is One, yet the sages call it by many names."

Before we leave this subject, I would like to propose a fourth meaning for *sunyata*, from the Sufic standpoint.

4. *In* and *of* themselves, all things in the physical world are empty of *meaning*. It is only as signs to what lies beyond them, as pointers to Ultimate Reality, that they possess meaning. They are like foam on the surface of the sea, and as we watch foam, we forget for a moment that it is intimately related with the sea, that it is the sea itself in another form. But when it vanishes, we remember that we were looking at the ocean all along. The foam, then—however beautiful and dear to our hearts—is bound to pass. It is only to the extent that it signifies the ocean that it possesses any meaning. I feel that deep down, this is what the Chinese actually intended by "emptiness."

Multiplicity is empty. This is what is meant by "Form is emptiness, emptiness is form." Forms are a mere husk.

By the same token, we can say: "Formlessness is fullness, fullness is formlessness." Form arises from formlessness (the Essence), which is Absolute Unity. Thus the Sufi poet Rumi:

"Form comes into existence from the Formless, just as smoke is born from fire." And he addresses God as: "Lord of lords! Formless Giver of forms!"[104]

Fullness resides in the One, the Essence.

Everything is empty with the emptiness of itself, and full with the fullness of God.

Which means: the One God is at the core of all things.

The Problem with Emptiness

Now, to repeat, we must also see that there is great danger in misunderstanding *sunyata* and *nirvana*, which can happen very easily. Because it is very easy for one who has not had mystical experiences to confuse *sunyata* with nihility or simple nothingness, and to conflate *nirvana* with death, or at least the denial of life. Not having had the experience which the terms refer to, one cannot help but fall back upon a concept readily available from common experience—nothingness as opposed to being, simple lack of existence. Once this has happened, it is very easy to reduce spirit and the sacred to nothingness, to argue them out of existence. And this is exactly what has happened in some modernizing Eastern countries. This may also explain why some of them have fallen easy prey to materialistic ideologies.

The problem with the concept of Emptiness, or Void, is that it is no substitute for the concept of God. Emptiness is passive. A jar left empty will remain empty forever unless someone fills it. Emptiness cannot even fill itself, let alone the entire universe. Emptiness does not possess life, let alone eternal life. It does not possess intelligence, let alone infinite intelligence. It does not possess anything at all. It is not a person, you cannot speak to it.

---

104. *Mathnawi* 6/3712 and *Diwan* 14964, quoted in William C. Chittick, *The Sufi Path of Love,* Albany, NY: State University of New York Press, 1983, p. 23.

It has no powers, you cannot ask anything of it. One cannot love emptiness, nor can one be loved by it. So emptiness may, perhaps, represent existence when compared to God, but it can never stand as a substitute for God. God is partially nonmanifest, but this is not the same as saying that He is identical with emptiness. He possesses qualities that are not emergent in the physical world. This does not mean that He is the same as nothingness.

If one is still not convinced, one can always perform a simple experiment. One can take an empty cup—disregarding the air in it, which is negligible for the purposes of this experiment—and from that emptiness, request whatever one wishes. One can pray to it, and then one can begin to wait for the requests to be fulfilled.

It's going to be a long wait. As Confucius said, "A man standing on a hilltop waits a long time for a roast duck to fall into his mouth."

And if this is the case, Emptiness is simply the wrong term to use for Ultimate Reality, and should not be used at all for that purpose, because it is confusing.

When one equates emptiness with Ultimate Reality, one sees form with one eye. But whereas the other eye should be seeing content, one sees only emptiness. One eye sees appearance, but the other eye sees not meaning, spirit, but simply emptiness.

Formlessness is not emptiness. With one eye one sees existence, but with the other one sees not God, but emptiness. With one eye one sees the mundane, with the other eye one sees not the sacred, but emptiness. The sacred is equated with emptiness, it is *reduced* to blackness, to nothingness.

There is a saying in English: "In the country of the blind, the one-eyed man is king." But in the country of one-eyed people, the one who can see with both eyes is the one who is truly king.

The *Sunyata* Shortfall

Why do the sages of the East speak, not of God, but of emptiness? Years ago, I obtained an answer to this puzzle, not from the Master himself, but from another Sufi master whom I shall call Saladin. We had been studying some books on Zen Buddhism that had recently been published in Turkish, and he was indicating the parallels with Sufism. At some point, as I remember, he said that the mystics in these traditions did not experience the full unveiling of God, because they started their Ascension from the level of the Contented or Serene Self. (This is further borne out by the fact that the prime characteristic of the Serene Self is tranquility, while the Japanese name for *nirvana* is *jakumetsu*. Here, *jaku* means tranquility and *metsu* means death, so that *jakumetsu*, "death of tranquility," is an appropriate term for *nirvana*.)

To recall the levels of selfhood in Sufic teaching, there are seven stages, with the Base Self at the bottom or everyday level, and the Purified Self at the top. The Tranquil Self is in the exact middle of these two, at Stage Four. Before this level, Ascension is impossible in any case: one can jump up and down, but no matter how high one jumps, one will fall down again. There are, however, two more levels before the Purified Self is reached, that can serve as a takeoff point for Ascension. This also means that not all mystics achieve the same level of realization, for there are different gradations of Attainment (*wuslat*). This is in no way meant to belittle anyone's Great Work, it is only a statement of fact. Even in Sufism, for example, there are those who get stuck at the level of Annihilation (*fana*), and cannot make the transition to Subsistence (*baqa*).

Nevertheless, I am convinced that the greatest among Eastern mystics did, in fact, experience the divine. The Buddha, for example, must have lived it. Being eminently practical, however, he must have seen that the goal of *nirvana*, as expressed by him, was more accessible to the multitude and more urgent in his time and place. His attitude seems to have been: "First attain *nirvana*, and then you will see what you will see." Perhaps this explains his deliberation for weeks on end about what to tell and how to tell it. As for other mystics, they probably chose to keep silent about it because there was no reference point in their traditions on which they could anchor an explanation.

Now the Ascension to God may be considered in two steps. Once the "Lote-tree of the Boundary"—the Uttermost Limit, i.e. the limit beyond which nothing finite can exist—is left behind, there is the emptiness of the Void. This is the first step. But this is not yet full Attainment. There is a second step, and it is when this step is taken that the fullness of God can be experienced. In other words, *sunyata* is not yet God, but an initial limbo region in transfinity that leads on to God. *It is like a corridor or hallway that leads to the Throne of the Emperor, an elevator shaft in which the ascent to God takes place.* The expression: "the clear light of the Void" is a reference to the divine light one is bathed in during this ascent (*meeraj*). The void is a necessary condition for the Ascension, but it is not a sufficient condition for attaining God. This is the fine point that has hitherto puzzled eveyone.

Picture this in terms of a trip to the moon. When a sufficient amount of kinetic energy is involved, one reaches "orbital (or critical) velocity," the speed at which the earth's gravitational pull is overcome. This is enough to place an object in stable circular orbit around the earth. But unless further energy is available, the object cannot break free from earth orbit and continue on its journey to reach the moon. At a higher level of kinetic energy, the object breaks completely free of the earth's gravitational attraction. This is called "escape velocity" (7 miles or 11.2 km per second at the surface of the earth), and has a value of 1.41 times the orbital velocity.

It is similar with the Ascension. If one starts from the stage of the Contented Self, one can reach the Void, but one has not yet accumulated enough energy to reach the God experience—and especially if the "God hypothesis" is not among one's working assumptions. This can be attained at stages beyond the Contented (Serene) Self. What I understood from the Sufi master was that although one can reach the stage of the Contented Self under one's own steam, by the utmost self-exertion, the stages beyond that are only attainable through techniques prescribed by God to enable His realization—such as Sufi practices and worship, of which by far the most important is the Formal Prayer.

What is really a pity is that a person who has taken the first step is already halfway there—not in terms of distance, since most of the way to the moon still remains, but in terms of the needed boost. For the stages between the Contented Self and the Purified Self are concatenated (as they are in the Koran—89:27-28), and follow with relative ease once the immense hurdle leading up to Stage Four is over. To continue with our analogy of a lunar trip, a person who has attained terrestrial orbit has already expended at least half the kinetic energy necessary for completing the trip—once in orbit, a comparatively smaller nudge might be sufficient to reach the moon. Thus, if the mystics had only accumulated enough energy before their great "jump" using God-given techniques, there would have been nothing to bar them from transcending the envelope of the Void and to attain its Core, namely, consciousness of God. The shortcoming here, perhaps, if one can call it that, is that if these worthies would void the Void, empty the Emptiness, they would directly attain the Fullness that is God.

The ground preparation for this, however, must be completed before the jump. Premature Unveiling always leaves something to be desired. Ideally, the "Great Teleportation" must be attempted only after the stage of the Purified Self has been reached. Nevertheless, this does not detract from the fact that genuine mystical experiences and insights are obtainable even in lesser realizations. I offer this insight of the Sufi master because it provides the most plausible account I have yet come across of the discrepancy between Western and Asian modes of mysticism.

Zeroing the Self

The sense of *sunyata* that is most fruitful in Sufic terms is the original sense it had in Buddhism. This is suggested by the question: What is the Void a void *of?* Alex Wayman explains:

Ananda asked the Buddha about the saying "The world is void." The Buddha explained: "Because it is void of self or of what belongs to self, therefore, 'The world is void'."…simply to say "The world is void" does not convey much comprehension to the hearer, and so the Buddha had to add: "void of self or of what belongs to self."[105]

Thus the problem of *sunyata* is reduced directly to that of *anatman* (non-self), for which see below. The term *sunyata* in the original Sanskrit means "zero, nothingness," and the Buddha is talking about "zeroing the self," annihilating individual consciousness (*fana*). If in fact the world is void of individual selves,

---

105.*Samyutta-nikaya,* 4.54 (Tathagata Sutra), quoted in Alex Wayman, "*Mula-Madhyamaka-karika,*" *Philosophy East and West,* vol. 38, no. 1 (January 1988), pp. 51-52.

if such selves are fictitious, one must "void oneself" in order to see that this is indeed so. The Ch'an masters have described Sudden Enlightenment as "the bottom of a tub falling out." When this happens, all its contents are suddenly gone.[106] Or, as the Sufi poet Niyazi Misri puts it,

> *We reached the water together, they filled their cups*
> *I reached it too, and my ocean destroyed my jug*

That is, whereas the others were able to obtain only as much water as their cups would hold, Niyazi's little local self (his "jug") was annihilated (*fana*) in the Ocean of Unity.

But there is more. For *sunyata* is not only the void, it is the pregnant void, because etymologically the term signifies swollenness as in pregnancy. Hence it depicts the fullness of being. The emptiness is also a fullness, it conceals a fullness—it is not emptiness pure and simple. Out of this "emptiness of individual selfhood" bursts (*falaq*)—as out of a pea pod—all that exists, along with all the fictitious, individual selves that appear so real to us. Here we are talking about nothing less than the formation of the universe. Yet there is only One Real Self, "the Originator of the heavens and the earth" (6:101), who is clearly perceived when one's self has been voided.

A Buddha is void (*sunya*) of own-nature (*svabhava*),[107] and *this* is Buddha-nature: lack of a self (*atma-sunya*) or being (*svabhava-sunya*) that is unique to someone/something as distinct from everything else. (What this implies is: the Self/Essence of all things is One.)

As for no-mind, D. T. Suzuki has pointed out that it is derived primarily from selflessness, non-ego (*anatman, wu-wo, muga*).[108] Indeed, the ideogram for mind (*hsin, shin/shên*) also

---

106. Fung Yu-lan, *Short History...*, p. 262.
107. Ibid. p. 53.

means self or soul, and can more appropriately be translated as "self-mind," so that no-mind (*wu-hsin, mushin*) can be directly identified with no-self. Again, when "mind control" and "control of desire" are equated in Zen Buddhism,[109] it is obvious that desire pertains to the self, so that "mind control" implies "self-control." Here, too, "no-mind" reduces to "no-self." Since thoughts are associated with minds, "no-thought" (*wu-nien, munen*) would more appropriately correspond to "no-mind," but then again, mind is a function of the human self/spirit. "No-thought" would thus indicate the cleansing of consciousness, emptying consciousness of its contents, which itself is based on self-purification. According to the Chinese sages, but according even more to Sufism, one must first still the self in order to bridle the mind. In order to stop thought, one must first bring the self to quiescence. Before the moon can be reflected, the surface of the water must be unruffled. What all these negations seem to indicate is a state radically different from mundane reality, rather than a state, for example, of unconsciousness.

This suggests that the Buddha's concept of *anatman* does not, after all, differ from the Hindu, Vedanta, Taoist, or Sufi conceptions. Perhaps the best way to define *anatman* is "the absence of subject and object," of self and other, attainable in Enlightenment. From the standpoint of Buddhism, the "Real I" is the one who has achieved Buddhahood, the self that dwells in *nirvana*. For example, Lin Qiuwu, a Taiwanese Buddhist of the twentieth century, spoke of "the no-self that is also the Great Self." In fact, we may view Hinduism and Buddhism as two sides

---

108. D.T. Suzuki, *The Zen Doctrine of No Mind,* New York: Samuel Weiser, 1972 [1949], p. 120.
109. Tang Yi-Jie, *Confucianism, Buddhism...,* www.crvp.org/book/ Series03/III-3/chapter_vii.htm, accessed September 2, 2004.

of the same coin, as complementary facets of the great legacy of India. But whereas the former was heavy on theory, the latter laid greater emphasis on practical experience, and discouraged all speculation as to the nature of enlightenment. After all, it was (and is) ineffable, as the Buddha said, and as all mystics have agreed throughout history. But we may, I think, justifiably equate the Buddha-nature with Brahman. According to Mahayana Buddhism, Buddha-nature is universal—all things possess Buddha-nature, which accords nicely with the Hindu/Taoist notion that Brahman/Tao is in all things. Now, when a student asks: "Does a dog possess Buddha-nature?" and a Zen master (Chao-chou) answers "Yes" on one occasion and "No" on another, this can be read as a statement that the Divine is both immanent and transcendent: in one case the first is emphasized, in the other, the second. For while Ultimate Reality is in all things, it cannot be limited to all things. So there really is no contradiction. As for Chuang Tzu, and here I paraphrase:

"There is nowhere the Tao is not to be found. It is in the ant, it is in the weeds, it is in this piece of tile... But why look for Tao by going down the scale of things, as if that which we call 'least' had less of Tao? Tao is Great in all things, Complete in all, Universal in all, Whole in All. These three aspects are distinct, but the Reality is One."

Similarly, when a Zen master (Tung-shan) answers the question: "What is the Buddha?" as: "Three pounds of flax," and when Nagarjuna says that the essence of the Buddha is "this mundane world," they both mean the same thing. Likewise, a master said in a Zen sermon: "When you know what this staff is, you know all, you have finished the study of Zen." For the "Suchness, Thusness" (*tathata*) of all things is One. And the Prophet prayed: "Oh Lord, show us the reality of things"—that reality being none other than the Real, Unity, the Essence.

According to the *Maitrayana Upanishad*, "Having realized his own self as the Self, a man becomes selfless... This is the highest mystery." And in the *Brihadaranyaka Upanishad* it is stated: "When there is consciousness of the Self, individuality is no more." The same holds with Chuang Tzu: "The Perfect Man has no self." "No-self is True-Self." The true sage "transcends the distinction between the self and the world, the 'me' and the 'non-me.' Therefore he has no self. He is one with the *Tao*."[110]

Selflessness also plays a central role in Sufism. In explaining the occurrence of this concept in Rumi, William Chittick remarks: "To find his true Self, man must pass beyond his illusory self." Selflessness "is the goal of the path, for it is nothing other than Selfhood." Rumi mentions selflessness in such verses as:

In absolute selflessness, how joyful I am with Self.
God calls... "Come out of your selves...to selflessness." Selflessness is
Meaning.
Oh lovers, go out from the attributes of selfhood. Obliterate yourselves
in the vision of the Living God's Beauty.
[God's] Self is the lamp within every selfhood.[111]

These verses from Rumi point the way to a correct appreciation of the Buddhist *anatman* doctrine. As Chittick indicates, when the Formula of Unification, "There is no god but God," is applied to a human being, it means "There is no self but the Self." Man's I-ness is unreal, what exists in truth is God's "I"— but this can be realized only when one's poverty (*faqr, wabi*), i.e., one's self-emptying or self-annihilation, has become perfect.

---

110. Quoted in Fung Yu-lan, *Short History...*, p. 110.
111. Chittick, *The Sufi Path of Love*, pp. 174-75. I have edited the text slightly.

Since another way to read the formula is "Everything that exists is God,"[112] we arrive at Rumi's enlightening thunderbolt:

I sought around the world for "others" and reached certainty:
There are no others.[113]

The Ethics of Unity

"There are no others!" As soon as we realize this, the difference between inner and outer, individual and social, evaporates. One sees that one can realize enlightenment not only by individual striving, but also by service to others. That is, by saving others, one saves oneself. "The person who comes to look on all creation as his very self comes to love it as he loves himself."[114]

In fact, service to others takes precedence, because personal striving can always be unconsciously tainted by egotism. This is why the Koran always mentions Formal Prayer, the most personal form of meditation, in the same breath with the alms-tax or charity, the most social form of worship. The full benefits of Formal Prayer cannot be obtained *unless* one has also fulfilled one's obligation to be charitable.

Two examples convey the importance of social duties in Sufism. One is a Sacred Tradition that shows how, in serving one's fellow human beings, one is serving God. The second is from Sheikh Saadi.

God will say to a man: "I was sick and you did not visit Me." He will reply, "How could I visit You, seeing that You are Lord of the worlds?" God will answer, "Didn't you know that

---

112. This should not be read as implying pantheism. Everything is an infinitesimal subset of God. Everything is (or is within) God, but God is not confined to everything.
113. Chittick, *Sufi Path...*, pp. 181, 183, 191.
114. Laurence G. Thompson, *Chinese Religion,* p. 109.

such-and-such a person fell sick? You did not care enough to visit him. If you had, you would have found Me with him."

God will continue, "I asked you for food and you did not feed Me." He will ask, "How could I feed You, seeing that You are Lord of the worlds?" God will answer, "Didn't you know that such-and-such a person asked you for food? You refused to feed him. If you had fed him, you would have found Me with him."

God will then continue, "I asked you to give Me water to drink and you refused Me." He will reply, "How could I give You water to drink, seeing that Your power holds the destiny of all things in its hand?" God will answer, "A person asked you for water to drink, but you refused him. If you had given him water, you would have found Me with him."[115]

The famous Sufi Sheikh Saadi of Shiraz tells the following story:

A dervish left the convent (*takka*) and became affiliated with the university (*madrasah*). I asked him why he had abandoned dervishhood for the sake of becoming a scholar. He said:
"A dervish tries to rescue his own prayer-rug out of the water. The scholar (scientist) tries to save other people from being drowned."

The following sayings of the Prophet, taken from the Six Books, suggest how to be considerate and human-hearted:

Visit the sick, feed the hungry, and help to relieve people's misery.

Every good deed is a charity. It is a good deed that you meet your fellow-men with a cheerful countenance, that you pour from your bucket into the vessel of your fellow. Answering a questioner with mildness is charity. Removing obstacles to

---

115. *Muslim,* 32/6232; *al-Wasa'il,* Vol. 2, p. 636.

wayfarers—such as thorns and stones—from the road is charity.

God has forbidden you disobedience of parents, miserliness, false claims, and disposing of female infants.[116]

Abuse no one, don't despise what is good, and speak clearly to your fellow-men.

God has no mercy for him who has no mercy for others.

Forgive your servant seventy times every day.

He who does not behave kindly towards younger people and does not show due respect to the elderly is not of us.

What is Islam? Purity of speech and hospitality.

Charity Stones

The Ottomans, as sincere Muslims, were so filled with compassion towards all beings that they instituted foundations—not just for the care of the poor and needy, but for the welfare of animals in the wild. In fact, Ottoman society may be characterized as a society of foundations. (A distinction must be made between the Ottomans as a society and as an empire, for the latter may be judged on the basis of its policies.) There were foundations for birds, foundations for wild beasts. There were foundations for leaving carrion in forests so that wolves in the mountains would not go hungry. Here we can also discern an ecological wisdom that aims to conserve species instead of sending them to extinction. Yes! What seems so inconceivable to us today was a daily fact of life for them. People in Turkey are not ordinarily told about such things, and I learned of them only by coincidence in later life. If a people themselves don't know their own heritage, others may well be excused for their lack of knowledge in this regard.

---

116. This was a practice at the time of the Prophet and banning it was a great achievement by him.

Another legacy of the Ottomans were—as mentioned briefly earlier—stone pillars, approximately the size of a human, which I am informed are still to be found in certain parts of Istanbul. (They are said to exist all the way from Central Asia to the Balkans.)

The purpose these stones served was not as mysterious as that of the monoliths at Stonehenge, but it may turn out to be more exciting by far in social terms. They were called "charity stones" (*sadaka tashi*). A rich person who wanted to make a donation would reach up to a niche at the top of the stone, where he would deposit his gift. Later on, a needy person would come along, reach up, take what was enough for his needs, *and leave the rest of the money where it was* so that another one in need may find solace. The purpose of this device was to preserve the anonimity of the poor, thereby saving them from shame and loss of face. As a Turkish Islamic saying goes, "The right hand should not know what the left hand is doing." This also saves the rich donor from ostentation, pride, and an inflated ego.

Does that sound too good to be true? Were there not, you may ask, any thieves? Well, it was either that, or the thieves themselves—unlikely as this may seem—would also be making donations. If they had thieves, this was the kind of thieves they had—the "Robin Hood" kind.

If all this sounds unbelievable, it is still a great consolation to learn that the descendants of such ancestors still preserve the meaning of the charity stones as a sort of atavism.

As I wrote this, at the beginning of the third millenium A.D., a clipping from the day's newspapers stood before me. It said in part:

"Climbing towards Galatasaray [in Istanbul], I saw a large box full of clothing on Yenicharsi Avenue. On it was a sign: 'Charity – if you need it, don't hesitate to take it.' I watched from afar. Those in need approached the box and examined its contents. Some took one or two pieces, others didn't take anything…[The person who instituted it] said: 'There are lots of poor people around here. People who have unused clothes bring them and place them in the box. People who need them take them and leave.'"[117]

This, at a time when even the rich in Turkey were having trouble staying afloat.

രു   രു   രു

The main problem with Emptiness is that it is easily confused with nihility, leading in turn to nihilism. Nor is this confusion unjustified. We have traced the evolution of the concept of void, from the psychological sense to the philosophical to the ontological. The singular wisdom of a Sufi sage has shed light on why there is so much emphasis on Emptiness rather than God in the East: the jump to Enlightenment is attempted at an early stage of selfhood, before the highest stage, the Purified Self, is reached. Thus, the seeker has not accumulated enough spiritual "energy" to complete the trip to God. What results, i.e. the Void, is the ante-chamber to the Emperor's throne room, the elevator shaft in which the Ascension (*meeraj*) to God takes place.

The most fruitful sense of the various meanings of Emptiness is the psychological one. For this, we have returned to the original sense in which the Buddha used the term, and seen its parallels with "selflessness," as employed by the Sufi sage Rumi, who also tells us: "There are no others."

All of a sudden, we find ourselves confronted with ethics. This happens because the inner and the outer, the esoteric and

---

117. G. Uras, *Milliyet,* Feb. 17, 2001, p.7 (www.milliyet.com.tr/2001/02/17/yazar/uras.html).

the exoteric, are ultimately one. This means that the inner state of a person is intimately related to his outward behavior. If a person claims he is a buddha but acts unethically, he is deluding either himself, or others, or both. In self-cultivation, there is always the danger of becoming too preoccupied with oneself. In service to others, there is no room for covert egotism to creep in—unless one becomes proud of one's deeds. This is why these are best done in a subdued way—almost secretly, with no fanfare.

We can now move on to a fuller treatment of ethics. In East Asia, wherever ethics is involved, the first name that comes to mind is Confucius. Hence, in the following chapter, we shall be investigating the parallels between Confucian ethics and Sufism.

9

CONFUCIUS: THE EXOTERIC DIMENSION

Confucian Divine Law

For the moment, we shall be concerned not with the later neo-Confucian synthesis of Confucianism with Taoism or Buddhism, but stripped-down Confucian ethics, pure and simple. For Confucius, the central moral virtue is benevolence or human-heartedness (*jen*). But what is benevolence? Confucius answers this question in several ways, of which three have been singled out for special mention below.

The first is the Golden Rule, which he calls *shu,* universally shared by moral systems all over the world. "The way of the Master [Confucius] consists in doing one's best and *shu.* That is all." (*Analects,* 4.15)[118] Also defined as "using oneself as a measure to guage others," *shu* is:

> "Do not impose on others what you yourself do not desire." (12.2, 15.24)

The same viewpoint is expressed by the Prophet: "No one of you is a believer until he desires for his brother what he desires for himself." The equivalent term used by him for *shu* is "comparing others to oneself" (*qiyas al-nafs*).

---

118. In the main, I have followed the translation by D.C. Lau: Confucius, *The Analects,* Hardmondsworth: Penguin, 1979.

The second characteristic of benevolence is love of one's fellow human beings:

"Love your fellow men." (1.5, 12.22, 17.4)

The Messenger puts it this way: "You cannot enter Paradise...unless you love one another."

The third characteristic is this: benevolence consists in overcoming the self. And this overcoming of self is accomplished through "observance of the rites."

Confucius said, "To return to the observance of the rites through overcoming the self constitutes benevolence." (12.1)

Now in Sufism, self-cultivation is the highest goal. And this is accomplished through overcoming the (Base) self. The Messenger said: "The greatest war/struggle is the war against the self." Sufism outlines an entire program for overcoming the self through self-purification. As God states in the Koran,

Whoever struggles, struggles only to his own gain. (29:6)
Whoever purifies himself does it only for his own good. (35:18)
Those who struggle for Our sake, surely We shall guide them in Our ways. (29:69)
By the moon when it is full, you shall surely ride from stage to stage. (84:18-19)
The reward of the self-purified is eternal Paradise. (20:76)
Who purifies his self has surely attained liberation/salvation. (87:14, 91:9)

It can be seen that up to this point, Confucius and Sufism are in full agreement. But even greater agreement can be observed if a new interpretation is made of what Confucius called "rites." Confucius attached the greatest importance to the observance of rites:

> "Do not look unless it is in accordance with the rites, do not listen unless it is in accordance with the rites, do not speak unless it is in accordance with the rites, do not move unless it is in accordance with the rites." (12.1)

Now of course, what Confucius meant here were the time-honored rites of the past. These rites needed to be adhered to meticulously. Similarly, the Divine Law, which consists of the explicit injunctions of the Koran plus the sayings and example of the Prophet, outlines a foolproof list of external observances that will lead to salvation. Among these are ethical requirements, details of bodily and spiritual purification, the Ritual Prayer (Formal Prayer), and techniques that will help in overcoming the self. Confucius simply advised:

> "Swerve not from the right path." (2.2)

So does the Koran: "Go straight, as you have been commanded." (11.112) And of course, one should ideally follow "the Straight Path" (*An.* 15.25, *Kor.* 3:51, 3:101, etc.) without any thought of recompense, simply because it is the Right Way. Nevertheless, it is a great reassurance and positive incentive that reward for Right Action is guaranteed by Heaven, as it is in Sufism.

Let me hasten to add that observing the Divine Law is only part of Sufism. But it is the foundation, the most essential part. No progress in cultivating the self can be made without this infrastructure to build upon.

Further Parallels

In addition to the above, there are other points where the teachings of Confucius coincide with those of Sufism. Some of the more outstanding examples are given below.

The sage is free of fear.

Confucius said: "The gentleman is free from worries and fears...If, on examining himself, a man finds nothing to reproach himself for, what worries and fears can he have?" (12.4)

Or, as the Zen master Rinzai put it: "The true aristocrat is the one who is free of anxiety." In the Heavenly Book, it is stated: "The Friends of God (the sages)—there is no fear for them, neither shall they sorrow." (10:62) In Sufism, one is called to engage frequently in self-examination. The Messenger of Heaven said: "Examine your self before you are called to account."

To the superior person, all human beings are brethren.

The famous Sufi poet Niyazi Misri wrote the following couplet:

I used to think that in the world, for me no friend was left
I abandoned me,[119] *and knew that no stranger was left*

According to Mencius, "The one who has no enemies in the realm is the vicegerent of Heaven." (*Meng Tzu* 2A:5) Is this not a different description of Confucius' words?—

---

119. To elaborate, in Sufism one abandons the world, renounces the afterworld, quits being (both self and other), and then abandons renunciation itself (*tark-i dunya, tark-i uqba, tark-i hasti, tark-i tark*). When one is stripped of all of these, one finds God.

"The gentleman is reverent and does nothing amiss, is respectful toward others and observant of the rites, and all within the Four Seas are his brothers." (12.5)

Government.

Confucius' ideas about government also find a resonant frequency with Sufism. He says:

"To govern is to correct. If you set an example by being correct, who would dare to remain incorrect?...If you yourself were not a man of desires, no one would steal even if stealing carried a reward." (12.17-18)

In the words of Lao Tzu, "I love quiescence and the people of themselves go straight." (*Tao Te Ching*, Ch. 57) And according to Chuang Tzu, the Perfect Man governs the world by rectifying his inner state. This is best explained by a Sufi story about the Grand Sheikh Abdulqader Geylani.

One day, a child's parents brought him to the Great Sage. The child was addicted to candy, and try as they might, they had not been able to cure him of this habit. They had even sought the help of doctors, but to no avail.

Now the Sage happened to have a sweet tooth himself. He told the parents: "Go now, and bring him back a week later."

When the week had passed, the parents brought the child back. The Sage simply told him, "My son, don't eat sweets from now on." The parents were mystified as to why such a simple command had not been issued the week before, but they said nothing.

After some time had passed, the parents came back to thank the Sage. They were both surprised and elated. The child had stopped eating sweets of his own accord. "O Sage, how did you accomplish this?" they asked. "And why didn't you give him the same order when we first brought him to you?"

The Sheikh smiled. "Before I could ask your child to renounce sweets," he said, "I had to do so myself. It was because I dropped my own habit that he was able to abandon his."

As Mencius observed, "There are great men who rectify themselves—and others are rectified." (7A:19) "So wherever the Superior Man passes through, people are transformed; the place where he stays is spiritualized and Heaven and Earth blend harmoniously." (7A:13) "The Superior Man concentrates on the cultivation of his own character. The common error of people is that they forget about their own garden and try to cultivate the other man's garden. They expect much from others and little from themselves." (7B:32) Or, as has been said, "The words of an unreformed reformer rarely inspire reform." According to Confucius, "If a man is correct in his own person, then there will be obedience even if orders are not given. But if he is not correct in his own person, there will be no obedience even if orders are given." (13.6)

This also suggests another meaning for "government" as the Chinese have conceived it. Obviously, only a sage can be capable of this kind of self-control. Ideally, then, the ruler should be a sage-king. But because authentic sages are so rare, it is extremely difficult to place one in political authority. In this case, political rule has to be distinguished from moral "government." Confucius explains this further: "Simply by being a good son and friendly to his brothers...a man is, in fact, taking part in government." (2.21) Or, as the Messenger put it, "Each one of you is a shepherd with respect to his duties. A ruler is a shepherd over those he rules. He is responsible for the dissemination of justice in his country. A person is responsible for his people and family, and is a shepherd to them. A woman is a shepherd in her home, and is responsible for everything within it. A servant is responsible for the property of those s/he serves, and for protecting it. Be aware that you are all shepherds, and are responsible for the duties you undertake."

Confucius also adds: "Do not concern yourself with matters of government unless they are the responsibility of your office." (8.14) If a society has many sages, many enlightened persons, the mere force of their own self-control will be echoed by the populace at large. It is not by attempting a near-impossibility, but by widespread self-cultivation, that social harmony and peace can be achieved.

Don't even try to make a sage the emperor. Instead, try to become a sage yourself.

Motives take precedence over results.

For Confucius, the motives of an action are more important than the results.[120] In Sufism, the collections of sayings of the Messenger are second in importance only to the Koran. These have been brought together in the *Six Books*. In the most important, called the *Bukhari* after the name of its collector, the very first saying is: "The reward of deeds depends upon the intentions and every person will receive reward according to what he has intended." For instance, if a person emigrates only with the intention of worldly benefit or finding a spouse, that will be his gain and nothing more, for God looks at the hearts of human beings and not at external appearances. It is also said that a good person never is able to do as well as he intends and a bad person is never able to do as wrong as he intends. But the recompense of a bad deed is only in its own measure, whereas the reward for a good deed is many times the measure of the deed itself, so the accumulation of merit (purification) is much faster than that of demerit (defilement). As Tung Chung-shu says: "Heaven has trust in the *yang* but not in the *yin;* it likes beneficence but not chastisement." A saying of God related by the Prophet is: "My

---

120. Laurence C. Wu, *Fundamentals of Chinese Philosophy,* p.18.

mercy takes precedence over My wrath." Likewise the Koran: "My mercy embraces everything."(7:156)

Doing what is beautiful.

In the *Analects,* it is stated that one should sacrifice to the deity as if the deity were present. (3.12) This is reminiscent of the Messenger's definition of "doing the beautiful" (*ihsan*): it is to "worship God as if you see Him, for even if you do not see Him, He sees you."

God.

As is often the case in China, God is called "Heaven" by Confucius. For example: "When you have offended against Heaven, there is nowhere you can turn to in your prayers." (3.13) Elsewhere, he calls God "Tao": "Set your heart on the Tao." (7.6)

Words and deeds.

Confucius said, "In antiquity men were loath to speak. This was because they counted it shameful if their person failed to keep up with their words." (4.22) In the same vein, the Heavenly Classic (the Koran) admonishes: "Why do you say what you do not do?" (61:1) A disciple of Confucius feared that he would be told something further before he could put into practice something he had heard. Likewise, it is related that the Companions of the Messenger would read a page of the Koran, and would not read another page until they had put in to practice what they had already read.

The Golden Mean.

Confucius said: "Supreme indeed is the Mean as a moral virtue." (6.29) Likewise, the Classic calls believers a "middle community" (2:143), because they walk a "middle way," and the Messenger was always careful to avoid excess in all things.

Knowledge.

Confucius and the Messenger alike placed the greatest value on knowledge. Confucius said: "I was not born with knowledge, but…I am quick to seek it." (7.20) Likewise, the Messenger said: "Seek, knowledge, even if it be in China" (i.e., that far away), and also: "Knowledge is the lost property of the believer. Wherever s/he finds it, s/he takes it at once."

Regarding moral knowledge, Confucius stated: "Even when walking in the company of two other men, I am bound to be able to learn from them. The good points of the one I copy; the bad points of the other I correct in myself." (7.22) In Sufi tradition, Loqman, an earlier sage, made it a point to "learn courtesy from the discourteous"—whenever he saw an immoral deed performed, he shrank away from that deed because of its intrinsic ugliness, and performed its exact opposite instead. As Mencius puts it, "To learn from others to develop one's goodness is also to develop goodness together with others." (2A:8)

Trustworthiness.

Confucius counted trustworthiness in word among the most important moral virtues (7.25, 9.25, 12.10, 15.6, 17.6). The Messenger was so truthful in what he said that he became known among his people as "Muhammad the Trustworthy."

Guaranteeing security to others.

The gentleman, Confucius said, "cultivates himself and thereby brings peace and security to his fellow men [and] to the people." (14.42) The Messenger defined the faithful in similar terms: "The believer is one such that others are safe from his hand, his lust, and his tongue."

Speech.

Confucius said, "To fail to speak to a man who is capable of benefiting is to let a man go to waste. To speak to a man who is incapable of benefiting is to let one's words go to waste. A wise man lets neither men nor words go to waste." (15.8) The Prophet said, "Speak to people according to the level of their undersatnding." Rumi, the famous Sufi, was saying the same thing when he observed: "A blade of grass cannot support a mountain."

Being industrious.

Confucius said, "Even playing games is better than being idle." (17.22)

> The Messenger was walking with his Companions one day when they came across a man sitting on the ground doing nothing. The Messenger passed by without a remark. On their way back, the man was fiddling with a stick, drawing patterns on the ground. This time the Messenger offered his greetings. When his Companions asked him why he had not greeted him the first time, the Messenger said, "Then, he was doing nothing at all. Now, at least he was occupied with something."

Love of Relatives.

In the *Doctrine of the Mean,* it is stated: "*Jen* is 'humanity' and its most obvious function is in love for relatives. 'Justice' means 'setting things right' and its most obvious function is in venerating the Good. The differing levels in loving relatives and venerating the good are expressed through propriety." (Section 20)[121] Likewise, the Koran states: "God calls you to justice, performing good deeds, and giving to relatives in need. He forbids fornica-

---

121. I am mainly following A. Charles Muller's translation: http://www.human.toyogakuen-u.ac.jp/~acmuller/contao/docofmean.htm.

tion, impropriety, and insolence. He advises you with commandments and prohibitions, so that you may heed" (16:90).

Gentleness to Visitors.

The *Doctrine* continues: "Being gentle to guests from afar, people will flock to you from all directions." This is echoed in the Classic: "It is due to mercy from God that you deal with them gently: had you been rough, hard-hearted, they would certainly have turned away from you and dispersed." (3:159)

Fate.

Usually translated as "Mandate of Heaven," *T'ien Ming* may better be termed "Heavenly Command" or "God's Will." It is this which gives rise to the destiny (*ming*) of human beings. The fate of every individual is determined by God's Will.[122] In the Koran, the nature of the Command is explained. The Heavenly Command is "Be!" (*kun*). "His only action, when He desires a thing, is to say to it "Be," and it is" (3:47, etc.). Chuang Tzu often speaks of "what cannot be evaded" or "that which cannot be made otherwise": "Man usually regards the ruler he serves as superior to himself. He is willing to die for him. If such is the case, how much more should he regard as superior to himself the true Ruler!"[123] The Heavenly Ruler, namely God, has issued commandments for all of us to follow. These are for our own edification.

The Prophet, however, discouraged his followers from thinking too deeply about matters of fate. The reason is that while God knows everything, we as human beings can know what our destiny is only after the event. Hence, brooding on fate

---

122. I owe this understanding of Ming-ming theology to Tienzen (Jeh-Tween) Gong. See his online article, "Confucianism: The greatest religion of mankind" (1994).
123. T. Izutsu, *Sufism and Taoism,* pp. 423-24.

should not lead to pessimism, fatalism, or laziness. Nor should it prevent us from carrying out God's commands for human beings. God only helps those who help themselves.

Sincerity and Unity

Mencius said, "The essentials of the Superior Man's character are *jen*, Righteousness, Propriety and Wisdom." (7A:21) "The feeling of concern for the well-being of others is *jen*. The sense of shame and disgust is Righteousness; the sense to treat others with courtesy and respect is Propriety. The sense of right and wrong is Wisdom." (6A:6)

Chu Hsi considered sincerity (*ch'eng*) all-important. If it exists, said he, the other four virtues will be manifested too: human-heartedness (*jen, ren*), righteousness (*yi*), propriety (*li*), wisdom (*zhi*). Again, we find in the *Doctrine of the Mean*: "Sincerity is the Way of Heaven. Making oneself sincere is the Way of Man. If you can be perfectly sincere without effort, without a mindfulness to its attainment, and walk embracing the Middle Way, you are a sage…The enlightenment that comes from sincerity is our own nature…If you are sincere, you will be enlightened. If you are enlightened, you will be sincere.

"Only the perfectly sincere person can actualize his own essence [nature: *hsing, fitra*]. Actualizing his own essence, he can fully actualize the essence of others. Fully actualizing the essence of others, he can fully actualize the essence of all things. Being able to fully actualize the essence of all things, he can assist Heaven and Earth in their transformation and sustenance. Able to assist in Heaven and Earth's transformation and sustenance, he forms a [bridge between] Heaven and Earth." (20-22)

"Sincerity is just 'perfecting' and the Tao is just 'following.' Sincerity is the beginning and end of all things. Without sincerity there is nothing. Thus the Superior Man values the process of 'becoming-sincere.'...[O]ur nature is...none other than the Tao by which inner and outer are merged." (25)

To actualize the essence of all things is Enlightenment. It is to realize that this essence is One, and that it is none other than God. This is the reason why Chapter 112 of the Koran, "Sincerity" (*ikhlas*), is also called "Unification" (*tawhid*). The chapter states:

> *Say: God is One*
> *God, the Eternal, the only One*
> *Who has not begotten, nor been begotten,*
> *Equal to Him is no one.*

This is the quintessential statement of Sufism: the Unity of Ultimate Reality. Why, then, has it been linked with sincerity? Because only those who earnestly believe it, who sincerely profess this Unity, will come to understand and eventually discover what it means, since they will be fully enlightened to the Truth that He is One and they are forever in His Presence. All others who are distracted by a multiplicity of idols, of attachments—in a word, those who are deluded by Multiplicity itself—will never find a path from untruths to Truth. Until, that is, they sincerely concede, in an act of what initially is faith, that God is One. That act of faith will lead to the Truth of Certainty (*haqq al-yaqin*)— "The journey of a thousand miles begins with one step." When sincerity is perfect, that is enlightenment.

If one has doubts about this, it is best to again consult the *Doctrine of the Mean.* "Where there is a lack in your understanding, or your study has not yet reached the point where it is effective, don't just leave it. When there is something you have investigated, or investigated but not understood, don't just leave it. When there is something that you have not yet discerned, or discerned but not yet clarified, don't just leave it. When there is something you have not yet practiced, or have practiced, but not yet universally, don't just leave it.

"'If someone else gets it in one try, I will try a hundred times. If someone else gets it in ten tries, I will try a thousand times.' If you are able to follow this Way, then even if you are stupid, you will become enlightened. Even if you are weak, you will become strong." (20) Likewise, a great Sufi sheikh counseled that a disciple should not despair just because of numerous failures on the path, and should not give up visiting his master or fulfilling the master's requirements. This is a path of hope.

ଔ   ଔ   ଔ

Confucian ethics overlaps Islamic Divine Law (*sharia*) at many points. The basis of it all is to measure others by reference to oneself (*shu, qiyas al-nafs*). Most important of all is sincerity. If one is utterly truthful to oneself, in the end one will discover the Truth. Through a chapter in the Koran, honesty is inextricably bound up with Unity—the all-encompassing Unity (*wahdaniyah*) of God, the unfathomable unity (*wahdah*) of objects with objects, subjects with subjects, and objects with subjects.

When one attains such a Unity—through Unification (*tawhid*) resulting in Fusion (*jam*)—how is the universe perceived? What is the experience of mystical consciousness? The next chapter is now devoted to this subject.

10

INDRA'S NET

If you hide a small thing in a large place, it still might escape and disappear.
If, on the contrary, you hide the whole world in the whole world itself,
nothing will find any place through which it might escape.

—Chuang Tzu

I am happy to the extent that I look at these mirrors.

—Niyazi Misri

Mutual Interdependence

I now wish to discuss the equivalents of the term *sunyata:*
"dependent origination," "dependent co-arising," or "interdependence" (*pratityasamutpada*), and "no self-nature or own-being"
(*nihsvabhavata*).[124]

According to Nagarjuna: "We declare that what is dependent co-arising, that is emptiness... Emptiness is by definition
absence of own-being (*svabhava*)."[125] The first of these is best

---

124. *Nihsvabhava* (dependent origination, non-self-existence) also ties in
with the Islamic term for created beings: *kaim bi gayrihi* (dependent on
another for its existence), as opposed to the attribute of God or the
Tao discussed earlier (*kaim bi nafsihi,* self-existent without dependence
on anything else). In Islamic and medieval philosophy, God has been
called Necessary Being (*wajib al-wujud*) and Substance (*gawhar*), while
the created world has been termed Contingent Being (*mumkin al-
wujud*) or Accident (*araz*). (This use of the terms "Substance" and
"Accident" do not quite correspond to their contemporary usage.)
All these terms and concepts shed light on the nature of *nihsvabaha,*
the "non-essential," which corresponds to the created world.

expressed by the Taoists. "The universe and I," said Chuang Tzu, "came into being together." The second, lack of self-nature, is a direct result of the first: if the "ten thousand things" come into being together, and if all are interrelated, none of them can stand on its own independently of the others.

Here we approach a concept of the utmost importance: lack of essence, or essencelessness. It is critically important to understand correctly what this means. When Nagarjuna, Lao Tzu, Chuang Tzu, and other East Asian thinkers say that things have no essence, what they actually mean is that they have no essence *of their own*, independently of other things. This is also what is meant by no-self (*anatman*) and no-mind (*wu-hsin*): there are no selves or minds independent of each other. In that case, however, the whole of Totality must constitute an incomprehensible unity. Similarly, things have no being of their own, no existence in and of themselves. A chair, for instance, has no "chair-being" unique to itself, and neither does it have a "chair-essence," as distinct from "catness" or a "cat-essence." *Yet this does not preclude their having a common, single essence.* And indeed, everything in the universe has, for nontheistic Eastern thinkers, at least one thing in common: they are united by *sunyata*, or else *tathata* (Suchness/ Thusness, Buddha-nature). But the main question remains unresolved: from what, then, is the entire universe spawned? And the answer to that question, an answer that is already implicit in all the philosophies we have been discussing, is: from a single Essence, from Undifferentiated Unity. That Essence is self-existent, it can stand by itself even in the absence of the universe. And it is at the root of every existing thing in the phenomenal world.

---

125. Quoted from the *Mulamadhyamikakarika* in Richard H. Robinson, "Some Logical Aspects of Nagarjuna's System," *Philosophy East & West*, 6, 4 (October 1957), p. 306.

Therefore, although things do not possess a multiplicity of individual self-natures, at their core there nevertheless lies a single self-nature, the Essence. If this did not exist, neither would the universe, and neither would Buddha-nature. There would then be no Buddha-nature to be realized, and the following way of translating a verse from the Heart Sutra would be true: "There is no suffering, no origination, no stopping, no path. There is no knowledge and no attainment, because there is nothing to attain."[126] In that case, what's all the fuss about? But this is to negate wisdom and all strivings after wisdom, including *nirvana* and the Buddha-nature.

I should add that strictly from the God's-eye point of view, this is actually true: nothing exists except God. As a Sufi poem states,

There is no comer and no goer,
No one who dies and no survivor

—it is only God that moves. Likewise the *Upanishads*: "There is no dissolution, no birth, none in bondage, none aspiring for wisdom, no seeker of liberation and none liberated. This is the absolute truth."[127] But from the standpoint of the formed universe, i.e. the differentiated universe, this is not obvious at all, and the attainment of that wisdom is the highest goal. (Once this is achieved, of course, there still remains the goal of enlightening others.)

---

126. Laurence G. Thompson, *Chinese Religion,* p. 89.
127. Gaudapada on the *Mandukya Upanishad,* 2.32.

Two Different Visions

At this point we may profitably recall, from Zen, the famous poem contest between Shen-hsiu and Hui-neng. Shen-hsiu wrote:

The body is the Bodhi tree,[128]
The mind a mirror bright,
Take heed to keep it always clean,
On it let no dust alight.

To which Hui-neng replied:

There never was a Bodhi tree,
Nor is there a mirror bright,
Since not a thing in truth exists,
On what should dust alight?

It is important to understand that what Shen-hsiu says is not wrong. It is stated from the standpoint of ordinary experience, of Multiplicity. Hui-neng's poem, on the other hand, states the situation from the standpoint of the One Essence, of Unity. The two poems are two sides of the same coin. They complete and complement each other.

This is but an explanation of a saying of the Prophet: in the Great Beginning, "God was, and nothing was with Him," to which the Sufi saint Junayd (or Ali) added the rejoinder: "He is even now as He was." In appearance, myriads of events occur each instant. In reality, it is He who comes and He who goes, forever and ever there is none other than He. As Chuang Tzu puts it, "Nothing has ever existed from the very beginning." The first proclamation of Hui-neng was: "From the first, not a thing

---

128. *Bodhi*: Enlightenment. Bodhi tree: The tree under which the Buddha achieved *nirvana*.

is."[129] It is also important to understand that "no thing" is not "nothing," for "no thing" (*la shay*) is God in His unmanifest state. We have seen that it is the gravest error, but unfortunately also the easiest, to confuse this with nothingness.

Here we approach a central problem of eastern philosophies: that *samsara* (the phenomenal world) is identical with *nirvana* (the Absolute, or its realization), that "form is emptiness and emptiness is form" (*Prajna-paramita-hridaya Sutra*). This might lead to the erroneous notion that enlightenment is nothing but the mundane, ordinary world, and that consequently there is no enlightenment to be striven for—enlightenment is no different from the state of ignorance.

As the Koran states: "He who knows and he who does not know—how can they be the same?" (39:9) There is a world of difference between ignorance and enlightenment. Some have claimed that to seek serves to distance you from what is sought. While they do have a point, it is also true, as a famous Sufi sage said, that "Not all who seek God find Him, but those who find Him are only those who seek."

In order to better understand this point, consider the following statement of Ch'ing-yüan:

"Before I had studied Zen for thirty years, I saw mountains as mountains, and waters as waters. When I arrived at a more intimate knowledge...I saw that mountains are not mountains, and waters are not waters. But now...I see mountains once again as mountains, and waters once again as waters."[130]

Now according to Sufism, there are two ways in which this can happen. The first is the experience of a state (*hal*), which is

---

129. Quoted in D.T. Suzuki, *The Zen Doctrine of No Mind*, New York: Samuel Weiser, 1972 [1949], p. 22.
130. Quoted in Watts, *Way of Zen*, p. 146.

impermanent. It is as if you go up in a plane, and then come down again. One first attains Annihilation in God (*fana fillah*), the stage where nothing exists except the Essence, but one cannot sustain the experience and descends back to the normal world.

But there is also a second possibility. One can go *through* this stage, go forth to the second stage of Unity, called Subsistence in God (*baqa billah*), where things again exist, but this time it is clearly perceived that all are mysteriously (to us) plunged in God. This is the difference between a temporary *nirvana* state and true realization ("reaching the moon," so to speak). And it is for this reason that we cannot treat the ordinary perception of the world and the perception of the-world-plunged-in-God as equal; a vast chasm separates the two. This is why the God's-eye statement, "there is nothing to be attained," is not applicable to the human-eye condition. How can ordinary cognition, everyday experience, be compared with Supreme Realization?

The Emptiness of Emptiness

We can treat the concept of Void (*sunyata*) in two ways: as an ontological descriptor, or as Nagarjuna defined it, as the dependent co-arising of things.

Let us first suppose that we are talking about Void or Emptiness in the ontological sense. If Emptiness is that in which nothing exists, then the "Emptiness of Emptiness" can only be that in which not even Emptiness exists.

Now, some have thought of the "Emptiness of Emptiness" as a return to the phenomenal world, as form or being. But if we look at things in the Hegelian sense, "the negation of the negation" is something higher. If the thesis is being (form) and its antithesis is nonbeing (emptiness), the "Emptiness of Emptiness" must be the synthesis, which includes and transcends both thesis and antithesis. Otherwise, we will simply be returning from antithesis back to thesis, and not going on to something higher. Hence, the "Emptiness of Emptiness" must be beyond both being and emptiness. We have already discussed this in the chapter on Emptiness.

Second, let us suppose that we are talking in Nagarjuna's terms, that Emptiness means the dependent origination of all things, as we are discussing in the present chapter. In that case, the "Emptiness of Emptiness" would mean the dependent origination of dependent origination. But what is the origination of dependent origination itself dependent on? Again, some have claimed that dependent origination is dependent on the existence of all things, thus treating the ruling principle as if it were subject to that which is ruled.[131] This reminds us of a work by Maurits C. Escher, where two hands are depicted drawing each other into existence.

What this picture neglects to say, of course, although it is tacitly implied by its very existence, is that such a situation cannot even be conceived, let alone depicted, without the presence of the artist. In order to even imagine two hands drawing each other, we have need of M. C. Escher himself. The two hands appear to depend on each other, but in reality both depend on Escher.

Here, too, the Hegelian principle holds. What is itself dependent, cannot give rise to that on which it depends. The child cannot give birth to the mother. Rather, the mother must be born of the grandmother—dependent origination must be spawned from something higher still. And that is the Essence of God, the Absolute, which is itself self-existent and independent, but on

---

131. Jay L. Garfield, "Dependent Arising and the Emptiness of Emptiness...," *Philosophy East and West, 44*, 2 (April 1994), p. 232.

which all things (including dependent origination) depend for their existence. Thus, whichever way we understand Emptiness, the "Emptiness of Emptiness" is seen to be equivalent to Nonspace (*la makaan*), and not simply a shuttling back and forth between space and its contents, between emptiness and form. (We already discussed Nonspace in an earlier section, "Kendo and 'The Sword of No-Abode.'")

Indra's Holographic Net

There is a simile in the *Avatamsaka Sutra* ("Flower Garland" Scripture, or *Huayen Jing*) of Mahayana Buddhism that beautifully illustrates the mutual interdependence and mutual interpenetration (nonobstruction, *wu-ai*) of all things:

> In the heavenly abode of Indra, there is a wonderful net that has been hung by some cunning artificer in such a manner that it stretches out infinitely in all directions. The artificer has hung a single glittering jewel in each "eye" of the net, and since the net itself is infinite in all dimensions, the jewels are infinite in number. There hang the jewels, glittering like stars of the first magnitude, a wonderful sight to behold.
> If we now arbitrarily select one of these jewels for inspection and look closely at it, we will discover that in its polished surface there are reflected all the other jewels in the net, infinite in number. Not only that, but each of the jewels reflected in this one jewel is also reflecting all the other jewels, so that there is an infinite reflecting process occurring.[132]

Indra's Net "symbolizes a cosmos in which there is an infinitely repeated interrelationship among all the members of the cosmos. This relationship is said to be one of simultaneous

132. Quoted in David J. Loy, "Indra's Postmodern Net," *Philosophy East and West*, *43*, 3 (July 1993), p. 481. Some small liberties have been taken with the text.

mutual identity and mutual inter-causality."[133] Thus it is that in one of the greatest classics of Sufi thought, *The Secret Rose Garden*, Mahmud Shabustari declares:

Know the world from end to end is a mirror;
in each atom a hundred suns are concealed.
If you pierce the heart of a single drop of water,
from it will flow a hundred clear oceans;
if you look intently at each speck of dust,
in it you will see a thousand beings...
The universe is contained in a mosquito's wing,
Through a single point in space the heavens roll.

Here, I cannot resist quoting from the great mystical poet William Blake:

To see the world in a grain of sand,
And heaven in a wild flower;
Hold infinity in the palm of your hand
And eternity in an hour.

This is very similar to the way in which the Neo-Confucianist Chu Hsi envisaged the Supreme Ultimate. In his view, the Supreme Ultimate is immanent in all things. Every particular thing has inherent in it the *Li* (principle) of its particular category of things, but at the same time the Supreme Ultimate in its entirety is inherent in it as well. In his *Recorded Sayings,* Chu Hsi states: "With regard to heaven and earth in general, the Supreme Ultimate is in heaven and earth. And with regard to the myriad things in particular, the Supreme Ultimate is in every one of them too."

---

133. Quoted in Ming-wood Liu, "The Harmonious Universe of Fa-tsang and Leibniz: A Comparative Study," *Philosophy East and West*, 32, 1 (January 1982), p. 65.

But in that case, wouldn't the Supreme Ultimate lose its unity? Chu Hsi's answer is no. We may call his approach "the Moon in Water." He says: "There is but one Supreme Ultimate, which is received by the individuals of all things. This one Supreme Ultimate is received by each individual in its entirety and undivided. It is like the moon shining in the heavens, of which, though it is reflected in rivers and lakes and thus is every-where visible, we would not therefore say that it is divided."[134] And, as Rumi cautions, "Look for the moon in heaven, not in the water!"

An example from biology may enable a better understand-ing. The entire human genome, coded into 23 chromosomes, is present in every cell of the body. Potentially, it is capable of expressing any kind of differentiation. Yet in practice, in accor-dance with position and need, only a specific aspect of the gene pool gets expressed: here a cell becomes skin tissue, there liver, and elsewhere part of an eye.

Here, too, we won't get lost as long as we recognize that beyond all the myriad reflections, there is the moon which is the One Real. In Islamic Sufism, God is both immanent and tran-scendent: He is both within all things and beyond all things. The Taoists, too, recognized that the Tao had an immanent aspect, an outward aspect facing the universe, which they called the Supreme Ultimate (*t'ai chi*), as well as an inward, transcendent aspect, the Non-Ultimate or Ultimateless (*wu chi*). These corre-spond, in Sufism, to the (immanent) Names and Attributes of God, and to the (transcendent) Essence, respectively. They are two sides of one coin.

---

134. Quoted in Fung Yu-lan, *Short History...*, p. 298.

The Room of Mirrors

Fa-tsang, the great systematizer of Hua-yen Buddhism, was very impressed by Indra's Net, and wrote about it himself. In order to illustrate the Net for the Empress Wu, Fa-tsang constructed an eight-sided room, lined with mirrors on all sides and on the ceiling and the floor. In the center of the room, he placed a candle. It is a long-known fact that two mirrors facing each other multiply the images of an object placed between them to infinity—the Sufi poet Rumi described infinity as "two mirrors and an apple." Not only was the candle reflected in each of the mirrors, but each mirror also reflected each other mirror, as well as itself being reflected in every other mirror, resulting in an infinite regress of images.

We now come to a crucial point. Given that any section of Indra's Net does not have any self-existence apart from all the rest, can the net itself exist without something beyond it? In other words: can the universe, for which the Net is a symbol, come into being of itself? If each part of something lacks independent self-existence, the whole, which constitutes the sum total of those parts, cannot have the quality of independent self-existence, either.

There are two things to consider. First, it is true that all the images are interdependent. *But they are dependent, above all else, on the candle in the center.* Remove the candle, which is the only Real One among the reflections, and all the illusory images will immediately be plunged into darkness.

The second point is this. Without the cunning artificer of Indra's Net—or the clever person who originated the simile—such an idea cannot even be conceived. Moreover, it takes a genius of Fa-tsang's caliber to actualize that idea in the real world. For the mirrors did not come into being of themselves, they did not place themselves on the walls of the room, and they emphatically did not light the candle in the center on their own. It was Fa-tsang who, with surpassing creativity, brought together and arranged all the hardware.

So we ask: Where is the artificer of Indra's Net? *Who is the Fa-tsang of the universe?*

The following excerpt by one of the greatest Sufi saints, Abdulqader Geylani, will help us to answer these questions.

The Mysteries of Unification

The following text is the pinnacle of mystical expression of all that we have discussed and can discuss. There are many Sufic technical terms and concepts involved, but I do not want to burden the reader with long, abstract explanations at this point. Instead, I would like you to sit back and simply savor the text:

God Almighty manifested Himself in the mirror of His Perfect Beauty, and the face of His Beloved appeared from every reflection therein.

[Each reflection is itself a mirror.] When the Beauty of Glory manifested in each mirror, God's Names appeared in this descent of Reality. That is, when His Beauty began to dance (manifest) in every reflection, this was termed His Names, and these are all loci of manifestation or emergence.

In these endless loci of emergence, He has brought forth His Attributes. Here are the works (of art). Who is the Great Artist that has created them?

These Attributes and Names—these works—are the world, the universe. Now this universe is the same as Essence. For God is the Uniter of all.

There is nothing but Reality in the field of existence. Everything is annihilated in the Essence of Unity. Other than Him there is no hearer, nor anything that is heard.

The sum total of light, darkness, the elements water, air and fire, and nature itself—is He.

The rule of causality, the command to Be, the exalted, the ruler and the debased—is He.

Word and meaning, everything that is manifested from the mind—is He.

He is the inventor of objects. He is also the same as objects.

Just as He is the Essence of everything, it is also He who keeps each in a state distinct from all others.

The light of the sun (that He is) shows itself from stars that are His Creation. But whereas this sun is always present and never sets, the rule of the stars is impermanent.

It is as if the universe emerged when your self separated slightly from its Essence.[135] This, however, is neither completely separate from you, nor is it entirely attached or connected to you.

Creation is like snow. And you are the water that produces and becomes manifest in that snow. But when snow melts, its rule is over, and the rule of water manifests itself. Now this is an unexpected situation.

Creation is like the snow. In other words, all creatures are representatives in the bodies in which they appear. But they are like snow; they have no independent existence of their own. For the existence of snow is the existence of water. And you are the water that gives rise to the snow, that is embodied in the snow.

But when snow melts, its rule is over... Cleansing, which is the rule and fame of water, is realized. For the rule of water has manifested itself.

Do not see ugliness in the world. For what you see is not ugly, but a beauty that intends to communicate the incomparable Beauty and Beatitude.

---

135. "Make a hairbreadth difference, and Heaven and Earth are set apart." Seng Ts'an, *Hsin Hsin Ming,* stanza 2.

Do not be veiled from it because of form or some other reason. That is, nothing should veil you from Reality. For behind every veil of sight shines the light [of Reality].[136]

ಌ   ಌ   ಌ

Nagarjuna defined Emptiness as mutual interdependence or dependent co-arising. In mystical states of consciousness, the entire universe is perceived as a stupendous whole. Every point of this whole simultaneously contains, like a holograph, all the other points, in a flow that occurs with dizzying speed (Ibn Arabi's *sarayan al-wujud*). This is Indra's Net. It was exemplified by a room lined with mirrrors, reflecting each other and each reflection *ad infinitum*. But who is the author of it all, the master of this show? Without God, such a design cannot even be conceived, let alone exist. And, as the excerpt from Geylani shows, God is indeed at the center of this house of mirrors.

But such visions of surpassing sublimity and beauty are not easy to come by. It comes at the end of a long period of self-cultivation. And how to cultivate the self is our next topic—from the standpoint of Sufism, naturally.

---

136. Quoted in www.geocities.com/henrybayman/fourbooks.htm, "The Mysteries of Unification."

SELF-CULTIVATION IN SUFISM

The ancients who wished to illustrate the highest virtue
. . . first cultivated their own selves.
Wishing to cultivate their own selves
. . . they first extended their knowledge to the utmost.

—The Great Learning (*Ta Hsüeh*)

Strive to be a full moon; you are now a fragment thereof . . .
the "Friend of God" ascend[s] above the heavens . . .
Take up your abode in heaven, O bright full moon!

—Rumi, *Mathnawi*

The Two Restrictions

It is stated in the Glorious Book: "Whoever . . . forbids their self its vain desires will have heaven as their abode." (79:40) Master Kayhan always said that at the basis of all self-cultivation, of all ethics, were two restrictions: illicit gain and illicit sex. The first is quite obvious: one should not break even a twig of a tree unless one is permitted by its owner. Otherwise, one will have the bad name of a shameless robber.

This is reminiscent of a Sufi story, concerning the father of Abu Hanifa, founder of one of the Four Schools of Law in Islam.

One day, he was traveling along a riverside when he became hungry. He saw an apple floating along on the water, so he reached out to pick it up. He had hardly taken a bite out of the apple when it occurred to him that apples don't grow in the wild, and consequently this apple must have an owner. He had bitten into it without the owner's permission. In order to find the owner, he went upstream, and presently saw the branch of an apple tree that was extending over the river. He found the owner.

"I want to repay you," he said, "for a bite I took out of an apple that belongs to you."

After the owner heard the details of how this had happened, he said: "I will let you go only if, in recompense, you work for me for seven years. And after that, you must marry my daughter, who is blind, deaf, and paralysed."

The man was stricken by this harsh verdict, but could not bring himself to walk away. So he worked for the owner of the apple tree for seven years, and when the day of marriage came, he found that the daughter, who had remained in hiding until then, was a ravishing beauty, not physically impaired at all. His surprise and happiness knew no bounds.

"This," said the owner, "is my daughter. She is blind to all that is evil, she is deaf to all that is evil, she is paralysed in reaching towards all that is evil. I give you her hand, and may you live happily ever after."

Such were the parents of the illustrious Abu Hanifa. Likewise, during the reign of the Ottoman sultan Suleiman the Magnificent, it is related that soldiers on the march, when they entered a vineyard and ate grapes, used to hang a bag of money where the bunch of grapes was missing.

As for the second restriction: one must content oneself with one's own mountain spring. One must not go beyond that. One must not scoop and soil the water of other springs, even if they are overflowing.

Islamic Sufism has the highest regard for family life, and takes special measures to preserve its sanctity. Moreover, it regards the rest of society—and, ultimately, humankind—as one's "extended family." Extramarital sex is prohibited, because nothing wrecks a marriage, and by implication a family, more than "forbidden lust." Indeed, it is deleterious to humanity as a whole, because not only is a particular family undone, but the very institution of marriage, the family concept, and the idea of a human being itself, all suffer injury. A durable family is the basis of a strong society. Dissolve the family institution, and an entire society will be ruined.

These two prerequisites, which the Master always emphasized, are beneficial to all human beings without exception. They are not for Sufis or Muslims alone. Because they are the primary methods by which the Base Self is to be seized and overcome. If you do not pull in these reins, you lose control of the wild horse. Self-cultivation is impossible without these two.

The Difficulty of the Way

The Master used to say that the Trust is "easy to give but hard to receive." As Chuang Tzu remarks in his chapter on "The Great Supreme": "You can hand it down but you cannot receive it." The Tao "may be transmitted, but cannot be received; It may be obtained, but cannot be seen." The teacher may be compared to a champion weightlifter, the student to a novice. If the teacher gives the barbell to the student before his muscles are fully developed, the student will not be able to support the weight but will simply drop it, possibly also being crushed underneath.

In visiting a Sufi master, one's heart must be empty, open, and receptive to the advice and the spiritual emanations of the teacher, if one wishes to derive maximum benefit from the visit.

The Man with Too Much Tea

A scholar of great knowledge once visited a Sufi sage. He was very pleased to be visiting the sage, and began talking and talking to show how much knowledge he had. Finally, the sage said: "Let me pour you some tea," and began pouring tea for his guest out of a teapot. He kept pouring until the teacup was full, and began to overflow onto the table.

The scholar was surprised. "What are you doing?" he asked.

"You are as full as this teacup," said the sage. "How can I put anything in it, when it is overflowing already?"

One must visit a Sufi sage with an empty heart, with a humility that is receptive to whatever the sage may choose to put in there. If one's heart is already full—of pride, of worldly concerns—one can receive nothing. The scholar in this story was obviously a person with too much tea in him.

The Cavity of the Heart

Whatever you put in your heart, that is your idol, your god.

In ancient times, people used to worship statues and effigies rather than Ultimate Reality. Nowadays things are a bit more subtle, but basically no different. Modern people may not worship graven images, but they have put money in their hearts. Or else they have put sex, or power, or something else there. The "cave of the heart," however, is the location which should be reserved only for God. This is the inner cavity, the inmost sanctuary of a human being. And only when it is filled with God can it resonate properly.

The formula of Islamic Sufism: "There is no deity but God, and Muhammad is His Messenger," needs to be understood in this light. The first part of the formula, "There is no god," denies reality to all finite idols. It empties the heart of all things other than God. Even if one achieves perfect Emptiness of the heart, however, this cannot be sustained for long. And why not? Because *nature abhors a vacuum.* The Void is unstable. If you do not grow flowers in your garden, pretty soon it will be infested with weeds and wild oats. Therefore, emptiness is not enough.

Weeding the garden and cleansing it of wild growth is not enough, for this will yield an empty field and nothing more. What you want is to cultivate your garden, to raise beautiful flowers and graceful trees in it. Once the throne of the heart is cleared, the second step is to place the Emperor on that throne. Which is the "except God" part of the formula meaning, "God is." God exists, God is the only Real.

This is also why we should practice *zazen* (sitting meditation) together with the Invocation of God. Nature abhors a vacuum. If you rid your garden of weeds but do not plant flowers therein, the weeds will just grow back. If the void of self-emptying is not filled with God, then it will be filled by other things.

Up to this point we have been talking about an abstract notion of God"—the God of the philosophers," as Pascal called it. And it is better, much better, than nothing. But we still have a further step to go. We need to move on from abstract theory to concrete practice. We need somebody to show us how to approach God, somebody who has already made the trip and is thoroughly familiar with the terrain. That is a different person in every religion, and in Sufism it is Muhammad, whom God called His "Beloved." Only with the aid of a true guide can we expect to discover God, to come closer to Him.

It is a sad fact of the human condition that information is subject to entropy with the passage of time. Lamentably, the pure, clean water of a prophet, buddha, or messenger tends to get polluted, and the same intensity and veracity cannot be carried on to succeeding generations. The utility of Islamic Sufism resides in the fact that all the elements of religion and philosophy have been brought together and constructed in such a fashion that *they mutually reinforce each other*. There is nothing out of place, and what is more, *everything interlocks* so that the result is a stable structure. There are no superfluous or incompatible elements. It is also fault-tolerant, because even if, by human error, one fails to implement all requirements completely, the structure will still stand. It is only when the most important pillars are omitted that it will fall apart. Because this is internal to everyone, because it is your own inner world that you are building or destroying, it cannot be assailed from outside. In this project, God is the architect—not only the Great Architect of the universe, but also the architect of your own inner salvation— Muhammad is the construction engineer who tells you how to implement the plans, and you are the worker who builds his/her own liberation step by step. If you can find one, a true sage—a faithful follower of the Messenger—will act as your foreman and help you, immensely easing your task. But even if you cannot, you have all the guidance you need in the legacy the Messenger has left behind: the Book and the Way.

The Heavenly Book

It is known that the Prophet (Muhammad) received the Heavenly Book (the Koran) over a period of 23 years. Yet it was initially sent down to him all at once, on the Night of Power, and its unfolding in time took place as appropriate occasions arose for its revelation. It was revealed to Muhammad by Gabriel, the Archangel or Great Spirit, who brought it from Heaven. And its manifest form remains unchanged to this day.

Today, there are millions of copies of the Book, all of them the same. They are published as any other book is published. Yet their original, the Mother of the Book, resides beyond time and space in Heaven, and is One. This is because the Book is a cosmic script, a heavenly blueprint. Although it was revealed on earth in the seventh century A.D. in terms of historical time, from another point of view it is older than the universe. It is the Oldest Classic, the Primordial Scripture, because it came before spacetime even existed. It is for this reason that, in a famous debate of the Middle Ages, those who claimed that the Koran is uncreated were right. They knew that the copies produced out of paper, pen, and ink were part of the phenomenal world, but they were thinking of the Mother of the Book in Heaven, totally beyond physical spacetime.

This original Master Record is eternal: it exists forever and is not destroyed. It is a Celestial Writing that is written with a Pen of Light on the Guarded Tablet, and it radiates shining beams in all directions that dazzle the eye and dizzy the mind.

When Tao, the universal principle, began to manifest itself, it produced the primordial matter-energy *qi* (*ki, ch'i*). This energy differentiated into the light energy of pure spirit which formed Heaven, and into dense, gross matter which formed Earth. The holy script was formed out of the same energy which formed Heaven, and embodied the Universal Law which dictated the formation of the universe. It is for this reason that it is the heavenly blueprint. It is inaccessible to all except the highest angels and immortals, let alone ordinary mortals. Only its earthly transcripts can be read by human beings. Since it precedes the universe, everything it contains about the universe should be regarded as the mandate of Heaven.

Because its original is inscribed in divine light, both the external appearance and the inward content—both the letter and the meaning—of the text are capable of raising the spiritual energy level of one who reads or contemplates it. By earnestly studying the Book, one becomes a living embodiment of its message. One's being becomes penetrated by its light, and one's behavior, like the Prophet's, becomes permeated by its underlying ethics. This is a fundamental stage in the process of self-transformation. When one has accumulated enough energy, one is able to ascend to Heaven and becomes a heavenly immortal.

Repeatedly reciting the Book can lead to transcending the mortal state, for the more closely one is identified with the celestial script, the closer one approaches its transcendent and primordial light. This does not necessarily mean that one must memorize every word of the holy blueprint, but that one's body, one's every pore, must become inscribed with its *meaning*. Confucius attained his wisdom, not by reading all the books in the world, but by understanding the essential meaning embodied in every book, since each—including those not yet written—is a commentary on the same Truth which is One. It is of this Truth which the Master Classic speaks.

The Way of the Prophet

Though all things may be contained in the Koran, it is heavy on theory and light on practice. The words and deeds (*sunna*: Way) of the Prophet, and of his closest followers after him, translate the meaning of the Classic into a form comprehensible to human beings. The details[137] of how Formal Prayer, Fasting, and Pilgrimage are to be performed, as well as how the Alms-tax charity is to be paid, are found in the Way. Formal Prayer is always preceded by an ablution where one's mouth is rinsed and one's face, arms, and feet are washed. The purpose of the bathing, the Formal Prayer itself, and of the Fasting, is to purify oneself in body and heart and thus become worthy to approach the Divine Presence. The object is to perfect the "pure heart" (26:89) so that no evil heart should result. Similarly, by undergoing the inconveniences and hardships of the Pilgrimage, one cancels one's errors (sins) and becomes assured of rebirth in the Pure Land after one dies. As for the Alms-tax, it is a form of

---

137. For a fuller treatment, see Henry Bayman, *The Station of No Station*, Berkeley, CA: North Atlantic Books, 2001.

charity that promises to eradicate hunger and poverty, not just from a society, but from the whole world.

The Way of the Prophet contains, in addition, many pointers as to how one's ethics may be improved and how one's self may be cultivated. But there is not enough space in this book to list them all.

One's own strength (*jiriki*)

The great traditions of the world have accepted two ways for progress in a spiritual path: self-power (*jiriki*) and other-power (*tariki*). In some traditions, the law is not something that is transmitted from teacher to student, but something the student *masters himself*. There is no utter devotion to the master. One should not depend on one's teacher. One should respect his realization, but not him as an individual. The principle is to rely on yourself, and not even on (for example) the Buddha. (Depend on the Law, not on a human being.) This is due to the acceptance of an abstract "law" instead of a specific person. The *Dhammapada*, for instance, counsels: "Work out your own salvation diligently."

Another's strength (*tariki*)

In the second way, one relies not on one's own strength, but the strength of another. This other may be God, or it may be a spiritually realized teacher. In such traditions, we find acceptance of, and absolute devotion to, a specific person. One should "Depend on man, not upon the Law."

As a result, in this path one attains spiritual progress solely on the strength of an already accomplished sage. For example, Dogen explains: "By practicing asceticism within a group, one attains the Way. It is like boarding a boat without knowing how to row. Since one trusts a good boatman, it makes no difference whether one knows how to row; one gets to the other side. Thus one should follow a good teacher and practice in a group. Then, since one is not relying on one's own resources, one naturally attains the Way."

The Synthesis in Sufism

If we now look at Sufism, we find that there is a combination of these two approaches. The following is an apt summary of the situation: "Work as if everything depended on you, and pray as if everything depended on God."

> There was a lame ant who decided to go on Pilgrimage. Mecca was far, far away, yet nonetheless it resolved to visit that holy place. After some time had passed on the road, an eagle soaring high above spotted the ant. The eagle watched as the ant, unlike other ants, made a sustained effort in one direction. Sometimes it would stray from its path, yet eventually it would keep moving towards some remote destination.
> The eagle became curious and swooped down, alighting near the ant. "Hello," said the eagle. "Where are you going?"
> "To Mecca to do the Pilgrimage," replied the ant.
> The eagle laughed. "You!" it said, "And with a lame leg, too! How can you ever expect to get there?"
> "Getting there isn't the most important thing," said the ant. "The point is to be on the path that leads there."

When one dies, one should die while on the right path. One can conjecture that as a result, the eagle told the ant to climb onto one of its claws, took off, and conveyed the ant to its destination with what would be lightning speed by comparison. Among the Sufi sages, there are just such eagles.

Just as there is no *yin* without its *yang* and vice versa, one should combine one's own strength, and struggle, with devotion to God and to a teacher, through whom divine aid reaches one. Or, if a teacher is unavailable (and even when one is present), one must supplement the abstract teaching of the Divine Law (generally embodied in the Koran) with the practical details transmitted through the Way of the Prophet.

This situation is exemplified through the following Turkish Sufi saying. The disciple says: "Father, help!" (*Baba, himmet*). The sage replies: "My son, serve!" (*Oghlum, hizmet*). One must rely on the saving, elevating power of the teacher, his spiritual blessing (*baraka, fayz*). But at the same time, one must actively strive to attain spiritual growth oneself, by diligently fulfilling the requirements of the spiritual path. The master may be in charge of the boat, but it is one's duty to participate in rowing or doing some other chore that is necessary.

When you come to think of it, isn't this also more in conformity with the requirements of courtesy? For when a master accepts a student, he is already taking on a significant burden. It is an unwritten pact between the teacher and the disciple that the teacher will do everything to assist in the disciple's progress. For his part, the disciple in turn must accept whatever "tests, exams, homework," and so on the teacher will set out for him.

The needs of every student are different. One may be spiritually strong in some areas but weak in others. No two persons are the same. Hence, it is the student's duty to assume his own burden, and not be a burden himself to the master.

The Koran says, "Every human being has only that which he strives for" (53:39). That is, one can only enjoy the fruit of one's work. We can immediately understand this for the material world, where results are linked to one's efforts, that is, one earns by the sweat of one's brow. The same holds in the spiritual world. A disciple who is lazy and a freeloader will stand in shame of his teacher and be unable to make any progress.

There is one fine point, however, that needs mention. Doing things on one's own leads to mastery and accomplishment. But it can also fill the student with feelings of arrogance, one of the greatest hindrances in a spiritual path. "Arrogance is the sign that one's advancement has reached its extreme limit. It is the first thing that one should avoid." (*Lao-tzu,* Ch. 9.) How is this danger to be avoided?

The Sufis have found a workaround for this. The thing to do is to attribute *even one's own accomplishments* to the blessing and power of the teacher. For it is the teacher who sets up a problem which is simple enough that a student is able to solve it. And frequently, the master, in giving a task, has also prepared the "answer," so that the disciple can find it—ready-made, as it were—with only a little effort. Hence, all success should be seen as a favor of the master, and not imputed to oneself. The moment the disciple begins to have feelings of personal superiority is also the moment when his downfall sets in, as illustrated by the following Sufi story.

The Flying Frog

There was once a frog who lived on the shore of a lake. This was no ordinary frog, for each time it saw birds lifting up after a drink, its heart would fly off with them. How it longed to fly as birds do, to be utterly free of the curse of gravitation!

Meditating long and deep on how to fly, the frog finally came up with a solution. But it would require the cooperation of the birds.

The next time some birds landed to drink their fill, the frog jumped over and politely introduced itself.

"I find your talent of flying enviable," it said. "How I wish I could fly too."

The birds looked at each other and smiled. "Well, you know," they said, "that's rather difficult. You don't have wings, and you're too heavy for one of us to carry you on his back."

"Oh, but there is a way," answered the frog. "What I propose is this: I will bite a stick, like this one over here, in the middle. Two of you will hold the stick at each end with your claws, and when you take off, we'll all be airborne."

That seemed like a feasible plan to the birds, and after they had debated it among themselves, two of them did exactly as the frog said. The frog clamped its jaw at the center of the stick, and they rose into the air.

"How glorious it is to fly like this!" thought the frog, thoroughly enjoying the trip. No frog had ever beheld an aerial view of the landscape before—it was breathtakingly beautiful.

By and by, another flock of birds appeared, flying towards them. The two flocks greeted each other, and hovered in the air for a moment's chat.

"What's that strange contraption you've got there?" asked an interested bird from the second party.

"Why, that's our friend the frog. We're teaching him how to fly," joked one of the birds.

"But how on earth is that possible?" The other birds had never seen a frog in flight before.

"Well, it's quite simple, really. Our amphibious friend holds on to this stick with his teeth, and two of us lift off grasping the ends."

The birds on the opposite side were impressed. "What an ingenious idea!" they exclaimed. "Whoever thought of it?"

"I," said the frog...

Stages of the Self

The symbol of Islam is the crescent moon. The Chinese symbol of perfection is the full moon. When one first enters Islam, one is as yet undeveloped. One gradually gains maturity, passing through phases like those of the moon. Ideally, the process culminates in the Perfect Human Being, who reflects God's light just as the full moon reflects the maximum light it receives from the sun. Rumi elaborates in his *Mathnawi*:

Since you have told the story of the new moon (hilal, crescent)
Now set forth the story of the full moon (badr).
That new moon and that full moon are now united,
Removed from duality and defect and shortcomings.
That new moon is now exalted above inward defect;

His outward defects served as degrees of ascension.
Night after night that mentor taught him grades of ascent
And through his patient waiting rewarded him with happiness.
The mentor says, "O unripe hastener, through patient waiting,
You must climb to the summit step by step.
Boil your pot by degrees and in a masterly way;
Food boiled in mad haste is spoiled." [138]

The Sufis have outlined seven stages through which one must pass before Enlightenment occurs. These are the stages of the self. At the bottom, everyday level is the Base Self. As self-purification proceeds, the self undergoes a metamorphosis, and finally the caterpillar is transformed into a beautiful butterfly. One must cultivate one's self to its highest perfection.

The levels of selfhood in Sufism are, in brief:

1. The Base Self: The seat of selfish passions and desires, the stage at which most people find themselves.

2. The Critical Self: The self is ashamed of its baseness and tries to improve.

3. The Inspired Self: The self begins to receive inspirations from the divine.

4. The Tranquil Self: The self has reached tranquility, contentment, serenity.

5. The Pleased Self: Pleased with everyone, everything, and with the mandate of Heaven.

6. The Pleasing Self: God Himself is pleased with this self.

---

138. Rumi, *Mathnawi,* abridged E.H. Whinfield translation, www.sacred-texts.com. I have edited the text slightly.

7. The Perfect, Complete, or Purified Self: The final level where the self has attained Enlightenment (Gnosis).

In Sufism, the Purified Self is the stage of utter selflessness. It is reached after the self has been cleansed of all individual accretions that mark it off as distinct from all other selves, lending specificity to a human being in terms of geography, time, culture, and so on. It is like erasing one's fingerprints from one's fingers. In terms of Zen, it is "the face you had before you were born."

Since the Base Self is the most difficult to overcome, we shall concentrate our attention on this level.

The Base Self

The *Dhammapada* states: "If one man conquer in battle a thousand times a thousand men, and if another conquer himself, he is the greatest of conquerors. One's own self conquered is better than all other people conquered."[139] Lao Tzu concurs:

> One who overcomes others is strong,
> But he who overcomes himself is mighty.[140]

On returning from a battle, the Prophet said, "We now go from the lesser battle to the greatest battle." He explained that the greatest battle is "the war against one's self." Spiritual warfare, therefore, is waged primarily against the Base Self.

One of the ways in which the Base Self operates is portrayed in *Rashomon* (1950), a famous movie by Akira Kurosawa. In a nutshell: three characters come together, something horrible

---

139. *The Dhammapada,* Ch. 8 (The Thousands), quoted in Edwin A. Burtt, *The Teachings of the Compassionate Buddha,* New York: New American Library (Mentor), 1955, p. 58.
140. *Tao Te Ching,* Ch. 33.

happens, each one of the three subsequently relates a completely different account from the others of what happened. It is impossible to determine what really took place.

At first, one might be inclined to view *Rashomon* as a precursor of Postmodernism—all truths are relative, there is no single, absolute truth. Yet this is precisely what Kurosawa himself has emphatically denied. In his following statement regarding the film, he lays bare certain key elements pertaining to the Base Self:

> Human beings are unable to be honest with themselves. They cannot talk about themselves without embellishing. [*Rashomon*] portrays such human beings—the kind who cannot survive without lies to make them feel they are better people than they really are. It even shows this sinful need for flattering falsehood going beyond the grave—even the character who dies cannot give up his lies when he speaks to the living through a medium. Egoism is a sin the human being carries with him from birth; it is the most difficult to redeem. This film is like a strange picture scroll that is unscrolled and displayed by the ego.[141]

Thus, the Base Self actively "edits" reality to suit its own taste, and this is done differently by each person, who quite naturally possesses a different Base Self.

The Goose as Model for the Base Self

Baso (Ma-tsu) was taking a walk with Hyakujo, one of his disciples. Spying a flock of white geese, Baso asked him: "Where are they flying?" The disciple answered: "They have already

---

141. Quoted from *Something Like an Autobiography* by A. Kurosawa. "On the Death of Akira Kurosawa: The Battle Against Egoism," www.hal-pc.org/~questers/Kurosawa/Kurosawa.html, accessed September 6, 2004.

flown away." Baso gave the disciple's nose a twist. "Who says they are flown away?" he asked. As D. T. Suzuki observes in his comment to this tale, Baso's purpose was to draw attention to the living goose that moves along with the disciple himself, not outside but within his person.

Because of its low intelligence and temperamental nature, the goose is one of the many symbols for the Base Self in Sufism. A Turkish poet, Kaygusuz Abdal, composed a poem entirely devoted to the goose, highlighting the difficulties of taming the Base Self:

> *I got a goose from the woman*
> *Its neck longer than a pipe*
> *Enough to feed Forty Sages*
> *Been boiling for forty years, and still it isn't cooked*
>
> *Eight of us hewing wood*
> *Nine of us stoking fire*
> *With raised neck the goose looks on*
> *Been boiling for forty years, and still it isn't cooked*
>
> *We paid a small sum for the goose*
> *Its flesh stiffer than its bone*
> *Outlived both ladle and caldron*
> *Been boiling for forty years, and still it isn't cooked*

If only the Base Self could be purified, it would be enough bounty for forty sages. The trouble is, even forty years may not be enough to bring it to the required purification. The difficulty of attaining a permanent transformation of the Base Self is illustrated in the following story.

Namik Kemal and the Cat

This story is about Namik Kemal, a Turkish poet of the late Ottoman period (no relation to Yahya Kemal). Although it is not a Sufi story, it was related to me in a Sufic context.

One day, Namik Kemal was strolling down the street when he came across a friend he hadn't seen in a long time. They exchanged greetings and inquired about recent developments. His friend gushed with enthusiasm about a cat he had recently acquired and trained. "It's so smart," he said, "the things I can't get it to do are few indeed. You simply must visit me at home so you can see for yourself."

His curiosity aroused, Kemal paid his friend a visit at his house a short while later. As they sat talking in their armchairs, the door opened, and in walked a cat. It was standing on its hind legs, with a waiter's napkin draped over its paw, and was primly balancing a tray on its forelimbs, on which there were two cups of Turkish coffee. It trotted over to the guest and served him, after which it served the host.

His friend beamed at his pet's accomplishment. "You see?" he said, all smiles. "Yes," said Kemal, "you do seem to have done a marvelous job with the cat." And he made an appointment to come back the following evening to see the cat's further tricks.

However, the next day he procured a mouse and put it in a box punctured with air holes.

When evening came, Kemal set off to see his friend. Again they were seated, and again the cat walked in with two cups of coffee. This time, though, Kemal reached into his pocket and, without attracting the attention of his friend, slipped out the box. He reached toward the floor with his arm and released the mouse.

The mouse scurried away, the cat went right after it. They went one way, the tray and the coffee went another, pandemonium reigned.

Which leads to the empirical rule: Only measurements made under actual test conditions can provide reliable results. This is why the true character, the level of selfhood, of a person is revealed not under ordinary conditions, but only under duress.

One of the methods used in subduing the Base Self is Fasting, spare eating, drinking and sleeping, as we shall see below. Before doing that, let us consider another phenomenon similar to Namik Kemal's cat.

Nitinol and the Base Self

Nitinol is a nickel-titanium alloy that comes under the general class of shape memory alloys (SMA). Forged at high temperatures to a specific shape, it has a crystalline structure called the austenite form. Upon cooling, it undergoes a phase transformation to the martensite form. At this lower temperature, it can be given a different shape. But upon reheating, Nitinol "remembers" its earlier shape and reverts to that shape with great force. The results can be quite spectacular. It is used in many areas, from catheter wires to spacecraft antennas.

In this respect, the Base Self is very much like Nitinol. It, too, has a "one-way shape memory"—its "shape" may be changed under intense concentration or with the *baraka* (spiritual power) of an authentic Sufi master. But this latter shape is unstable, and the Base Self will spring back to its original shape upon the slightest disturbance. Only a small provocation is enough to cause the self of John Smith to snap back to John Smith.

The solution to this is low nutrition and reduced sleep time. What cooling does for Nitinol, reducing food and drink intake does for the Base Self. Then, slowly, the new self can gradually become permanent, at "cooler temperatures" as it were. This is called Stabilization or Settling (*tamkin*) in Sufism.

The human body is an excellent and efficient organism—it can survive without food and drink for longer periods than many of us would think possible. One should not go overboard, of course, and wreck the constitution of the body in the process. One must proceed intelligently. The technique is to *gradually* accustom the body to less food and drink, plus breath control: less food and more oxygen input, or substituting oxygen for food. The "fuel" in the body is thus utilized more efficiently.

A good model here is the carburetor, which mixes air and fuel in a car. Too much gas (or food), and it is liable to "choke." (Modern "computerized" cars have all but eliminated this problem.) But if air and fuel are mixed in just the right proportion, optimum combustion of the gasoline is possible. One should practice deep inhalation, breath retention for a not excessive period, and deep exhalation (to harness the unused capacity of the lungs).

Breath retention also helps to keep the Base Self at bay, which thinks it is dying and goes into panic mode. Such breath control is especially effective during Formal Prayer. To cancel the benefits of Formal Prayer, the Base Self floods the heart/mind with mental distractions, agitations, and impressions (*hawatir*) that prevent it from being brought under control. One is performing the Formal Prayer, but one's mind is elsewhere. With breath retention, the Base Self becomes preoccupied with its own survival, and so cannot distract the mind.

Even without breath control, greatly reduced food intake is a possibility, and is the process by which many of the great sages have conquered the Base Self. It is a bit like cutting off the power going to the evil computer HAL in the sci-fi movie *2001: A Space Odyssey* (though only its modules were removed there).

The thirty days of Fasting during the month of Ramadan, properly applied (not overindulging when one breaks the fast!) is an emulation of more concentrated efforts to corner the Base Self, and the Festival (*eid, bayram*) at the end of Ramadan is symbolic of the supreme Realization (*tahqiq*) that follows this conquest—a great cause for rejoicing and celebration.[142] That is the great liberation, the supreme triumph (*fawz al-azim,* a phrase which occurs numerous times in the Koran). But any step taken in that direction, however small, is also a triumph.

Sleep Less, Wake Up to God

As for reduced sleep, this requires little explanation. The goal is to "be awake," and the less time we spend in sleep, the better off we are. Taking an Ablution with cold water before starting on a Formal Prayer ensures that the Prayer is entered in a marvelously conscious state. (One can take it at other times as well to enhance wakefulness. It's okay to take an Ablution even when you already have an intact Ablution.[143])

The Ablution is not just a physical cleansing. When done in the right state of mind, it is a spiritual purification as well. At this point, one cannot help but remember Princess Shikishi's[144] following lines:

---

142. Of course, this is not meant to reduce Fasting solely to this interpretation. It has other aspects, beginning with the fact that it is a Pillar of Islam, a Commandment of God that has to be obeyed.
143. An Ablution is breached and has to be renewed when anything emerges from the front or rear orifices. (Also when one vomits and when there is bleeding that exceeds the thumbnail in area.)
144. Or Shokushi——Japanese nature poet, died 1201 B.C. The lines are from a poem about summer.

the sound
of mountain water
cleanses my heart.

The poetess has become so attuned to nature, and to her own true nature, that even the sound of mountain water is enough to induce this feeling of purification. One should engage in Ablution with a similar mind. As we rinse our mouth and wash each limb, we should meditate on cleansing them spiritually also, plus purifying and awakening our Heart, which is the higher goal. And we should gratefully thank God for water, this wonderful source of life and cleanliness. Wakefulness, higher consciousness, happiness—all come with what is Clean. Sorrow and bad dreams are the result of the Unclean.

In their battle with the Base Self, the great Sufi sages would take a Bodily Ablution (bath) whenever they were overcome by sleep, although this is not at all obligatory. We have already mentioned in the first chapter that in his struggle to stay awake, the great Zen Patriarch Bodhidharma is said to have cut off his eyelids, which became the seeds for a plant called tea—an interesting way of highlighting the wakeful influence of tea. For us, there is no need to go to drastic measures, but the less sleep, the easier it is to control the Base Self. The goal is explained by the Prophet: "I sleep, too, but my Heart is awake when I sleep."

Sufis attach special importance to worship and Invocation during the early morning hours, between four a.m. and the Dawn Prayer-call, when the beneficial effects of wakefulness are heightened. The gentle breeze of dawn is regarded an auspicious sign, a message from the Beloved. If one is conducting a night-long vigil and drowsiness sets in around, say, three a.m., brewing a cup (or two) of tea at this time and imbibing it will make sure that one remains wide awake.

Sufism and Biotech

Dolly the cloned sheep was talking to a Sufi sage.

"What," asked the sage, "is the secret of your existence? How did you happen to come about?"

"Well," said Dolly, "I'm not sure I understand it fully. But here's the way my cloners explained it to me. As you no doubt know, sir, every cell in an organism contains enough information to reproduce that organism in its entirety. But once each cell has differentiated into a unique form, it loses its ability to turn into anything else. A cell that has become part of my wool, for instance, cannot turn into a bone cell any more. My cloners called this *gene expression*—certain genes are expressed, but all the remaining genes are suppressed."

"And?"

"Their great discovery was that this one-way process could be reversed. What they did was, they took cells and put them under nutritional stress. That is, they starved them of nutrients. Under these conditions, the cells entered a latent quiescent state, where they were once again able to express all the genes that had been switched off. It was this dedifferentiation of cells that made me possible."

"I see," said the sage. "Undernourishment caused the cells to revert to an earlier stage that was not achievable otherwise. Even so, fasting brings the ordinarily boisterous self to a quiescent state, where it is again able to express the ten thousand things. It reverts to nondifferentiation, and travels from multiplicity to Unity, something that the less-well-informed deem impossible. The state of Unity then allows redifferentiation, and hence a new multiplicity. Not everyone who fasts achieves this, but it can be achieved only by fasting, by spare intake of food and drink. The creation of every new organism, no matter how small, mimics in some way the original creation of the universe.

"That reminds me," the sage went on, "of a recent study where mice kept on a low-nutrition diet lived 30 to 60 percent longer than their control group. The ancient sages, in their quest for immortality, hit upon fasting as a way to increase longevity. Even if you can't become an immortal, fasting at least contributes toward a long and healthy life.

"Furthermore, your cloners would no doubt have heard of John Cairns' directed-mutation experiments. He took bacteria lacking the genes to digest lactose, starved them for several days, then put them into a solution where lactose was the only nutrient. Under these conditions, the bacteria entered a trans-mutable state, and presto!—they were able to develop the genes necessary to digest lactose.

"Such is the Way of God (48:23).[145] He has hidden signs of Himself and His processes everywhere. All you need to reach wisdom is to look with a discerning eye, for the laws that govern the unfolding of the universe are written no matter where you look."

Unveiling

The Ch'an Masters called enlightenment the "vision of the Tao." Here, "knowledge and truth become undifferentiable, objects and spirit form a single unity, and there ceases to be a distinction between experiencer and experienced [subject and object]."[146] Only a person who experiences the non-distinction of the experiencer and the experienced knows what it really is.

---

145. *Sunnat-Allah,* where *sunna(t)* has the same meaning as the customary translation of the Tao.
146. *Recorded Sayings of Ancient Worthies, chüan* 32, quoted in Fung Yu-lan, *Short History...,* p. 262.

Likewise, the Sufis are elevated by self-cultivation to a vision of God (*ruyat Allah*). Geylani, for example, uses the term in his *Mystery of Mysteries*. This is also called Unveiling (*kashf*), for the veils are lifted from one's eyes and one beholds Reality. But one must beware of forcing this. One must do the right things and be patient. The mystical flower takes its own time to bloom. Otherwise, one will be placed in the position of the man from Sung, as related by Mencius:

> There was a man from Sung who was worried about the slow growth of his crops and so he went and yanked on them to accelerate their growth. Empty-headed, he returned home and announced to his people: 'I am so tired today. I have been out stretching the crops.' His son ran out to look, but the crops had already withered. (2A:2)

Until Gnosis occurs, the Sufi saint Bahauddin Naqshband cautioned, "the wayfarer on the Path should always think that he is at the first step." As Tao-sheng observed, Sudden Enlightenment "is an instantaneous act, like the leaping over of a deep chasm. Either one makes the leap successfully, in which case one reaches the other side and thus achieves Buddhahood in its entirety in a flash, or one fails in one's leap, in which case one remains as one was...Oneness means oneness with the whole of it. Anything less than this is no longer oneness."

If one is able to find a perfect master, one must submit to the teacher's instructions wholeheartedly and with no reservations, "like a corpse in the hands of the corpse-washer." Of course, this presupposes that one has found a truly realized and accomplished master, worthy of being followed. One must "throw away the world," detach oneself from everything-other-than-God (*masiwa*). The goal can only be reached by dying to one's self and, in the words of Bunan Zenji, "living as a dead man."

Quantum Sufism

The little proton had reached an impassable barrier. It scurried to and fro, trying to reach the nucleus that was its goal, but could find no way through. "What business have I," it thought, "with you over there and me over here?"

So it went to the quantum physicist for advice.

"What," it asked, "happens when an irresistible force meets an immovable object?"

"I see," said the physicist. "You wish to attain the nucleus, to merge your existence with that core. Your love, your will to reach your Attractor is the irresistible force, and the barrier that repels you is the immovable object. Well, I'm glad to say," he continued, "that our laws—meaning the laws of the universe as quantum physics has been able to discover them—allow your admittance under certain circumstances. Here it is," he exclaimed triumphantly, opening a big book with a flourish. "Statute 5, article 10. It's called quantum tunneling."

"Oh, really?" asked the little proton.

"But of course. If you don't have enough energy to climb over the barrier, there's still a small but finite probability you can pass through it. The tunnel effect is used a lot in modern technology, from tunnel diodes to scanning tunneling microscopes."

"And how," asked the proton, "am I supposed to tunnel through the barrier? Do I drill a hole, or what?"

"Well," said the physicist, and here his face assumed a grave expression, "it isn't easy, I'll grant you that."

"Tell me! Tell me!" The proton began to jump up and down, all excitement.

"Very well, then. In order to pass through the barrier, you have to *cease to exist on this side* first."

"Cease to exist?" The little proton paled, to the extent that protons can be said to turn pale. "You mean I have to *die?*"

"Yes!" said the physicist. "Unless you cease to exist on this side of the barrier, you cannot begin to exist on the other side." As he said that, could one have detected a mischievous gleam in his eye?

"That reminds me of a nice Sufi story," he continued. "There was once a Sufi, and he would visit his teacher. So one day he arrived, and knocked on the door. 'Who is it?' came the teacher's voice from inside. 'It is I,' the student replied. 'Go away,' the voice answered. 'There isn't enough room in here for the two of us.' And the door remained closed.

"So the student went away, and meditated on this a lot, and tried to adopt his teacher's traits. After a while he came back. 'Who is it?' the voice asked again. 'It is you,' the student replied this time. With that reply, the door swung open, and his teacher stood there, beaming. 'Since there is nobody here but me,' he said, 'welcome in, so that I can have a chat with myself!'

"That's how you're supposed to reach the nucleus," the physicist went on. "Once you become annihilate on this side of the barrier, you will be instantaneously teleported, beyond space and time, to the other side of the barrier. And that's what's called quantum tunneling. It's very much like what your sister, the electron, does when she jumps from one energy level to another. She really can't be said to exist between levels—she disappears from one orbital, and then rematerializes instantaneously at her destination."

"But- but- but," stammered the proton, "How do I do all that?"

"Haven't you read your *Jonathan Livingston Seagull?*" the physicist asked gently. "In order to get anywhere, you have to start by thinking that you've already arrived. I'm not saying that you should delude yourself," he added as an afterthought, "but there are situations in life where this really helps."

And with that he bade the little proton farewell.

The end result of Enlightenment (Gnosis) is the perfection of one's courtesy. For while the inner state (temporary) or station (permanent) of a person can never be known, his inner condition is invariably reflected in his outward behavior.

Loqman's Last Lesson

In the Koran, Loqman is mentioned by name. According to my Master, he was a sage rather than a prophet. He is regarded as the patron saint of doctors. In fact, legend has it that by the grace of God, he even discovered the medicine of immortality. But since it would not do to have immortal human beings, the Great Spirit Gabriel assumed human form and, walking toward Loqman when he was crossing a bridge, knocked the prescription out of his hand. It fell into the river and was lost forever.

But enough of this. The story that concerns us now is the last lesson of Loqman.

Loqman had a teacher who taught him wisdom, of whom he was very fond and who was very fond of him. One day, the teacher was presented with a melon,[147] and he decided to give it to his star pupil.

"I have something for you," he said when Loqman next came by, and sliced up the melon for him. Loqman was delighted. "What a delicious melon," he said as he took his first bite.

The teacher watched in satisfaction as Loqman consumed the melon, enjoying every bite. Finally, as they came to the last slice, the teacher's own appetite was aroused, and he decided to have some himself.

---

147. According to Rumi in the *Mathnawi*, it was a watermelon.

His face contorted with disgust as he realized that the melon, contrary to its appetizing appearance, had gone bad and was so bitter it was unedible. He spat it out immediately.

Then he looked at Loqman. "You ate that entire melon," he said in wonder.

"You are my teacher and my mentor," said Loqman. "You have nurtured me with your wisdom so much and for so long, I was ashamed to say that what you gave me was bitter. If I can't stand even this much hardship, it would be the height of discourtesy and ingratitude."

The next day his master gave Loqman his diploma (certificate authorizing the person to teach, *ijaza*). "I have nothing more to teach you," he said. "From now on, you are a teacher yourself."

☙ ☙ ☙

The very basis of self-cultivation, not just for Muslims and Sufis but for everyone, is to shun two things: illict gain and extra-marital sex. Without these, nothing is possible, and the way to sagehood in any religion or tradition is opened only when these two are accomplished. The Trust is easy to give but hard to receive. And to receive it, one must first of all be receptive— empty, and hence capable of reception. Only when the Heart is empty can it receive the Light of God. For a Sufi, the prerequisites of progress are adherence to the precepts of the Koran and those of the Way exemplified by the Prophet. In Sufism, one uses both self-power and other-power—that is, one must both struggle on one's own, and be lifted up by the liberating power (*baraka*) of the master. Under no circumstances must one fall victim to arrogance, a danger that is averted by ascribing any and all progress to one's teacher.

There are seven levels of selfhood in Sufism. These levels have not been explained, or even recognized, in other traditions, but if one wishes to attain the highest reaches of Gnosis, progress from the Base Self to the Purified Self prior to the

Ascension (*meeraj*) process is a must. One has to die to the little local self in order to reach the Great Self. When one's spiritual state (*hal*) is established as a permanent station (*maqam*) to the highest degree, this is observable in the perfection of one's courtesy (*adab*), at which point one's every action becomes infused with pure beauty. One's entire life then becomes an embodiment, as it were, of the Tea Ceremony.

The culmination of this process is now the subject of our final chapter.

12

THE END OF THE JOURNEY

The ten thousand things are complete within us.

—Mencius (7A:4.1)

What is in the universe, that is in man.

—Sufi saying

Only that day dawns to which we are awake. There is more day to dawn.
The sun is but a morning star.

—Henry David Thoreau[148]

The Peak of Unification

We can now proceed to a comparison between the esoteric essence of the East Asian philosophies and that of Sufism. For this purpose, we shall make use of a prime text of Chinese alchemy, *The Secret of the Golden Flower.*[149] The book itself repudiates the mundane claim that the purpose of alchemy is to make gold: "worldly people who do not understand the secret words...have misunderstood...in that they have taken it as a means of making gold out of stones. Is not that foolish?" Nor is the secret of longevity to be found in swallowing a pill: "the

---

148. Thoreau, *Walden (Spring, Conclusion).*
149. Richard Wilhelm/Cary F. Baynes (tr.), *The Secret of the Golden Flower* (*T'ai I Chin Hua Tsung Chih*), New York: Harcourt, Brace & World, 1962 [1931]. Another text, "The Book of Consciousness and Life" (*Hui Ming Ching*) is also included in this volume (henceforth referred to as *SGF*).

ancients really attained long life by the help of the seed-energy in their own bodies, and did not lengthen their years by swallowing this or that sort of elixir."[150]

What, then, is it all about? "The Golden Flower is the light…It is the true energy of the transcendent great One." It is equivalent to the "thousand-petalled lotus" in Yoga that blooms in the *Sahasrara* chakra. The light is white gold: "the golden color is white, and therefore white snow is used as a symbol."[151]

> If man attains this One he becomes alive; if he loses it he dies. But even if man lives in the energy…he does not see the energy (vital breath), just as fishes live in water but do not see the water. Man dies when he has no vital breath, just as fishes perish when deprived of water.[152]

> Which brings to mind the famous Sufi story about the fishes in the sea who did not know the sea. They finally went to the Sage Fish, who told them, "You are surrounded, at this very instant, by the sea. Inside you is its water, outside you is its water. You do not see it precisely because it is so all-pervading. How shall I show you the sea, when it is everywhere?" The sea being, of course, a metaphor for God. As the *Doctrine of the Mean* observes, "Nothing is more seen than what is hidden, and nothing is more manifest than what is concealed." (1:3)

In order to understand *The Secret of the Golden Flower*, we first have to know something about intelligence. According to the ancient Egyptians, the seat of intelligence and man's being was, not the head, but the heart. Upon death, the heart would be weighed against the feather of Truth, and too bad if it was heavy with dirt and impurities. One should strive above all else to purify one's heart.

---

150. *SGF* pp. 62-63.
151. Ibid.
152. *SGF* p. 21.

Now the Chinese word for consciousness or intelligence, *hsin* (Jap. *shin, kokoro*), stands for both heart and mind. In these two traditions, therefore, we have an association of intelligence with the heart. It should come as no surprise, therefore, that in Sufism as well, the intellect is associated with both the heart and the head. Memories and thoughts (*hatarat*), for example, are described in the literature as flooding the heart. Far beyond mere intelligence, however, in Sufism the Heart (*qalb, fouad, dil*) is the seat of God. As a Holy Tradition states: "The heavens and the earth cannot contain Me, but the Heart of My faithful servant does." The Heart is where God always looks.. And the spiritual organ that perceives the light of God, and indeed all Truth, is the Eye of the Heart (*ayn al-basirah*). A saying attributed to the Prophet goes: "Beware the discernment of the faithful, for he sees by the light of God."

The Sufis aim at the rectification of mind and heart (*hsin*). The Master never tired of exhorting his followers to have a "sound mind, sound heart" (*aql al-salim, qalb al-salim*—the latter is mentioned in the Koran, 26:89), and to connect and unify the mind with the heart. To unpack the meaning of the word *salim* a little bit, it means the sound judgment of one who has surrendered to God. Such a person always goes with the flow of things, obeying only the advice of God. He never pushes the river, because to push against its flow is futile, and to push in the same direction is equally senseless. Thus, he never engages in unnecessary action, which is the true meaning of "non-action" (*wu wei*). A Sufi master was asked: "If you had the power, how would you change the world?" He replied: "I would leave everything at its center (as it is)," for which reason he was called Center Master (*Merkez Efendi*) thereafter. (This sentiment is echoed by Chuang Tzu: "Let it be, let things be.")

This does not mean that such a person is lazy or indolent. It only means that he doesn't waste his energy—he doesn't "row in vain," with his oars raised in the air. When the chaos of the heart is quieted and the perturbations of the mind are stilled, sound judgment arises naturally, of itself. Because it is not the frenzy of the Base Self, but an intelligence that sees by divine light, which then shines through.

We can now return to our discussion of *The Secret of the Golden Flower.* "The heavenly heart," it says, "lies between sun and moon (i.e. between the two eyes)."

The square foot house is the face. The square inch field in the face: what could that be other than the heavenly heart? In the middle of the square inch dwells the splendour...the primal spirit [Tao] dwells in the square inch (between the eyes), but the conscious [human] spirit dwells below in the heart.[153]

We are told that the Confucians call it the Center of Emptiness; the Buddhists, the Terrace of Living, or the Center in the Midst of Conditions; the Taoists, the Ancestral Land, the Yellow Castle, the Yellow Middle, the Dark Pass, or the Space of Former Heaven. It is known as the Third Eye in the West. Whatever name it is called by, it is the point on the forehead lying exactly between the two eyes.

The Primal Spirit (Tao) dives down and fertilizes the human spirit, as a result of which the holy "embryo of the Tao" or "Immortal Fetus" is formed. In time, the energy-body of the spirit-child is born out of the top of the head and returns to Emptiness. The body is born into pure light.

---

153. *SGF* p. 22, 25.

In this summary, we have passed over certain practices mentioned in the text which are not germane to the present discussion. Now, it will be clear that the purpose of it all is to *unite the heart and the mind*. The result is the heartmind, and out of this synthesis is born the embryo of the Tao. What does Sufism have to say about this?

Chapter 53 of the Koran is called "the Star." The "Star" has been interpreted by Sufis as the "Most Sacred Effusion" (*fayz al-aqdes*). It is on the uppermost horizon, at the zenith. "Then he drew near and came down, until he was at the distance of two bows or even nearer (as close as possible), and He revealed to His servant what He revealed." (53:7-10) The Sufis have claimed that "the distance of two bows" (*qaaba qawsayn*) refers to the center of the eyebrows ("bows"), and "even nearer" (*adna*) refers to the Heart.

We are here being told, according to the Sufis, of the process by which the Ascension (*meeraj*) of the Prophet took place. The point is to connect, and then unite, the Mind (the center of the two eyebrows) and the Heart. The psychic center (*latifa*: Subtlety) in Sufism appropriate to the present sense is the Universal Intellect (*Aql al-Kull*), and also the Total (*Kull*), representing Totality. Then, the "Child of the Heart" or the "Child of Meaning/Spirit" (*walad al-qalb, tifl al-maani*) is formed. Once it is born, *meeraj* (the Ladder of Heaven) follows automatically.

It is here that the saying: "Formal Prayer is the Ascension of the faithful" assumes paramount importance. For the linkage and union of the Mind and Heart is an extremely difficult achievement for ordinary people. *The Formal Prayer acts as a spiritual lens that focuses the Mind and the Heart into a single point.* This occurs effortlessly and without conscious concentration. When the Formal Prayer is performed properly, this effect is felt especially on the forehead.

This is not to say that this is the *only* benefit of the Formal Prayer. Like the Supreme Ultimate Exercise (*Tai Ji Quan*), it is beneficial to one's health, keeping one spry and limber into old age. And it has many other positive effects besides. But it must be performed diligently for many years before the results manifest themselves. One invokes the name of God a million times, say the Sufis, in order to say "God" once, properly. It is that single utterance that yields the desired result, but it cannot be properly uttered before all that preparation in advance. This also resolves the "gradual" versus "sudden" approaches in Zen—the "sudden" result must be approached by gradual means.

Formal Prayer

To those accustomed to thinking of churches as the places where formal worship is performed, the locations for Formal Prayer would be the mosques, which have facilities for frequent prostrations and ablutions. But the Formal Prayer can be performed almost anywhere. People have been known to spread out their Prayer-mats on the streets of New York. The Prophet himself said, "The whole world has been made a mosque [*masjid*, lit. "a place of prostration"] for me." While congregational Prayer is encouraged and is performed in mosques, the facility for prostrations is usually one's bedroom, or any other room. The facility for Ablutions (which are prerequisite) is the nearest faucet. While on this subject, let me add that there are forty cycles of required Prayer per day. And the truly essential part is 17 cycles. At a cycle a minute, that's 17 minutes. Add 5 minutes for an ablution, 22 minutes. And if one can't do even that, just 2 cycles per day is better than none.

Under the present circumstances of life, one can lump together these Prayers as one wishes and perform them whenever one wishes during the day. The Master also made allowance for non-Arabic speakers to recite the prayers of Formal Prayer in their own language, even to say "God" or "Dieu" instead of "Allah." Though not many orthodox *hodjas* would agree with this, it makes perfect sense. For those who have difficulty in memorizing and correctly reciting long Arabic formulas, their "translations" in different languages is a feasible option. What is lost in terms of accuracy is made up for by the involvement of the reciter in meanings that are readily understood. And, unlike us, God understands all languages.[154] (See the Appendix for a brief description of how the Formal Prayer is performed.)

Chuang Tzu Visits a Sufi Physicist

Chuang Tzu went to visit a Sufi physicist—on the spiritual plane, of course.

"Honorable Sir," said Chuang Tzu after the usual exchange of greetings, "I am here to learn about this new theory of yours. Apparently, you find certain aspects of the mystical experience to be quite similar to the energy processes that take place within the interior of stars."

"Oh, yes," said the Sufi physicist. "The union of the Mind and Heart is not unlike thermonuclear fusion."

"How so?" asked Chuang Tzu.

"Well," said the physicist, "let us begin by considering that in some science museums, there are rooms in the shape of an ellipsoid. A person speaking at one of the two focal points (foci) of the ellipsoidal room cannot be heard properly by anyone else in the room, except by a person who has his ear at the other focus. This is because all the sound waves emerging from one focal

---

154. On how to Pray and how to take an Ablution, two of the many
    descriptions on the Internet (as of this writing) can be found at:
    http://islam.about.com/c/ht/01/03/How_Pray0985072209.htm
    http://islam.about.com/c/ht/00/07/How_Wud0962933372.htm

point are focused and concentrated on the other focal point. And the same goes for light."

"Ah," said Chuang Tzu, "I have visited such a museum during my spiritual wanderings, and seen how people enjoy this amazing phenomenon. But what does all this have to do with mystical experience?"

"That's the really interesting part," replied the physicist. "A similar thing happens in the unification of the Heavenly Mind on the forehead and the Heart within the breast. And the Formal Prayer is the means whereby this fusion is brought about. Spiritual light from the first is focused and concentrated on the second. Bathed frequently in this sunlight, the Heart blooms. It is this process that gives rise, first, to the Child of the Heart, and—when it comes to term—to the spiritual rebirth that is not different from the Ascension.

"As the two foci of an ellipse approach each other, the ellipse becomes more and more like a circle. When the foci coincide and become a single center, you have a perfect circle, totally round. This happens during Kowtow (*sajda*) in Formal Prayer. God has said, 'One is closest to Me during prostration (touching the forehead to the floor).' When the Universal Mind and the Heart in the chest fuse like two deuterium nuclei, great spiritual energy is released that makes the Ascension possible. From all this, I conclude that the Formal Prayer stands in the same relation to other forms of worship and spiritual techniques as the full moon does to a star."

"But," protested Chuang Tzu, "doesn't that make Formal Prayer too powerful, and therefore dangerous?"

"On the contrary," replied the Sufi physicist, "it is inherently safe—much safer than other spiritual techniques. This is because it is entirely natural. Unlike other techniques, it doesn't force the blooming of the Golden Flower, leading to premature—and hence partial or incomplete—Unveiling. Certain spiritual techniques that appear promising actually hinder the full blooming of the Golden Flower."

Chuang Tzu bowed in respect. "I see," he said, "that both physics and spirituality have progressed some ways since my time on earth—although, of course, since the Ten Thousand Things and I came into being together, it was all built into the universe from the Great Beginning."

☙　☙　☙

The Secret of the Golden Flower, that most abstruse and esoteric classic of Eastern meditation, tells us that the Heavenly Mind (or Heart) should descend and establish itself in the human Heart. The most effective way to achieve this is the Formal Prayer (*salat, namaz*), which was described by the Prophet as "the Ascension of the faithful." It is the two restrictions outlined in the last chapter, then, plus the requirement of Formal Prayer, that will propel the wayfarer from the World of Multiplicity to the Realm of Unity. It is impossible to exaggerate the importance of this. For those who can't find a master, the Master said: "Your master is the Formal Prayer, the Five Daily Prayers." The Formal Prayer focuses the Mind and the Heart into a single point. The Fusion (*jam*) of the Mind with the Heart provides the thrust that will elevate the student to the Utmost Limit (the "Lote-tree of the Boundary") and beyond.

The Sufis have alluded to the highest mystical experiences by allegories and metaphors. For example, the Turkish poet Yunus Emre sang:

Within a mountain, I beheld
The eighteen thousand worlds

where the "mountain" is the human frame (mind and body) and the "18,000 worlds" correspond to the ten thousand things—Totality itself.[155]

And what of the Beyond? There, words fail us, for there is no language and no discrimination in the Beyond for a description to be possible. It is not without reason that the following saying is shared by Taoism and Sufism alike:

Those who know do not speak, those who speak do not know.

---

155. In the Heavenly Classic, God is mentioned as "the Lord of the worlds" (1:1). "The eighteen thousand worlds" is a term current among the Sufis. Like "the ten thousand things," it is to be regarded as a figure of speech denoting manyness, rather than a numerically exact "body count."

CONCLUSION

A lamp...kindled from a Blessed Tree...
an olive that is neither of the East nor of the West,
whose oil well-nigh would shine, even if no fire touched it;
Light upon Light.

—The Koran (24:35)

An oil that is neither of the East nor of the West, and hence is able to nourish both: that is Sufism. A lamp lit from that oil can enlighten everyone. To unite the mind and the heart is to unite knowledge and love. Once this is done, it is realized as an immediate perception that truth, beauty, and goodness are inextricably intertwined. A teaching that combines them all has the best chance of serving humankind.

On the southern coast of Turkey, there is a spot called Ulash near Alanya, where the beauty of rock mingles with the softness of sand. As one walks down the narrow path, one is suffused by the fragrance of figs in the wild. Inhale deeply enough and, if one sniffs one's hand later, one may find the aroma coming, as if by miracle, from one's finger. The horizon is occupied by the azure sea; closer by, the reflection of sun under water paints the surface the color of pure jade.

Watching closely, one will see the sea shimmer. Each instant, hundreds of flashes of light are reflected from the wavelets, to be replaced by an entirely different set of scintillations an instant later. It is always the same sun that the gleams take their light from. Whitecaps break against the beach every now and then, while foam, white and pure, is sprayed from the rocks.

Faced with beauty of such magnificence, a sigh of gratitude escapes inaudibly through one's lips:

Thanks be to God, the Lord of the Worlds,
The Compassionate, the Merciful,
Master of the Judgment Day.

You alone we worship, and you alone we ask for help.
Guide us along your Straight Path,
The path of those whom you have blessed,
Not of those who incur your wrath, nor of those who go astray.[156]

Amen.

Of course, one doesn't need Ulash for this—every sight of breathtaking beauty will do. By thus expressing our gratitude, we ensure that our probability of enjoying similar moments of happiness in the future is increased. For if we give thanks to God, He will improve our circumstances even further, will give us even more reasons to be grateful. Because He has stated: "Give thanks to Me, and I will increase your thanks."

This is a great and wonderful secret, for it promises to improve our lot both physically and spiritually, both in this life and the next. "He who does not give thanks for what little he has," said the Master, "cannot find the much. Nowadays, people have much, but they don't give thanks for even that." The best way to illustrate the situation is by the following Sufi story.

Moses is one of the greatest prophets, and is known to have conducted extended conversations with God (though he could not see Him). He often did this by ascending Mount Sinai.[157]

---

156. The Heavenly Classic, 1:1-7.

One day, he set out again for the mountain as usual. On his way he came across a famous merchant. Everybody knew and respected Moses, of course, so the merchant greeted him. "O Moses, where are you going?" he asked.

"I'm going to visit God on Sinai," Moses said.

"Is that so?" said the merchant. "If you get the chance, could you please relate to God a wish of mine?"

"Sure thing," said Moses. "What do you want?"

"God has been so generous to me all my life," said the merchant. "He's granted everything I desired. I'm so rich, with many ships and caravans, that lately I've got to thinking. Could you please tell God that I thank Him with all my heart, that I really don't need anything more, and could He please divert His gifts to the poor and needy from now on?"

"All right," said Moses, and departed from the merchant. Reaching the desert, he continued on his way until he saw a man sitting in the sand. Curious, Moses approached. The man was stark naked, except for some sand covering his private parts. "Hello there," Moses said. "Hi, O Moses," the man replied.

"What are you doing out here like this?" asked Moses.

"I'm destitute," said the man. "All my life I've kept on losing and losing, until this covering of sand is all I have left."

"I'm sorry," said Moses, "I feel for you."

The man, upon hearing that Moses was going for an audition with God, also had a favor to ask. "Could you please ask God," he said, "to divert a small part of His infinite bounty in my direction?" Moses nodded.

Moses proceeded to Sinai with no further encounters. During his discussion with God, he raised the subject of the merchant at a suitable point. The following exchange ensued.

"My Lord, on my way over here, I met such-and-such a servant of Yours, a merchant. He had a wish he wanted me to relate to You."

"Speak, O Moses."

"He says You've been so generous to him up to now, he's wealthy beyond his dreams. He thanks You, says he doesn't

---

157. We disregard the "cosmic mountain" implications of this for the moment.

need anything more, and asks whether You could give the gifts You intend for him to the poor and needy from now on."

"Why, Moses, I really can't do that. I have vowed to Myself that I shall increase the lot of a servant who is thankful. That servant has been so full of gratitude for even the smallest things, to cut him off like that would go against My Way which I have chosen for Myself. Tell you what you can do, though. Why don't you tell him to stop his thanksgiving, and that will block his inflow."

"Thank you, Dear God. I also met another of your servants who had exactly the opposite wish. All his life he's been a loser. He asks that you change his destiny and save him from destitution."

"You know, Moses, his case is also covered by what I just told you. That man has always been an ingrate. He never gave thanks for even the greatest blessings. Just as the merchant attracted My gifts, that man practically repelled them. When you see him, tell him he should give thanks to Me if he wants to see his lot bettered."

After their interview had ended, Moses returned home. On his way, he first came across the destitute man, and explained what God had counseled. When the man heard God's advice, he flew into a rage, and shouted: "Look at me! I have nothing left but this sand covering my loins! How can anyone expect me to be thankful under these circumstances!"

At that moment, a sudden gust of wind blew away the sand that was covering him, and the man was left completely naked.

Next, Moses saw the merchant, and told him what God had suggested. The merchant listened silently with bent head. When he looked up again, there were tears in his eyes. "How can I fail to give thanks to God," he said. "I'm so grateful for all His gifts, I have been incapable of proper gratitude for even the least of them. Forgive me, Dear Lord," he cried, "for not having thanked you enough!"

Just then, one of the merchant's servants ran up, all excitement. "Sir," he said, "one of your ships pulled in a large fish, and when the crew split its belly, here is what they found."

He held out a pearl between two fingers. It was a black pearl —rarest of the rare, worth more by itself than all the wealth of the merchant put together.

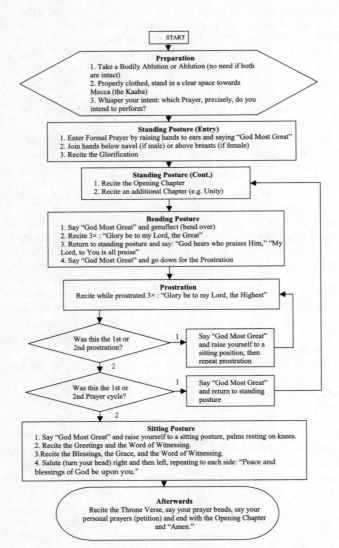

START

Preparation
1. Take a Bodily Ablution or Ablution (no need if both are intact)
2. Properly clothed, stand in a clear space towards Mecca (the Kaaba)
3. Whisper your intent: which Prayer, precisely, do you intend to perform?

Standing Posture (Entry)
1. Enter Formal Prayer by raising hands to ears and saying "God Most Great"
2. Join hands below navel (if male) or above breasts (if female)
3. Recite the Glorification

Standing Posture (Cont.)
1. Recite the Opening Chapter
2. Recite an additional Chapter (e.g. Unity)

Bending Posture
1. Say "God Most Great" and genuflect (bend over)
2. Recite 3× : "Glory be to my Lord, the Great"
3. Return to standing posture and say: "God hears who praises Him," "My Lord, to You is all praise"
4. Say "God Most Great" and go down for the Prostration

Prostration
Recite while prostrated 3× : "Glory be to my Lord, the Highest"

Was this the 1st or 2nd prostration? — 1 → Say "God Most Great" and raise yourself to a sitting position, then repeat prostration

2

Was this the 1st or 2nd Prayer cycle? — 1 → Say "God Most Great" and return to standing posture

2

Sitting Posture
1. Say "God Most Great" and raise yourself to a sitting posture, palms resting on knees.
2. Recite the Greetings and the Word of Witnessing.
3. Recite the Blessings, the Grace, and the Word of Witnessing.
4. Salute (turn your head) right and then left, repeating to each side: "Peace and blessings of God be upon you."

Afterwards
Recite the Throne Verse, say your prayer beads, say your personal prayers (petition) and end with the Opening Chapter and "Amen."

Figure 1. Flow Chart of Basic 2-Cycle Formal Prayer (see text for details).

APPENDIX

HOW TO PERFORM A FORMAL PRAYER

Formal Prayer is the Ascension of the faithful.
—The Prophet Muhammad

The Formal Prayer embodies the highest form of worship and spiritual techniques. It includes bodily postures, concentration, meditation, and Invocation (in a loose sense, mantras). Together with Fasting, Pilgrimage, and the Alms-tax, it constitutes a comprehensive program for self-cultivation and spiritual elevation.

It is a well-known fact that the Five Pillars of Islam are: the profession of faith by repeating the Word of Witnessing (or the Word of Unity), Formal Prayer, Fasting, the Alms-tax, and the Pilgrimage. The profession of faith means that we accept everything taught us by God and His Prophet. It is a once-in-a-lifetime affair. The Pilgrimage, too, is done once in a lifetime by those who can afford it (though many go back more than once). The Alms-tax is paid once a year, the Fasting is for one month every year.

By contrast, the Five Daily Prayers comprise 40 cycles of Formal Prayer per day. (At the rate of 1 cycle per minute, that's 40 minutes in 24 hours.) 17 of these are mandatory. In addition to the 40, there are Extra, Thanksgiving or Repentance Prayers which are optional. This highlights how important the Formal Prayer is, compared to the other Pillars: its necessity and frequency lies far beyond the others'.

The Formal Prayer is performed in services or "batches" of 2, 3, or 4 (rarely 6 or 8) cycles. Only the Mandatory part of the Dusk Prayer and the last part of the Night Prayer—called the "Odd-numbered Prayer," it concludes the Daily Prayers—are performed as 3 cycles. The norm is 2 or 4 cycles, and the 2-cycle Prayer constitutes the building block for the others.

There are many details to performing the Formal Prayer, though all can be mastered easily. Since this is not a full-fledged Formal Prayer manual, we shall here be concerned to outline the basic 2-cycle Prayer.

Normally, the recitations during Formal Prayer are conducted in Arabic, the language of the Koran. My Master, however, gave permission for those who could not memorize the Arabic formulas to recite these prayers in their own language. For the benefit of English-speaking readers, they are presented here in English.

The best way to learn how to perform the Formal Prayer is to have someone who knows it well teach you. Here, we have to remain content with a written description. Information can also be found on Internet websites: www.sufism.org/society/salaat/index.html is a good place to start.

The main steps in performing a two-cycle Formal Prayer are summarized in the accompanying flowchart (Figure 1). In what follows, we shall move through the steps shown therein the chart. It is recommended that one perform at least these two cycles per day. This will protect one and provide continuity of contact with the Divine.

Preparation

Leaving all worldly considerations behind, Formal Prayer is the occasion for communion with God. Ideally, all else should disappear from one's attention and the performer should be left alone with his Lord.

God, who is all purity, cannot be aproached in a state of defilement. Hence, it is first necessary to prepare for this encounter by bodily, spiritual, and mental purification.

To this end, one performs a Bodily (Full) Ablution and/or an Ablution.

Bodily Ablution

1. Declaration of intent: Say, "I now intend to take a Bodily Ablution."

2. Wash your hands, rinse your mouth three times, sniff water into your nose and blow your nose 3×, wash your face 3×. Then wash your head and your whole body. No part of the body must remain untouched by water.

Since an Ablution is a subset of a Bodily Ablution, a separate Ablution need not be taken unless something has happened that voids an Ablution (see below).

Things that void (annul, cancel) a Bodily Ablution:

-sexual intercourse,
-wet dreams,
-menstruation in women,
-childbirth.

Ablution

Provided you already have an intact Bodily Ablution, you can take an Ablution.

1. Declaration of intent: Say, "I now intend to take an Ablution."
2. Wash your hands, rinse your mouth three times, sniff water into your nose and blow your nose 3×, wash your face 3×.
3. Wash the right arm and then the left up to and including the elbows.
4. Wet your right hand and wipe the top of your hair (head).
5. Wet the fingers of both hands and wipe the inner sides of the ears with the forefingers and their outer sides with the thumbs.
6. Wet both hands and wipe the back of the neck with their backs.
7. Wash the right foot and then the left up to the ankles.

Things that void an Ablution (making it necessary to take a new Ablution):
-discharges from the body (urine, stools, gas),
-the flow of blood or pus from the body,
-vomiting,
-falling asleep,
-becoming intoxicated.

Symbolic Ablution

If water is not available or you cannot take a Bodily Ablution or Ablution for reasons of health, perform a Symbolic Ablution.

1. Declaration of intent: Say, "I now intend to take a Symbolic Ablution."
2. Pat earth or a clean surface with both hands and wipe your face with your palms as if washing it.

3. Pat again and wipe your right and then left arm up to and including the elbows as if washing them.

Anything that voids the other Ablutions voids the Symbolic Ablution as well. In addition, it is canceled when water becomes available or health impediments are removed.

You are now ready to perform the Formal Prayer. Your clothing should properly cover you (from the waist to below the knees for men, from the neck down to the wrists and ankles for women—the latter should also wear a headscarf to cover their hair).

Stand at any clear, clean spot facing Mecca (the Kaaba), which is roughly 70 degrees NE in the northeastern USA. If you are in doubt as to the direction, make your best guess and proceed accordingly. A prayer mat is useful but not essential. Stand erect, head slightly lowered, eyes looking at the place where your forehead will touch the ground. Your feet should be separated about the width of a hand. State your intent: for example, "I intend to perform two cycles of Thanksgiving Prayer."

Standing Posture (Entry)

1. Enter Formal Prayer by raising hands to ears and saying "God Most Great," palms facing forward and thumbs touching earlobes.
2. Join hands below navel (if male) or above breasts (if female). The right hand should grasp the left wrist in such a manner that the little finger touches the pulse area and three fingers remain extended.
3. Recite the Glorification:

Glory to You, My God, and to You belongs praise
And blessed is Your Name, and exalted is Your Majesty,
And there is no deity other than You.

Standing Posture (Continued)

Recite the Refuge and the Naming:

I take refuge in God from the accursed Satan
In the Name of God, the Compassionate, the Merciful.

1. Recite the Opening Chapter (first Chapter of the Koran):

Praise be to God, the Lord of the worlds
The Compassionate, the Merciful, Master of the Judgment Day.
You alone we worship, and You alone we ask for help
Guide us along the Straight Path,
The path of those who receive Your bounty;
Not the path of those who earn Your wrath,
Nor of those who go astray.

2. Recite an additional Chapter from the Koran. This can be either part of a long chapter or one of the 20-25 short chapters located at the end of the Koran. To illustrate, the Chapter of Sincerity (Unity) is presented below. Though very short, the Prophet Muhammad stated that it is equivalent to a third of the Koran in terms of importance. The same chapter can be recited in one or more cycles.

Say: He is God, He is One
God, the Everlasting
Unborn, unbearing,
Comparable to Him is no one.

Bending Posture

1. Say "God Most Great" and genuflect (bend over). Your back parallel to the ground, place your hands on your knees. Look at the big toe of your right foot.
2. Recite 3× : "Glory be to my Lord, the Great."
3. Return to standing posture, hands not clasped but left loose on both sides, and say: "God hears who praises Him," "My Lord, to You is all praise."
4. Say "God Most Great" and go down for the Prostration.

Prostration

Placing hands on knees, descend slowly to kneeling position; when knees touch the ground, keep going. Place forehead, nose and palms (but not elbows) on the ground. Place feet together, heels touching, bend toes so tops of feet face forward.
Recite while prostrated 3× : "Glory be to my Lord, the Highest."

Say "God Most Great" and rise to sitting position, looking at your lap. Men turn up heel of right foot, right toes bent, and sit on their left foot; women keep both feet, soles up, under their body. Wait until all your organs are settled, then, saying "God Most Great," prostrate again. Recite while prostrated 3× : "Glory be to my Lord, the Highest."

Say "God Most Great" and rise to standing posture. This completes the first cycle of the Formal Prayer, and the second cycle begins.

Second Cycle

The second cycle is a repetition of the first. One recites the Opening chapter plus another short portion of the Koran, genuflects and does the threefold recitation, stands up, descends to prostration and does a double prostration as before, all the while reciting the appropriate formulas.

After the second prostration of the second cycle, one rises to the sitting posture, which is the same as the position between two prostrations.

Sitting Posture

1. Say "God Most Great" and raise yourself to a sitting posture, palms resting on knees.

2. Recite the Greetings. This is the exchange between the Prophet Muhammad and God during the Ascension of the Prophet. The Five Daily Prayers were themselves bestowed on believers as a gift at the time of the Ascension, so that the faithful are enabled to participate in the Ascension by performing them.

All greetings to You, my God, and blessings and good deeds are from You
Greetings to you, O Prophet, and the mercy and blessings of God
Peace be upon us and the righteous servants of God

Raise right forefinger briefly and recite the Word of Witnessing:

I bear witness that there is no deity but God
And I bear witness that Muhammad is His servant and messenger

3. Recite the Blessings:

My God, bless Muhammad and the family of Muhammad,

as You blessed Abraham and the family of Abraham.
Surely You are the Praiseworthy, the Glorious.

(N.B.: "The family of Muhammad" means that blessings are pronounced on the Prophet's Household (the Ahlul Bayt and Twelve Imams), and "The family of Abraham" means that blessings are pronounced on Jews and Christians.)

Recite the Grace:

My God, grace Muhammad and the family of Muhammad,
as You graced Abraham and the family of Abraham.
Surely You are the Praiseworthy, the Glorious.

Raise right forefinger briefly and repeat the Word of Witnessing:

I bear witness that there is no deity but God
And I bear witness that Muhammad is His servant and messenger

(At this point, instead of the Word of Witnessing, many people recite the following:

My Lord, grant us goodness both in this world and in the world to come,
and protect us from the pain of the Fire.
My Lord, forgive my sins, and those of my parents and those of the faithful,
when the Day of Reckoning comes.)

4. Salute (turn your head) right and then left, repeating to each side: "Peace and the blessings of God be upon you."

This concludes two cycles of Formal Prayer.

Afterwards

Pronounce Blessings on the Prophet:

My God, bless Muhammad and the family of Muhammad

Recite the Throne Verse (Verse 2:255 of the Koran):

    God
There is no god but He, the
Living, the Everlasting.
Slumber seizes Him not, neither sleep;

To Him belongs
All that is in the heavens and the eartth.
Who is there that shall intercede with Him
Save by His leave?
He knows what lies before them
And what is after them, and they comprehend not anything of His knowledge
Save such as He wills.
His Throne comprises the heavens and the earth;
The preserving of them oppresses Him not;
He is the All-high, the All-glorious.

Say your prayer beads. Repeat

33× "Glory to God,"
33× "Praise be to God,"
33× "God Most Great."

Say your personal prayers (petition) and end with Blessings on the Prophet, the Opening Chapter and "Amen."

The Sufic Dimension

What we have presented above is the rote procedure of the Formal Prayer. To this, my Master added details of a Sufic nature, the most important of which are the following.

Distractions and stray thoughts flood the mind during Formal Prayer. These are induced by the Base Self, making it particularly difficult to concentrate.

Remedy 1:

In the standing posture, use your arms and clasped hands to squeeze your abdomen from the sides.

Remedy 2: Breath Control

Hold your breath while reciting the Opening Chapter, exhale, and repeat for the additional chapter. This can be continued throughout the Formal Prayer. The important thing is not to hold it so long that you run out of breath.

If the Formal Prayer is performed double the daily amount (75-80 cycles), the Base Self is kept totally at bay.

GLOSSARY

Many special and technical terms from half-a-dozen languages have been used in this book, yet it would have hopelessly complicated matters, in the heat of the argument, to indicate which term belonged to which language. The present glossary addresses this shortcoming. Almost every special term given in the book is listed, together with its meaning and its equivalent or proximate terms (also in the book) in other languages. It is hoped that this will provide a ready and easy reference.

Many of the Arabic and Persian terms have also found their way into Turkish. This is so pervasive that in many cases, I have not deemed it necessary to indicate their use in Turkish separately. The abbreviations used are as follows: Arabic: Ar., Chinese: Ch., Japanese: Jp., Persian: Prs., Sanskrit: Skt., Turkish: Trk.

abdest (Prs., Trk.) ablution; literally, "hand-water." *temizu* (Jp.)
adab (Ar.) courtesy.
adam (Ar.) Not-being, non-being, void emptiness, nonexistence. *sunya / sunyata* (Skt.)
Ahad (Ar.) Unity.
alam al-ghayb (Ar.) Invisible Realm.
anatman (Skt.) non-ego, selflessness. *la ana / la nafs* (Ar.), *bi-khudi* (Prs.), *wu-wo* (Ch.), *muga* (Jp.)
anjin (Jp.) true peace. *salaam* (Ar.)
anwar (Ar.) lights.
apratistha (Skt.) Nonspace, "no-abode." *la makaan* (Ar.), *wu-chu* (Ch.)
Aql al-Kull (Ar.) Universal Mind, Universal Intellect.
aql al-salim (Ar.) sound mind.
ashq / hubb (Ar.) Love.
asunya (Skt.) nonvoid.
atman (Skt.) self. *nafs* (Ar.)
atma-sunya (Skt.) lack of a self. See *anatman* (Skt.), *la nafs* (Ar.)
ayn al-basirah (Ar.) Eye of the Heart.

badr (Ar.) full moon. See *hilal.*
baqa (Ar.) Subsistence.
baqa bi-Allah (Ar.) subsistence in God.
baqa billah (Ar.) See *baqa bi-Allah.*
baraka / fayz (Ar.) spiritual power, effusion and blessings. *te* (Ch.)
Batin (Ar.) esoteric, inward. Opposite of *Zahir.*
bayram (Trk.) festival. *eid* (Ar.)
bi-khudi (Prs.) no-self. *la ana / la nafs* (Ar.), *wu-wo* (Ch.), *muga* (Jp.),
anatman (Skt.)
bodhi (Skt.) enlightenment. *satori* (Jp.), *wu* (Ch.)
butsu (Jp.) sage, enlightened person. *fo* (Ch.)
ch'an (Ch.) meditation. *tafakkur* (Ar.), *zen* (Jp.), *dhyana* (Skt.)
ch'eng (Ch.) sincerity. *ikhlas* (Ar.)
chi jen (Ch.) Ultimate Man. Synonym for Perfect Human, *jen ren.*
chia (Ch.): school, philosophy.
chiao (Ch.) religion. *din* (Ar.), *kyo* (Jp.)
dharma (Skt.) 1. Divine Law. *shariah* (Ar.) 2. the real nature of
things. *haqiqa* (Ar.)
dhikr (Ar.) invoke, remember, Invocation.
dhyana (Skt.) meditation. *tafakkur* (Ar.), *ch'an* (Ch.), *zen* (Jp.)
dil (Prs.) Heart. *qalb / fouad* (Ar.)
din (Ar.) religion. *chiao* (Ch.), *kyo* (Jp.)
edo (Jp.) Impure Land, the realm of suffering and prolonged woe,
Hell. *jahannam* (Ar.)
eid (Ar.) festival. *bayram* (Trk.)
falaq (Ar.) burst.
fana (Ar.) annihilation, extinction, oblivion. *tso wang* (Ch.), *jakumetsu* (Jp.), *nirvana* (Skt.)
fana fi-Allah (Ar.) annihilation in God.
fana fillah (Ar.) See *fana fi-Allah.*
fana fi-sheikh (Ar.) mind-meld with the Sufi master.
faqr (Ar.) spiritual poverty. *wabi* (Jp.)
fath (Ar.) conquest. *kyo* (Jp.)
fayz / baraka (Ar.) spiritual power, effusion and blessings. *te* (Ch.)
fayz al-aqdes (Ar.) Most Sacred Effusion.
fitra (Ar.) essence, nature, human nature. *hsing* (Ch.)
fo (Ch.) sage, enlightened person. *butsu* (Jp.)
fouad / qalb (Ar.) Heart. *dil* (Prs.)
gaws (Ar.) Helper.
ghayb (Ar.) hidden.

hal (Ar.) spiritual state.

halwat (Ar.) (from *hala'*, emptiness) solitude. *sabi* (Jp.)

haqiqa(h) (Ar.) Truth, Reality, the real nature of things. *dharma* (Skt.)

Haqq (Ar.) the Real, the Truth.

haqq al-yaqin (Ar.) Truth of Certainty.

hasan (Ar.) good, beautful

hasrah (Ar.) longing.

hatarat (Ar.) memories and thoughts.

hilal (Ar.) crescent, new moon. See *badr*.

hilm (Ar.) gentleness. *wa* (Jp.)

hiranya-garbha (Skt.) Golden Child/Embryo. *walad al-qalb* (Ar.), *tifl al-maani* (Ar.)

hsin (Ch.) mind, heart-mind. self, soul. *shin / shên / kokoro* (Jp.)

hsing (Ch.) essence, nature, human nature. *fitra* (Ar.)

hubb / ashq (Ar.) Love.

hurmah (Ar.) reverence. *kei* (Jp.)

ifrat (Ar.) too much. Opposite: *tefrit*.

ikhlas (Ar.) sincerity. *ch'eng* (Ch.)

insan al-kamil (Ar.) Perfect Human. *jen ren* (Ch.)

ishraq (Ar.) sunrise, enlightenment.

jahannam (Ar.) Hell, the realm of suffering and prolonged woe, Impure Land. *edo* (Jp.)

jaku (Jp.) tranquility. *Sukuun / tatmin* (Ar.)

jakumetsu (Jp.) "death of tranquility." *fana* (Ar.), *nirvana* (Skt.)

jalal (Ar.) Majesty or Wrath.

jam (Ar.) Fusion.

jamal (Ar.) Beauty or Bliss.

Jamil (Ar.) Most Beautiful.

janna (Ar.) Paradise, the realm of supreme happiness, Pure Land. *jodo* (Jp.)

jen / ren (Ch.) humanity, benevolence or human-heartedness.

jen ren (Ch.) Perfect Human. *insan al-kamil* (Ar.)

jihad al-manawi (Ar.) spiritual warfare.

jijimuge (Jp.) Transmutation/mutual interpenetration. *sarayan al-wujud* (Ar.), *wu hua* (Ch.)

jiriki (Jp.) self-power, own strength. Compare *tariki*.

jodo (Jp.) Pure Land, the realm of supreme happiness, Paradise. *janna* (Ar.)

k'ung (Ch.) emptiness. *adam* (Ar.), *wu* (Ch.), *sunya / sunyata* (Skt.)

kamal (Ar.) perfection.
kami (Jp.) god, sacred, sacredness.
karma (Skt.) Baggage of one's past deeds and misdeeds.
karuna (Skt.) compassion.
kashf (Ar.) discovery or Unveiling.
kei (Jp.) reverence. *hurmah* (Ar.)
kowtow (Ch.) prostration. *sajda* (Ar.)
Kull (Ar.) Totality, the Total.
kyo (1) (Jp.) conquest.. *fath* (Ar.)
kyo (2) (Jp.) religion. *din* (Ar.), *chiao* (Ch.)
la ana (Ar.) "no-I". *la nafs* (Ar.), *wu-wo* (Ch.), *muga* (Jp.), *bi-khudi* (Prs.), *anatman* (Skt.)
la makaan (Ar.) Nonspace, "no-abode." *wu-chu* (Ch.), *apratistha* (Skt.)
la nafs (Ar.) no-self. *la ana* (Ar.), *wu-wo* (Ch.), *muga* (Jp.), *bi-khudi* (Prs.), *anatman* (Skt.)
la taayyun (Ar.) nondelimitation.
latifa (Ar.): Subtlety, psychic center. Plural: *lataif.* See *chakra* (Skt.)
li (1) (Ch.) Principle.
li (2) (Ch.) propriety.
lisan al-hal (Ar.) language of states.
maarij (Ar.) Stairways. Singular: *meeraj.*
madrasah (Ar.) school, university.
maqam (Ar.) permanent station.
marifa Allah (Ar.) God-knowledge.
Marifa(h) (Ar.) Gnosis.
masiwa (Ar.) everything-other-than-(God).
masjid (Ar.) mosque, lit. "a place of prostration."
meeraj (Ar.) ladder, spiritual Ascension, the Ladder of Heaven. Plural: *maarij.*
ming (1) (Ch.) destiny. *qadar* (Ar.)
ming (2) (Ch.) illumination. See enlightenment (*satori* and *ishraq*).
muga (Jp.) non-ego. *la ana* / *la nafs* (Ar.), *wu-wo* (Ch.), *bi-khudi* (Prs.), *anatman* (Skt.)
mushahada (Ar.) Observation.
mushin (Jp.) no-mind. *wu-hsin* (Ch.)
nafs (Ar.) self. *atman* (Skt.)
nafs al-ammara (Ar.) Base Self (Stage 1)
nafs al-kamila (Ar.) Perfect, Complete Self (Stage 7)
nafs al-lawwama (Ar.) Critical Self (Stage 2)

nafs al-marziya (Ar.) Pleasing Self (Stage 6)

nafs al-mulhimma (Ar.) Inspired Self (Stage 3)

nafs al-mutmainna (Ar.) Tranquil, Serene, or Contented Self (Stage 4)

nafs al-raziya (Ar.) Pleased Self (Stage 5)

nafs al-safiya (Ar.) Purified Self (Stage 7)

nafs al-zakiya (Ar.) Purified Self (Stage 7)

namaz (Prs., Trk.) Formal Prayer. *salat* (Ar.)

nihsvabhava / pratityasamutpada (Skt.) other-dependence, non-self-existence. *qiyam bi-ghayrihi* (Ar.)

nirvana (Skt.) extinction, annihilation. *fana* (Ar.), *jakumetsu* (Jp.)

Nur (Ar.) Light.

pratityasamutpada / nihsvabhava (Skt.) other-dependence, non-self-existence. *qiyam bi-ghayrihi* (Ar.)

qadar (Ar.) destiny. *ming* (Ch.)

qalb / fouad (Ar.) Heart. *dil* (Prs.)

qalb al-salim (Ar.) sound heart.

qi / ki / ch'i (Ch.) primordial matter/energy.

qiyam bi-ghayrihi (Ar.) other-dependence, non-self-existence. *nihsvabhava / pratityasamutpada* (Skt.)

qiyam bi-nafsihi (Ar.) self-existence. *svabhava* (Skt.)

qiyas al-nafs (Ar.) the Golden Rule. *shu* (Ch.)

qutb (Ar.) Pole.

rabita (Ar.) connection or binding.

ren / jen (Ch.) benevolence, being human or human-heartedness.

ruyat Allah (Ar.) vision of God.

sabi (Jp.) modesty/solitude. *tawazu* (Ar.) / *halwat* (Ar.)

safiyah (Ar.) purity. *sei* (Jp.)

Sahasrara (Skt.) thousand-petaled (lotus). Refers to the highest *chakra*. See *latifa* (Ar.).

sajda (Ar.) prostration. *kowtow* (Ch.)

salaam (Ar.) true peace. *anjin* (Jp.)

salat (Ar.) Formal Prayer. *namaz* (Prs., Trk.)

sarayan al-wujud (Ar.) Transmutation/mutual interpenetration. *wu hua* (Ch.), *jijimuge* (Jp.)

satori (Jp.) enlightenment. *wu* (Ch.), *bodhi* (Skt.)

sei (Jp.) purity. *safiyah* (Ar.)

shariah (Ar.) Divine Law. *dharma* (Skt.)

shin (1) (Jp.) intimacy, parents.

shin (2) / *shên* (Jp.) mind, self, soul. *hsin* (Ch.)

shu (Ch.) the Golden Rule. *qiyas al-nafs* (Ar.)

sukuun (Ar.) tranquility. *jaku* (Jp.)

sunna(t) (Ar.) Way, course, order, law. Compare *tao* (Ch.)

sunya / sunyata (Skt.) void. *adam* (Ar.), *wu* (Ch.), *k'ung* (Ch.)

svabhava (Skt.) self-existence. *qiyam bi-nafsihi* (Ar.)

svabhava-sunya (Skt.) lack of being.

t'ai chi (Ch.) Supreme Ultimate.

taayyun (Ar.) delimitation.

tafakkur (Ar.) meditation. *ch'an* (Ch.), *zen* (Jp.), *dhyana* (Skt.)

tahqiq (Ar.) Realization.

Tai Ji Quan (Ch.) Supreme Ultimate Exercise.

takka (Ar.) convent.

talwin (Ar.) "coloring," variation. Opposite of *tamkin*.

tamkin (Ar.) Stabilization or Settling. Opposite of *talwin*.

tanasub (Ar.) harmony. *wa* (Jp.)

tanzih (Ar.) incomparability. Corresponds to transcendence. See *tashbih*.

tao (Ch.) Way. Compare *sunna* (Ar.)

tariki (Jp.) other-power, outside strength. Compare *jiriki*.

tariqah (Ar.) Spiritual Paths/Schools.

tashbih (Ar.) similarity. Corresponds to immanence. See *tanzih*.

tathata (Skt.) suchness, thusness.

tawazu (Ar.) modesty. *sabi* (Jp.)

tawba (Ar.) repentance.

tawhid (Ar.) Unification.

te (Ch.) spiritual power, virtue. *baraka / fayz* (Ar.)

tefrit (Ar.) too little. Opposite: *ifrat*.

temizu (Jp.) ablution; literally, "hand-water." *abdest* (Prs., Trk.)

tifl al-maani (Ar.) Child of Meaning/Spirit. *walad al-qalb* (Ar.), *hiran-ya-garbha* (Skt.)

tso wang (Ch.) sitting in oblivion, annihilation. *fana* (Ar.)

wa (Jp.) harmony, gentleness. *hilm* (Ar.)

wabi (Jp.) spiritual poverty. *faqr* (Ar.)

wahdah (Ar.) union, unity.

wahdah al-shuhud (Ar.) "Unity of Observers"unity of selves, spirits, subjects.

wahdah al-wujud (Ar.) "Unity of Being"unity of things, bodies, objects.

wahdaniyah (Ar.) Unity.

walad al-qalb (Ar.) Child of the Heart. *tifl al-maani* (Ar.), *hiranya-gar-*

bha (Skt.)

wu (1) (Ch.) enlightenment. *satori* (Jp.), *bodhi* (Skt.)

wu (2) (Ch.) nonbeing. *adam* (Ar.), *k'ung* (Ch.), *sunya / sunyata* (Skt.)

wu chi (Ch.) Non-Ultimate or Ultimateless.

wu hua (Ch.) Transmutation/mutual interpenetration. *sarayan al-wujud* (Ar.), *jijimuge* (Jp.)

wu wei (Ch.) "Not forcing." Usually translated as non-action.

wu-ai (Ch.) nonobstruction, mutual interpenetration. See *sarayan al-wujud* (Ar.)

wu-chu (Ch.) Nonspace, "no-abode." *la makaan* (Ar.), *apratistha* (Skt.)

wu-hsin (Ch., no-mind. *mushin* (Jp.)

wu-nien (Ch.) no-thought. *munen* (Jp.)

wuslat (Ar.) union, arrival, attainment.

wu-wo (Ch.) non-ego. *la nafs / la ana* (Ar.), *muga* (Jp.), *bi-khudi* (Prs.), *anatman* (Skt.)

yi (Ch.) righteousness.

Zahir (Ar.) exoteric, outwardly manifest. Opposite of *Batin*.

zat (Ar.) Essence.

zat al-mutlaq (Ar.) the Essence of the Absolute.

zazen (Jp.) sitting meditation. See *tso wang* (Ch.)

zen (Jp.) meditation. *tafakkur* (Ar.), *ch'an* (Ch.), *dhyana* (Skt.)

zhi (Ch.) wisdom.

INDEX

Chinese and Japanese names are listed "as is." For example, Lao Tzu is listed as "Lao Tzu". Arabic names are listed in the generally accepted way. For instance, Muhyiddin Ibn Arabi is listed as "Ibn Arabi, Muhyiddin". With few exceptions, footnotes have not been indexed.

Absolute x,xv,xxiii,xxx,14,26-27,29, 44-45,78,86-87,89,91,95-99,105,109, 115,117- 119,129,152,154, 156,172, 179
Adab (see also Courtesy) 2-3,146,193
adam (Non-Being, Void) 107,112,113
Akira Kurosawa 178-179
Ali (the Fourth Caliph) xix,37,153
Anatman (non-self, Pali anatta) 53-54,76,104,124-127,129,151
Annihilation (fana) 89,100,113,122, 129,155
Ascension (meeraj) xxix,48,52-53,98-99,122-124,134,177,193,198,201-202
Asunya (nonvoid) 106,115
Attainment (wuslat) xxviii,55,122-123
Attributes, Divine 84-85,87-88,106, 159,161
ayn al-basirah (Eye of the Heart) 196

Bankei xxi
baqa bi-Allah (subsistence in God) 102,155

Base Self xvii,xxxiii,11-12,37-38,56, 122,137,166,177-180,182-185,192, 197
Baso (Ma-tsu) 179-180
Bodhidharma 6-7,185
Brahman xxxii,54,100-102,107,109, 111,128
Buddha xxix,1,4,28,49,92,101,104, 107,115,123,125,127-128,134,153, 172
Buddhism ix-x,xii,xviii,xix,xxx,7, 18,40-41,43-44,54,76,91-92,95,100-102,104,106,108-109,111-114,117-118,122,125,127-128,136,157,160
Bunan Zenji 188

Ch'an (Zen) xxii,9,102,126,187
Ch'ing-yüan 154
Chang Tsai 48
Chao-chou 14,128
Charity xv,xxi,xxvi,46,49-51,130-133, 171-172
charity stones (sadaka tashi) 46,132-133
Child of the Heart (walad al-qalb) 106n,198,201
Chou Tun-yi xix
Chu Hsi 79,147,158-159
Chuang Tzu xi,xvii,12,23, 37,67,80,86-89,93,102,116,118,128-129,140,146,150-151,153,166,196, 200-202
Confucianism x,xii,xxx,88,136
Confucius xxi,xxv,80,88,121,135-145, 147,149,171
Courtesy (adab) x,24,7,13,46-47,49, 52,56,85,144,147,174,191,193

Daio 26
Dhammapada 18,172,178

Divine Law (shariah, dharma) 24,58, 96,136,138,149,173
Dogen 4,118,172

Emptiness xxxii,11,13,36,83,95,97, 101-102,105-107,110-123,125-126, 134,150,154-157,163,167,197
Emre, Yunus xx,61,202
Enlightenment xxii,xxviii-xxix,xxxiv, 40-41,43-44,52-53,92,96,98-99,102, 106,126-128,130,134,147-148,153- 154,177-178,187-188,191
Erzurum, Ibrahim Hakki of xxiv
Erzurum, Osman Bedreddin of 98
Essence, Divine xv-xvi,9,26-27,36, 40,42-43,51,61,82,89,93,96-97,100n, 104,106-107,117-120,126,128,152- 153,155-156,159,161-162
Eye of the Heart 9,61,64,66,196

Fana (annihilation) 13,89,100,103, 111,113,122,125-126,155
Fana fi-Allah (annihilation in God) 100,109,111
Fasting xv,171,182,184,186-187
Fa-tsang 105,160-161
Formal Prayer (salat, namaz) xv,10, 12,23,30,52-53,56,99,124,130,138, 171,183-184,198-202
Formlessness 114,117,119,121

Galib, Sheikh xviii
Geylani, Abdulqader xxiii,13,55,89, 94-96,140,161,163,187
Ghaybi 64-65
Glorious Book (the Koran) 164
Gnosis (marifah) xxviii-xxxiv,58,89, 94,96,98,178,188,191-192

Heart (qalb, fouad, dil) 196
Heavenly Book (the Koran) 139,169

Heavenly Classic (the Koran) xxi,24, 143
Hinduism 17,101-102,111,127
Hsiang Hsiu 116
Hsün Tzu xv,80
Huang-po 117
Hui Shih 78,80
Hui-neng 41,79,153
Hulusi, Father xx-xxi
Hyakujo 179

Ibn Arabi, Muhyiddin xi,12,26-27,40, 54,56n,82,85-87,89,97,163
Ibrahim, Sheikh 64
Indra's Net xxxiii,150,157,160-161, 163
Insan al-kaamil (see also Perfect Human) xxii,87
Invocation (dhikr, zikr) 14,58,109n, 168,185
Islam x,xiii,xviii,xxv,22,25-26,39,48, 79,84,109,119,132,164,176
Izutsu, Toshihiko xi,86-87,89

jam (Fusion) 94,149,202
jen (benevolence, human-hearted- ness) 136,145,147
Jijimuge 41,43,87
Junayd (of Baghdad) 153

Kakuzo Okakura 44
Kami 7,78,90,92-93,98
Kayhan, Ahmet (see also Master, the) x,xiii,xx,19,58,163
Koran, the (see also Glorious Book, Heavenly Book, Heavenly Classic, Master Classic)124,130,137,138,142- 143,145-146,148-149,154,169-171, 174,184,191-192,196,198,204
Kukai 91
K'ung Ying-ta 80

Kuo Hsiang 116

Lao Tzu ix,xi,xv,15,23,86,102,118-
119,140,151,175,178
Latifa (Subtlety) 198
Li T'ung-hsüan 41
Lin Qiuwu 127
Loqman 144,191-192
Love (ashq, hubb) 54

Master Classic (the Koran) 171
Master, the (see also Kayhan, Ahmet)
x,xxiii,20,23,30-31,35,49-50,53,65,74,
122,166,196,199,202,205
Meditation (tafakkur, dhyana, zen) 1,
15,53,56,130,168,202
Meeraj (ladder, Ascension) xxix,48,
53,98,123,134,193,198
Mencius (Meng Tzu) xv-xvi,xxii-xxiii,
19,139,141,144,147,188,194
Merkez Efendi 196
Messenger, the (see also Muhammad
and Prophet, the) 47,49,51-52,56,
59,98,100,137,139,141-145,167-169
Misri, Niyazi xvii,28,64,83,126,139,
150
Mo Tzu xxiii
Muhammad (see also Prophet, the,
and Messenger, the) xxv,18,20,23-25,
98,100,108,144,167-169
Multiplicity 10,14,40,42,51,57,59,66,
83,94,119,148,152-153,186,202

Nagarjuna 107,115,117,128,150-151,
155,163
Names, Divine xviii-xix,26-27,35,43,
81-82,87-88,159,161
Naqshband, Bahauddin 188
Nichiren 18
Nihilism 111,114-115,134

Nirvana xxxii,13,72-73,92,99-104,
106,109,111,113,115,117,120,122-
123,152,154-155
Nonempty (asunya) 106,109
Nonspace 136,157

One (Ahad) x,xxxin,39,43,47,78,80
Ottoman 46,68-69,132,165,181

P'ang-yun 64
Pantheism 65,85,104,107,130
Paths, spiritual (tariqah) 96
Peace (anjin, salaam) 47
Pen, the (Qalam) 98,170
Perfect Human xxi-xxii,11,19-21,29,
36-37,58,92,176
Plato 25,82
Pole (kutb) xxxii,23,58
Prophet, the (see also Muhammad
and Messenger, the) 45,47-48,51-53,
60,95-96,98-100,103,108-109,117,
128,131,132n,136,138,142,145-146,
153,169-172,174,178,185,192,196,
198-199,202

Reincarnation xxxii,71-76,99
Renyo 4
Rikyu 2,14
Rinzai 139
Rumi, Mawlana Jalaluddin ix,xi,xix,
xxviii,11,36,66,94,112-113,119,129,
134,145,159-160,164,176

Self-cultivation xvi,27,58,79,135,137,
142,163-164,166,187,192
Seng Ch'üan 95,97
Seng Chao 112
Seng Ts'an 82
Shabistari, Mahmud 94,113
Shao Yung 82
Shen-hsiu 153

Shikishi, Princess 184
Shinran 18
Shinto xxx,90-92,109
Shiraz, Hafiz of 4
Shiraz, Sheikh Saadi of 4,130-131
Shotoku, Prince xix,xxv
Shuko 2
Sincerity (ch'eng, ikhlas) 2-3,7,147-149
Sirhindi, Ahmed (Imam Rabbani) 40, 74
Spiritual power and blessings (baraka, fayz) 2,13,15,97,105,174,182,192
Straight Path, the 85,98,138,205
Su Tung-po xxviii
Subtlety (latifa) 198
Sunya (empty) 115,117,126
Sunyata (Void) 102,104-105,107,112-117,119-120,122-123,125-126,150-151,155
Suzuki, Daisetz Teitaro 16,30,35,126,180

Tao Sheng 9,188
Tao Te Ching 14n,15n,86,114,119,140,178n
Taoism ix-xii,xxx,7,86,89,102-103, 109,136,146,203
Tawhid (Unification) 47,94,148-149
Truth of Certainty (haqq al-yaqin) 148
Truth, the Real (al-Haqq) xxiv,xxvii-xxix,10,20,26,31,47,59,78,83,96,99,148-149,171,195-196
Tseng Lao-weng 24
Tsung-mi xviii,111
Tung Chung-shu 142
Tung-shan 128
Tustari, Sahl 94

Ultimate Reality xxviii,41,43,47,53, 99,101-102,104,106107,119,121,128, 148,167
Unity xxii,xxvii,7,9,14,36,38-40,42, 48,51-52,54-55,57,59,87,89,92-94, 104,118-119,126,128,130,147-149, 153,155,161,186,202
Universal Mind (aql al-kull) 103,201
Unveiling (kashf) 98,122,125,187,202
Upanishads 54,112,118n,152

Vedanta 102,127
Vision of God (ruyat Allah) 187
Void xxxiii,97,100,107,112,115,117-118,120,123-126,134,155,167-168

Wan Ch'ung-tsung 79
Wang Pi xvii,79
Way of the Prophet (sunna) 171

Zen ix-x,xii,xxi-xxii,xxx-xxxi,1-2,4,6, 7,9,14,26,33,35,64,79,102,106,118, 122,127-128,139,153-154,178,185, 189